# Financing Health Care in Sub-Saharan Africa

**Recent Titles in**
**Contributions in Afro-American and African Studies**

# Financing Health Care in Sub-Saharan Africa

## Ronald J. Vogel

Contributions in Afro-American and African Studies,
Number 164

**Greenwood Press**
Westport, Connecticut • London

**Library of Congress Cataloging-in-Publication Data**

Vogel, Ronald J.
  Financing health care in sub-Saharan Africa / Ronald J. Vogel.
    p.    cm.—(Contributions in Afro-American and African
  studies, ISSN 0069-9624 ; no. 164)
  Includes bibliographical references and index.
  ISBN 0-313-28993-X (alk. paper)
  1. Medical care—Africa, Sub-Saharan—Finance.  2. Medical
economics—Africa, Sub-Saharan.  3. Medical policy—Africa, Sub-
Saharan.  I. Title.  II. Series: Contributions in Afro-American
and African studies ; no. 164.
RA410.55.A357V64  1993
338.4'33621'0967—dc20        93-7713

British Library Cataloguing in Publication Data is available.

Library of Congress Catalog Card Number: 93-7713
ISBN: 0-313-28993-X
ISSN: 0069-9624

First published in 1993

Greenwood Press, 88 Post Road West, Westport, CT 06881
An imprint of Greenwood Publishing Group, Inc.

Printed in the United States of America

The paper used in this book complies with the
Permanent Paper Standard issued by the National
Information Standards Organization (Z39.48-1984).

10 9 8 7 6 5 4 3 2 1

  Much of the analytical content in this volume reflects the thinking that the author has done
in the last six years on health-financing missions in Sub-Saharan Africa for the World Bank,
the U.S. Agency for International Development, and the African Development Bank. Any
views expressed herein represent those of the author alone and should not be interpreted as the
official views of the World Bank, the U.S. Agency for International Development, the African
Development Bank, or any of the governments in Sub-Saharan Africa. The research assistance
of Marisa E. Domino is gratefully acknowledged.

For my daughters, Jaya and Samira Vogel

Critics of the market often argue that people in less developed countries are unable or unwilling to respond to prices and market signals generally. This is not so.

—P. T. Bauer, *Reality and Rhetoric*
(Cambridge, MA: Harvard University Press, 1984).

# Contents

# Tables and Figures

## FIGURES

# Preface

The ultimate purpose of expenditures upon health is to purchase inputs for slowing or retarding the rate of depreciation of the human body and mind; in this respect, health, or "healthy time"[1] has both consumption and investment aspects that are highly pertinent within a developmental context. All other things being equal, a healthy (and educated) population should be able to produce more goods and services over the long run than an unhealthy (and uneducated) population. And, if economic development were to be defined less materialistically than in the preceding sentence, but as an increase in human welfare, then the consumption of more healthy time should increase human welfare.

Expenditures on health can take many forms. At the individual level, they can range from seeking and paying for formal medical care from a highly qualified physician, to making nonmonetary expenditures in time and physical effort upon a self-conducted exercise and fitness program. At the governmental level, they may consist of such diverse activities as offering and trying to supply free formal medical care to all of the population, or of sanitizing drinking water sources, or of providing nutritional information for mothers and their children. Just as the definition of good health can be broad,[2] so too can the definition of the inputs (expenditures) that go into producing or maintaining it. Some of these inputs are medical and some are not, and, as will be shortly shown in the chapters that follow, some are cost-effective and some are not.

It has often been said that health cannot have a price, but as modern medical technology has made rapid and costly advances in recent years, governments and individual families all over the world have painfully begun to learn that financing expenditures upon medical care, as just one of the inputs into producing health, can be quite expensive on a per person basis. As a consequence, economists are increasingly being asked to study governmental health budgets and national health financing mechanisms, in order to find ways to save resources. The economist's approach to such a problem is to ascertain first what are the national objectives with respect to health; for example, a major national objective might be to drive down the national infant mortality rate (IMR) from 75 to 70 per 1,000 live births within the next two years. The next step would be to determine the set of feasible inputs for the production of an output such as the five-death reduction in the IMR; this step revolves around the question of technical efficiency. Finally, the economist tries to determine the least-cost combination of the feasible inputs for the output of an IMR that is five deaths less; this consideration has to do with economic efficiency.

The choice of health financing arrangements is extremely important for the eventual efficient achievement of the national objectives, simply because differing financing arrangements give differing incentive signals to the agents involved (the producers and consumers of health care) about choosing technically and economically efficient inputs for the production of the desired output. In the markets for most goods and services, prices provide the technical and economic efficiency-signal functions; in the medical marketplace, however, the role of prices is muted by varying types of health insurance.[3] Moreover, in the medical market, there is a large asymmetry in information between producers and consumers, and some financing arrangements (e.g., Health Maintenance Organizations) better serve to attenuate this asymmetry in information than other financing arrangements.

What has thus far been written in this preface could have been written for the United Kingdom, for France, for Japan, or for Benin or Zimbabwe, but it has served hopefully, to place this study on health financing in Sub-Saharan Africa within the context of the general paradigm of economics; this paradigm revolves around the necessity of making informed choices in situations of scarcity. With respect to scarcity, Sub-Saharan Africa, as a whole, remains the poorest region on earth.[4] And, despite the health improvements that have taken place there over the last twenty-five years, health status, as measured by such indicators as infant mortality rates, maternal mortality rates, and life expectancy at birth, remains the worst in the world. More recently, even though Sub-Saharan Africa only contains about 10 percent of the world's people, it has been estimated that about 60 percent of the world's AIDS cases can be found there (Barnett and Blaikie, 1992).

From the point of view of concern for human welfare, such statistics lend great urgency to the subject of this study.

The plan of analysis is as follows. The first chapter considers the current state of affairs in the health sector by asking three pertinent questions: what is the state of total financial resources available in each country; what is the state of health resources; and what is the rate of progress or decline in health outcomes? In the second chapter, we consider the issue of health resource efficiency by analyzing insufficient spending upon cost-effective programs, inefficient government programs, and who benefits from these programs, given the stated distributional objectives of these governments. Following Akin, Birdsall, and De Ferranti (1987), Jimenez (1987), and Vogel (1988), the third chapter considers four aspects of resource mobilization for the Sub-Saharan health-care sector: cost recovery and pricing; health insurance coverage and risk-sharing mechanisms; the role of the private sector; and the issue of decentralization. Finally, chapter four considers health-reform options for Sub-Saharan Africa, with respect to resource efficiency and resource mobilization.

## NOTES

1. The original coining of the term "healthy time" as well as the theoretical foundations for the investment and consumption aspects of health can be found in Grossman (1972).

2. The Preamble to the 1946 Constitution of the World Health Organization (WHO, 1986) defined health as a "state of complete physical, mental and social well-being and not merely the absence of disease or infirmity." Clearly, this definition has little economic or operational content.

3. Even in a country with no formal health insurance, where government provides "free" health care for all, and where the health care is financed through the general tax fund, there *is* health insurance, although not on an actuarial basis. In this kind of country, typical of many Sub-Saharan countries, government has provided "national health insurance." In effect, government bears all of the financial risk for health care, and the consumers of the health care face zero deductibles and coinsurance.

4. Of the forty-two countries classified by the World Bank as "low income," twenty-eight are in Sub-Saharan Africa. However, on a population-weighted basis, China and India, with a combined

population of 1.9 billion persons, and respective GNP per capita of $290 and $300 in 1987, are both low income and more important in terms of number of people.

# Financing Health Care
# in Sub-Saharan Africa

# 1

# The Current State of Affairs in Sub-Saharan Africa

## TOTAL FINANCIAL RESOURCES AVAILABLE

In a joint publication recently issued, the World Bank and the United Nations Development Programme (1989) paint a somewhat dismal picture for Sub-Saharan Africa:

During the first part of the 1980s, the region's economy grew much more slowly than its population. It then recovered in 1985 and 1986, but declined in 1987. Export value has fallen by nearly half, while capital inflows have shrunk. The debt burden has reached crisis proportions in more than half the Sub-Saharan Africa countries. External shocks, rapid population growth, war, and other internal disturbances have contributed to the crisis, but weak economic management has also been a major cause.

Given the appraisal above, in this section of this chapter, we make an effort to present the macroeconomic data that would have a bearing upon the ability of the countries in Sub-Saharan African to finance their health care, both in the public sector and in the private sector. Following Dunlop (1983), we use his format of analysis and the data that he used for 1960-1979, and contrast those data with data for 1980-1988, or for later years, when the data are available. As did Dunlop, we first range the countries of Sub-Saharan Africa by order of population size. Figure 1-1 shows the twenty-five most populous countries; these twenty-five nations consist of all of those with populations over five million persons as of 1990, and together comprise 93 percent of the population of Sub-Saharan Africa. In Figure 1-1, Nigeria has 23.3 percent of the total population; five countries (Nigeria, Ethiopia, Zaire, Sudan, and Tanzania) have 51.1 percent of the total population. An important lesson to be remembered from these data is that what happens in Nigeria is more important, on a

**Figure 1-1**
**Size of Selected Sub-Saharan Countries as a Percentage of Total Population of Sub-Saharan Africa, 1990**

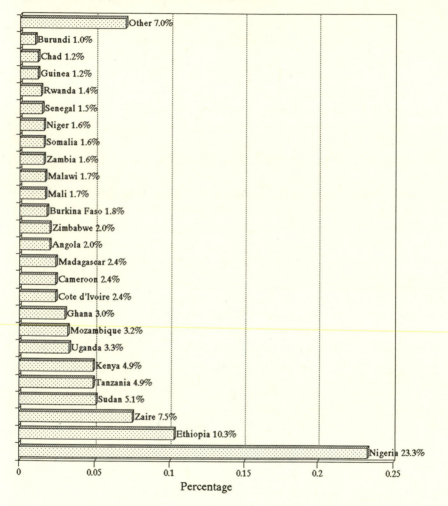

*Source*:   World Bank (1992).

population-weighted basis, than what happens in Burundi (1.0 percent of the total Sub-Saharan population).  While this point may seem obvious, it is almost always implicitly ignored in official-document, cross-country comparisons.[1]

### GNP per Capita

Table 1-1 shows the average annual growth rates of GNP per capita for the two comparison periods.  The period 1980-1988 was a time of widespread per capita income decline for the majority of the Sub-Saharan countries.   In some countries, these declines were accelerations of the declines that occurred in the period 1960-1979 (Zaire, Uganda, Ghana, Madagascar, Somalia, and Niger).   In other countries, the decline in GNP per capita in the 1980s reversed the growth experienced in 1960-1979 (Nigeria, Sudan, Tanzania, Kenya, Mozambique, Cote d'Ivoire, Zimbabwe, Zambia, and Rwanda).  Only five of these twenty-five Sub-Saharan countries saw an increase in the growth of their per capita GNP in the period 1980-1988 (Ethiopia, Cameroon, Burkina Faso, Mali, and Senegal).   Five Sub-Saharan countries are oil exporters (Nigeria, Angola, Cameroon, Congo, and Gabon).  The GDP[2] of these countries is highly dependent upon world oil prices, and oil prices were low during 1980-1984.  Thus, the per capita GDP of the oil exporters grew at an average annual rate of -2.8 percent during those years, while the per capita GDP of the non-oil exporters grew at an average annual rate of +1.1 percent (World Bank and UNDP, 1989).  However, for 1988, the per capita GDP of the oil exporters was growing at a +4.5 percent average annual rate; and that of the non-oil exporters at a +2.2 percent average annual rate.

### Food Production

From a health perspective, perhaps a more stable, long-run indicator of an economy's ability to provide basic sustenance, and thus avoid the disease-inducing debility caused by malnutrition, is the rate of growth of per capita food production.  Table 1-2 contains such data both for the period studied by Dunlop (1983), and for the more recent time period.  For the twenty-five countries for which data were available for 1979-1990, only five had positive per capita food growth

**Table 1-1**
**Average Annual Growth Rate GNP per Capita**

| Country | 1960-1979 | 1980-1988 |
|---------|-----------|-----------|
| Nigeria | 3.7 | -4.3 |
| Ethiopia | 1.3 | 5.8 |
| Zaire | -1.3 | -2.1 |
| Sudan | 0.6 | -4.2 |
| Tanzania | 2.3 | -1.3 |
| Kenya | 2.7 | -0.2 |
| Uganda | -2.2 | -2.5 |
| Mozambique | 0.6 | -7.5 |
| Ghana | -0.8 | -1.4 |
| Cote d'Ivoire | 2.4 | -3.7 |
| Cameroon | 2.5 | 3.0 |
| Madagascar | -0.4 | -3.4 |
| Angola | 0.6 | N/A |
| Zimbabwe | 0.8 | -0.1 |
| Burkina Faso | 0.3 | 2.4 |
| Mali | 1.1 | 1.8 |
| Malawi | 2.9 | 1.3 |
| Zambia | 0.8 | -4.9 |
| Somalia | -0.5 | -2.2 |
| Niger | -1.3 | -4.2 |
| Senegal | -0.2 | 0.3 |
| Rwanda | 1.5 | -1.5 |
| Guinea | 1.3 | N/A |
| Chad | -1.4 | N/A |
| Burundi | 2.1 | 1.2 |

*Sources*:  Dunlop (1983); UNDP (1991).

**Table 1-2**
**Average Annual Rate of Growth of Total Food Products per Capita**

| Country | 1970-1979 | 1979-1990 |
|---------|-----------|-----------|
| Nigeria | -0.8 | 1.3 |
| Ethiopia | -1.7 | -1.8 |
| Zaire | N/A | -0.5 |
| Sudan | 0.5 | -2.4 |
| Tanzania | -1.5 | -1.6 |
| Kenya | -0.5 | 0.0 |
| Uganda | N/A | -0.9 |
| Mozambique | N/A | -1.4 |
| Ghana | -3.1 | 0.1 |
| Cote d'Ivoire | -0.9 | -0.8 |
| Cameroon | 1.1 | -1.2 |
| Madagascar | -0.7 | -0.8 |
| Angola | N/A | -2.2 |
| Zimbabwe | -0.7 | 0.3 |
| Burkina Faso | 0.4 | 0.3 |
| Mali | -1.6 | -0.2 |
| Malawi | 0.3 | -2.0 |
| Zambia | 0.0 | -1.4 |
| Somalia | -1.7 | -0.4 |
| Niger | -1.5 | -2.6 |
| Senegal | -1.6 | 0.8 |
| Rwanda | 1.1 | -2.5 |
| Guinea | N/A | -0.8 |
| Chad | -1.0 | -0.5 |
| Burundi | -0.7 | -0.8 |

*Sources*:  Dunlop (1983); UNDP (1991).

rates (Nigeria, Ghana, Zimbabwe, Burkina Faso, and Senegal); however, only Nigeria had a growth rate that was greater than 1.0 percent. The food growth situation worsened in nine of the countries for which data were available for the two time periods (Ethiopia, Sudan, Tanzania, Cameroon, Madagascar, Malawi, Zambia, Niger, and Rwanda). In general, the contents of Table 1-2 give an impression of decline for both time periods. The World Bank and UNDP (1989) report that, starting in 1985, per capita Sub-Saharan *agricultural production* moved above the trend line for 1970-1984, and, by 1988, had reached a level 13 percent higher than would have been predicted from an extrapolation of the trend line for 1970-1984. However, because per capita *food production* did not increase at as rapid a rate as did per capita agricultural production between 1985-1988, the food production index only rose at a rate sufficient to maintain per capita food output between 1985-1988. Figure 1-2 shows an index of food production per capita for select countries between 1979-1990; 1979-1981 = 100.

### Export Earnings

Another source of food is to import it using export earnings. Table 1-3 shows exports as a percent of GDP for 1979 and for 1990. For the fifteen countries for which data were available for both years, one sees that exports as a percent of GDP increased in six countries (Nigeria, Tanzania, Ghana, Cote d'Ivoire, Malawi, and Somalia), but declined in nine countries. A comparison of the data in Tables 1-2 and 1-3 shows that, of those nine countries that experienced a decline in exports as a percent of GDP in 1990, six (Ethiopia, Kenya, Cote d'Ivoire, Cameroon, Mali, and Rwanda) also had zero (Kenya) or negative average annual rates of growth of total food products per capita between 1979 and 1990. On both counts, with 10.3 percent of the Sub-Saharan population, Ethiopia was particularly hard hit; its per capita food products declined by 1.7 percent per year in 1970-1979 and by 1.8 percent per year in 1979-1990, while exports as a percent of GDP dropped by 54.2 percent between 1979-1990. On the other hand, Nigeria, with 23.3 percent of the Sub-Saharan population had the highest average annual rate of growth of per capita food products (1.3 percent), and had exports as a percent of GDP increase by 63.8 percent.

**Figure 1-2**
**Index of Food Production per Capita, Selected Countries**
**1979-1981 = 100**

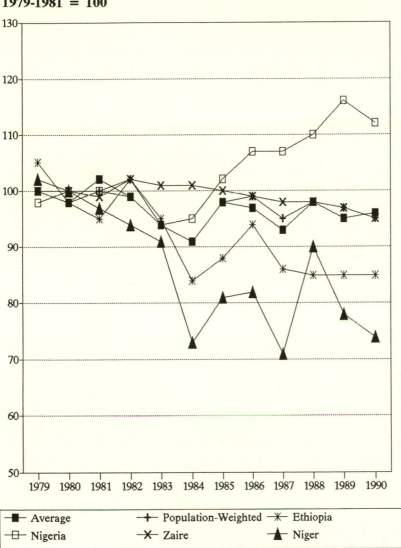

Legend:
- ■ Average
- ╋ Population-Weighted
- ✳ Ethiopia
- ☐ Nigeria
- ✕ Zaire
- ▲ Niger

**Table 1-3**
**Exports as a Percent of GDP**

| Country | 1979 | 1990 |
|---|---|---|
| Nigeria | 24.0 | 39.3 + |
| Ethiopia | 11.8 | 5.4 - |
| Zaire | N/A | 13.3 |
| Sudan | 7.6 | N/A |
| Tanzania | 12.7 | 14.6 + |
| Kenya | 20.9 | 13.7 - |
| Uganda | N/A | 5.4 |
| Mozambique | N/A | N/A |
| Ghana | 10.8 | 11.8 + |
| Cote d'Ivoire | 27.5 | 34.2 + |
| Cameroon | 21.2 | 10.8 - |
| Madagascar | 14.0 | 12.2 - |
| Angola | N/A | 39.0 |
| Zimbabwe | 32.8 | N/A |
| Burkina Faso | 9.4 | 5.2 - |
| Mali | 14.5 | 14.2 - |
| Malawi | 19.1 | 24.8 + |
| Zambia | 42.5 | N/A |
| Somalia | 10.8 | 14.6 + |
| Niger | N/A | 17.3 |
| Senegal | 17.0 | 13.4 - |
| Rwanda | 13.4 | 5.3 - |
| Guinea | N/A | N/A |
| Chad | N/A | 18.2 |
| Burundi | 14.4 | 7.5 - |

*Sources*:  Dunlop (1983); World Bank (1992).

### Balance of Trade

As shown previously, many countries experienced a decline in the importance of exports in their national economy. Although health care is labor intensive, and therefore not dependent upon foreign exchange to the extent that it is labor intensive in any given country, many of the important inputs into preventive and curative care are not manufactured or produced to any great degree in any of these countries. These inputs are vaccines, drugs and pharmaceuticals, and medical supplies and equipment. To the extent that the balance of trade is unfavorable, to that extent will countries not be able to import these important medical commodities, at the margin. Table 1-4 shows the balance of trade for these countries for 1979 and for 1990. Again, Nigeria is the exception to the general trend. Nigeria went from a trade surplus of $5.7 billion in 1979 to $8.0 billion in 1990. The Cote d'Ivoire increased its trade surplus from $24 to $500 million between 1979-1990. At the other extreme, Mali went from a trade deficit of $3 million in 1979 to a deficit of $293 million in 1990, and Ghana went from a trade surplus of $103 million in 1979, to a trade deficit of $460 million in 1990. Only three countries for which data for the two years were available (Sudan, Madagascar, and Malawi) reduced their trade deficits; Sudan reduced its trade deficit by 68 percent.

### Debt Service

Just as a negative balance of trade reduces a country's ability to purchase medical supplies and equipment, at the margin, so too do large debt service obligations. The burden of the debt, estimated to be about $129 billion in 1987 (or 100 percent of GNP and 3.5 times the value of exports) for Sub-Saharan Africa (World Bank and UNDP, 1989) has made it necessary for twenty-five of the Sub-Saharan countries to reschedule their debt with official and private creditors ninety-nine times during 1980-1988. Table 1-5 contains data on debt service as a percent of GNP for the two years 1979 and 1990. In 1990, four countries (Nigeria, 8.3 percent of GNP; Cote d'Ivoire 11.2 percent; Madagascar, 5.9 percent, and Malawi, 5.5 percent) led the list of debtors, in terms of how much of their GNP they had to pay in order to service their debts. For countries for which both the 1979 and 1990 data are available, one sees relatively large increases in debt service burdens, particularly in Nigeria and in the Cote d'Ivoire. The

**Table 1-4**
**Balance of Trade (Millions of Dollars)**

| Country | 1979 | 1990 |
|---|---|---|
| Nigeria | 5,674 | 7,983 |
| Ethiopia | - 149 | - 784 |
| Zaire | N/A | 111 |
| Sudan | - 619 | - 200 |
| Tanzania | - 561 | - 635 |
| Kenya | - 554 | -1,091 |
| Uganda | N/A | - 307 |
| Mozambique | N/A | N/A |
| Ghana | 103 | - 460 |
| Cote d'Ivoire | 24 | 500 |
| Cameroon | - 142 | - 100 |
| Madagascar | - 247 | - 145 |
| Angola | N/A | 1,800 |
| Zimbabwe | 254 | N/A |
| Burkina Faso | - 173 | - 320 |
| Mali | - 3 | - 293 |
| Malawi | - 166 | - 164 |
| Zambia | 622 | N/A |
| Somalia | - 176 | - 230 |
| Niger | N/A | 205 |
| Senegal | - 335 | - 837 |
| Rwanda | - 75 | - 167 |
| Guinea | N/A | N/A |
| Chad | N/A | - 250 |
| Burundi | - 47 | - 160 |

*Sources*:  Dunlop (1983); World Bank (1992).

**Table 1-5**
**Debt Service as a Percent of GNP**

| Country | 1979 | 1990 |
|---|---|---|
| Nigeria | 0.4 | 8.3 |
| Ethiopia | 0.7 | 1.6 |
| Zaire | N/A | 1.9 |
| Sudan | 4.5 | N/A |
| Tanzania | 0.9 | 2.9 |
| Kenya | 1.8 | 3.9 |
| Uganda | N/A | 2.3 |
| Mozambique | N/A | N/A |
| Ghana | 0.5 | 4.4 |
| Cote d'Ivoire | 6.0 | 11.2 |
| Cameroon | 2.5 | 2.3 |
| Madagascar | 0.7 | 5.9 |
| Angola | N/A | N/A |
| Zimbabwe | N/A | N/A |
| Burkina Faso | 0.8 | 0.3 |
| Mali | 0.7 | 1.7 |
| Malawi | 2.1 | 5.5 |
| Zambia | 9.7 | N/A |
| Somalia | 0.2 | 1.6 |
| Niger | 0.8 | 4.4 |
| Senegal | 5.0 | 3.0 |
| Rwanda | 0.1 | 0.7 |
| Guinea | N/A | N/A |
| Chad | 3.3 | 0.9 |
| Burundi | 0.4 | 2.9 |

*Sources*:  Dunlop (1983); World Bank (1992).

only exceptions are Cameroon, Burkina Faso, Senegal, and Chad, where debt service ratios actually declined.

The increase in the levels of indebtedness will have a substantial impact on the structure of expenditure patterns over the next decades. As interest accrues on these loans, an increasing obligation is placed on these governments to devote more funds towards paying off their debts. Figure 1-3 provides a dramatic picture of the burden of debt service compared with health expenditures as a percentage of central government expenditures. The alternatives for dealing with the current crisis level of debt include: (1) increasing reliance on aid from other countries, (2) increasing tax revenues, strapping already overburdened economies, or (3) decreasing funds devoted to other expenditures, often in societally beneficial health and education programs. Many of the Sub-Saharan nations have begun to experiment with these three options.

## Official Development Assistance

Sub-Saharan Africa as a whole now receives more official development assistance (ODA) and debt relief relative to its GDP and population than any other region in the world (World Bank and UNDP, 1989). Its share of worldwide ODA increased from about 16 percent in 1970 to almost 30 percent in 1988, even though its population is only about 12 percent of the total population of developing countries. Table 1-6 contains data, by country, on ODA as a percent of GNP for the years 1977 and 1990. In 1990, ODA in Mozambique amounted to 65.7 percent of its GNP, or $60.20 per capita. Somalia and Tanzania had ratios of 45.9 percent and 48.2 percent, or $54.80 and $47.10 per capita, respectively. Nigeria received the least ODA as a percent of GNP. When the data are compared for countries where the data for both years are available, no clear-cut pattern emerges. While the trend in ODA is upward for most of the countries, five countries (Cameroon, Burkina Faso, Mali, Senegal, and Rwanda) actually saw ODA decline as a percentage of GNP. Returning to Table 1-5, it can be seen that Cameroon, Burkina Faso, and Senegal were three of the only four countries where debt service as a percent of GNP actually declined between 1979 and 1990. One might expect ODA as a percent of GNP to be negatively correlated with GNP per capita, but that is not the case at all. For example, Sudan is ranked forty-second in the World Bank's list of low income

**Figure 1-3**
**Comparison of Debt Service and Health Expenditures as a Percentage**
**of Central Government Expenditures, 1989 or Latest Year Available**

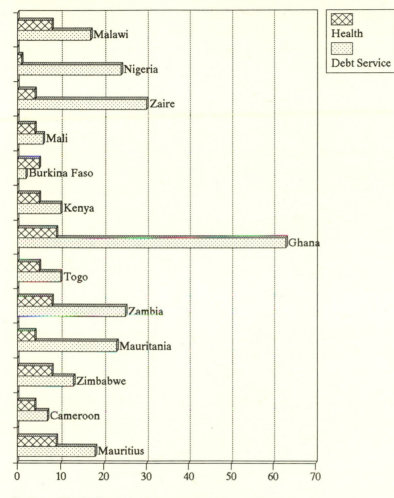

*Source*:  World Bank (1992) and UNICEF (1992).

**Table 1-6**
**Official Development Assistance as a Percent of GNP**

| Country | 1977 | 1990 |
|---|---|---|
| Nigeria | N/A | 0.7 |
| Ethiopia | 4.4 | 14.6 |
| Zaire | N/A | 10.9 |
| Sudan | 8.5 | 9.3 |
| Tanzania | 12.4 | 48.2 |
| Kenya | 6.0 | 11.4 |
| Uganda | N/A | 18.4 |
| Mozambique | N/A | 65.7 |
| Ghana | 3.8 | 7.4 |
| Cote d'Ivoire | 1.9 | 6.9 |
| Cameroon | 5.9 | 4.3 |
| Madagascar | 5.1 | 12.3 |
| Angola | N/A | N/A |
| Zimbabwe | 0.5 | 5.5 |
| Burkina Faso | 19.8 | 9.9 |
| Mali | 19.9 | 19.4 |
| Malawi | 12.0 | 25.7 |
| Zambia | 7.6 | 14.0 |
| Somalia | N/A | 45.9 |
| Niger | 12.3 | 14.2 |
| Senegal | 13.1 | 12.7 |
| Rwanda | 15.0 | 13.4 |
| Guinea | N/A | 10.4 |
| Chad | 18.0 | 28.6 |
| Burundi | 12.8 | 24.0 |

*Sources*:  Dunlop (1983); World Bank (1992).

countries (World Bank, 1992), but it received ODA of $31.50 per capita in 1990; Nigeria is ranked seventeenth, but it only received ODA of $2.00 per capita in 1990.[3]

### Food Aid Imports per Capita

Food aid imports are another dimension of ODA that are important for nutritional status and physical well-being in general. Table 1-7 shows data on food aid imports for 1979 and 1990. A comparison of the two years for countries where the data are available shows that nine countries had less food imports per capita in 1990 than they had in 1979. Seven countries increased their food imports per capita; of these seven, Ethiopia and Sudan have had prolonged civil conflict. There are no data for Mozambique for 1979, but its 31.4 kilograms per capita import of food aid in 1990 almost certainly reflects the civil conflict that has existed there. Although data for Nigeria for 1990 were not available, the data in Table 1-2 indicate that the average annual rate of growth of total food products per capita was 1.3 percent during 1979-1990, so it is doubtful that Nigeria has been receiving any food aid. In Malawi, it is difficult to explain why the per capita food aid import kilograms increased from 0.4 in 1979 to 20.6 in 1990, although Malawi's average annual rate of growth in food production per capita was a negative 2.0 percent during 1979-1990 (Table 1-2).

### Recapitulation on Total Financial Resources Available

As the World Bank and UNDP (1989) document understates in the conclusion of its executive summary, "The large variations in recent trends among (Sub-Saharan) countries preclude strong conclusions," it is difficult to predict the future for these economies. The one basic conclusion of the World Bank and UNDP (1989) stems from comparing the performance of "reforming" (structural adjustment) countries that have received increased ODA assistance with that of "non-reforming countries" that have not received such assistance. The reforming countries have done better with agricultural growth, export growth, GDP growth, and larger investment, despite the less favorable terms of trade facing reforming countries.

Perhaps, though, again following Dunlop (1983) and UNICEF (1992), we can add one more updated element for consideration. As

**Table 1-7**
**Food Aid Imports per Capita (Kilograms)**

| Country | 1979 | 1990 |
|---|---|---|
| Nigeria | 0.0 | N/A |
| Ethiopia | 5.1 | 10.5 |
| Zaire | N/A | 2.9 |
| Sudan | 5.1 | 13.4 |
| Tanzania | 3.0 | 0.9 |
| Kenya | 0.6 | 2.6 |
| Uganda | N/A | 2.2 |
| Mozambique | N/A | 31.4 |
| Ghana | 6.5 | 4.9 |
| Cote d'Ivoire | N/A | 2.2 |
| Cameroon | 0.9 | N/A |
| Madagascar | 1.0 | 2.7 |
| Angola | N/A | 11.3 |
| Zimbabwe | N/A | 1.3 |
| Burkina Faso | 8.7 | 4.9 |
| Mali | 3.7 | 4.5 |
| Malawi | 0.4 | 20.6 |
| Zambia | 8.9 | 0.4 |
| Somalia | 22.5 | 11.5 |
| Niger | 4.5 | 4.6 |
| Senegal | 11.8 | 8.2 |
| Rwanda | 2.1 | 1.0 |
| Guinea | N/A | 4.4 |
| Chad | 5.9 | 4.7 |
| Burundi | 4.0 | 0.4 |

*Sources*:  Dunlop (1983); FAO (1990).

UNICEF (1992) points out, with the seeming end of the Cold War, the Super Powers will no longer need to use Africa as a surrogate battlefield of ideology. While this will mean that the countries of Africa and Sub-Saharan Africa will no longer receive much aid in the form of armaments, it will also mean that they will no longer have to supplement such aid from their own financial resources.

Table 1-8 contains data on the percentage of total central government expenditures for recent years that were spent upon defense, education, and health. The data were only available for eleven of the twenty-five countries. Figure 1-4 shows the change in the percent of the budget spent for defense, education, and health for the same countries for the two periods 1975-1979 and in the late 1980s. Figure 1-4 is to be interpreted as follows; we use Nigeria as the example. Dunlop (1983) reports that, in 1977, Nigeria spent 17.9 percent of its central government budget on defense, 9.6 percent on education, and 2.2 percent on health. The data in Table 1-8 show that in 1987, Nigeria spent 2.8 percent of its central government budget on defense, 2.8 percent on education, and 0.8 percent on health. Thus, over the eleven-year period, defense declined by 15.1 percentage points as a percent of the total budget, education declined by 6.8 percentage points, and health by 1.4 percentage points. Figure 1-4 shows these changes for the eleven countries. For these countries at least, the preponderance of changes in defense, education, and health as a percentage of the central government budget have been on the negative side of the ledger. Dunlop (1983) indicated that scatter diagrams (not published) showed a negative correlation between defense as a percentage of the total budget and health and education as a percentage of the total budget. We calculated simple regressions for the data in both periods. The $R^2$ for the 1970s was -.30 and for the 1980s, it was -.14. From these calculations, it would seem that the negative relationship between the defense and health and education budgets is becoming more tenuous.

The last column in Table 1-8 shows the increase in central government health expenditures that would be possible for each country if the defense budget were decreased by 10 percent and all of these funds were reallocated to the health budget. For most of the countries, this would produce a sizeable increase in the health budget. Moreover, many defense expenditures use scarce foreign exchange. As just one example, a military tank requires more than one gallon of gasoline per mile; a ministry of health ambulance requires one gallon of gasoline per twenty miles. In an oil-importing country, for every

**Table 1-8**
**Central Government Expenditure Patterns, Latest Year**
**Available (1986-1990)**

| Country | % of Total Central Government Expenditures on | | | Ratio of Defense to Health Plus Education | % Increase in Government Health Expenditures if Defense Expenditure Were Reduced by 10%, All Allocated to Health |
|---|---|---|---|---|---|
| | Defense | Education | Health | | |
| Nigeria | 3 | 3 | 1 | 0.75 | 30.00 |
| Ethiopa | N/A | 11 | 4* | N/A | N/A |
| Zaire | 14 | 6 | 4 | 1.40 | 35.00 |
| Sudan | N/A | N/A | N/A | N/A | N/A |
| Tanzania | 16 | 8 | 6 | 1.14 | 26.67 |
| Kenya | 8 | 19 | 5 | 0.33 | 16.00 |
| Uganda | 26 | 15 | 2 | 1.53 | 130.00 |
| Mozambique | 35 | 10 | 5 | 2.33 | 70.00 |
| Ghana | 3 | 26 | 9 | 0.09 | 3.33 |
| Cote d'Ivoire | 4 | 21 | 4 | 0.16 | 10.00 |
| Cameroon | 8 | 13 | 4 | 0.47 | 20.00 |
| Madagascar | N/A | N/A | N/A | N/A | N/A |
| Angola | 34 | 15 | 6 | 1.62 | 56.67 |
| Zimbabwe | 16 | 23 | 8 | 0.52 | 20.00 |
| Burkina Faso | 18 | 14 | 5 | 0.95 | 36.00 |
| Mali | 17 | 17 | 4 | 0.81 | 42.50 |
| Malawi | 7 | 11 | 7 | 0.39 | 10.00 |
| Zambia | N/A | 9 | 7 | N/A | N/A |
| Somalia | 38 | 2 | 1 | 12.67 | 380.00 |
| Niger | N/A | N/A | N/A | N/A | N/A |
| Senegal | 9 | 15 | 4 | 0.47 | 22.50 |
| Rwanda | N/A | 26 | 5 | N/A | N/A |
| Guinea | 29 | 11 | 3 | 2.07 | 96.67 |
| Chad | N/A | 8 | 8 | N/A | N/A |
| Burundi | 16 | 16 | 4 | 0.80 | 40.00 |

*Source*:  UNICEF (1992) and *IMF (1992).

**Figure 1-4**
**Change in Percentage of Budget for Defense, Education, and Health Expenditures, Selected Sub-Saharan Countries, 1980s over 1970s**

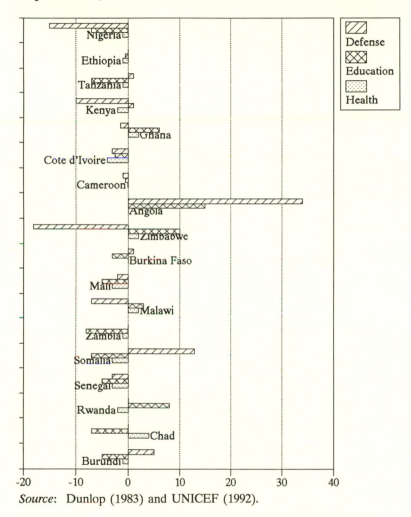

*Source*:  Dunlop (1983) and UNICEF (1992).

1,000 mile reduction in military-tank miles, many more ambulance-miles can be bought.    In the next section of this chapter we consider government health budgets and their components more closely.

## PUBLIC HEALTH CARE RESOURCES AVAILABLE

### A Cross-Sectional View

Table 1-9 contains the basic indicative data for forty countries in this study.  These data come from the World Bank documents listed in the reference section, from Summers and Heston (1988), and from the *World Development Report 1988*.  The first column in Table 1-9 gives the MOH recurrent budget in the local currency for the latest year for which the data were available.  Column 2 shows the MOH recurrent budget as a percent of the total government recurrent budget.  Here, we observe a wide variation in this measure.  In Somalia in 1984, the MOH budget was only 2.7 percent of the government budget, whereas it was 9.8 percent in Burkina Faso in 1981, 9.0 percent in Sierra Leone in 1984, and 9.0 percent in Ghana in 1988.[4]  Although this comparison gives some information about government budgetary priorities in each country relative to other countries on the African continent, it does not relate the MOH expenditure to population size nor does it give information about the absolute level of MOH recurrent expenditures in some common currency per population (nor does it relate the MOH expenditures to private-sector expenditures for health care).  For example, in mid-1986, Nigeria is estimated to have had a population of 103.1 million people, while the population of Botswana was 1.1 million.  If individual human welfare is assumed to be additive, if MOH expenditures per capita in a common currency are much lower in Nigeria than in Botswana, and if private expenditures per capita are also lower in Nigeria than in Botswana, than the welfare implications for Africa as a whole are entirely different than if it were Nigeria that had the better health expenditure profile per capita than Botswana.[5]  Column 3 contains the mid-1986 total population estimates for each country and Column 4 gives the MOH dollar recurrent expenditures per capita for each country, deflated by purchasing power parity ratios, for the countries for which the World Bank health expenditure data were available for 1985.  As can be seen, there is a wide disparity in the MOH dollar

# Table 1-9
## Government Health Financing Indicators: Sub-Saharan Africa

| Country | MOH Recurrent Budget (currency as indicated) | MOH Recurrent Budget as % of Govt Recurrent Budget | Population Size (mid 1986) (million) | US$ MOH Budget per Capita (PPPR) (1985) | US$ GDP per Capita (PPPR) (1985) | MOH Budget as % of GDP |
|---|---|---|---|---|---|---|
| Angola | | | 9.0 | | 609 | |
| Benin | 3.3 bil FCFA (1984) | 5.8 (1984) | 4.2 | | 525 | |
| Botswana | 6.4 mil Pula (1982) | 7.1 (1984) | 1.1 | 46.70 | 1,762[a] | 2.10 |
| Burkina Faso | 2,967 mil FCFA (1982) | 9.8 (1981) | 8.1 | 4.40 | 377 | 0.75 |
| Burundi | 1,077 mil FBU (1983) | 5.2 (1983) | 4.8 | | 345 | |
| Cameroon | 57.5 mil $ (1983) | 4.8 (1981) | 10.5 | 13.33 | 1,095[a] | 2.10 |
| Central Africa Republic | 3,731 mil FCFA (1988) | 6.4 (1988) | 2.7 | | 434 | |
| Chad | | | 5.1 | | 254 | |
| Congo | | | 2.0 | | 1,338[a] | |
| Cote d'Ivoire | 34.3 bil FCFA (1987) | 7.1 (1987) | 10.7 | | 920[a] | |
| Ethiopa | 90 mil $ (1982) | 4.4 (1985) | 43.5 | | 310 | |
| Gabon | | | 1.0 | | 3,103[a] | |
| Gambia | 11.29 mil $ (1986) | | .8 | | 526 | |
| Ghana | 3,992 mil C (1988) | 9.0 (1988) | 13.2 | | 349 | 1.94 |
| Guinea | 2,151 mil GNF (1986) | 5.6 (1986) | 6.3 | | 452 | |

# Table 1-9 (continued)

| Country | MOH Recurrent Budget (currency as indicated) | MOH Recurrent Budget as % of Govt Recurrent Budget | Population Size (mid 1986) (million) | US$ MOH Budget per Capita (PPPR) (1985) | US$ GDP per Capita (PPPR) (1985) | MOH Budget as % of GDP |
|---|---|---|---|---|---|---|
| Guinea-Bissau | | | | | | |
| Kenya | 3,147.9 mil Ksh (1984) | 6.2 (1985) | 21.2 | 12.40 | 598 | 1.72 |
| Lesotho | 14.1 mil M (1984) | 8.7 (1987) | 1.6 | 44.58 | 771 | 2.90 |
| Liberia | | | 2.3 | 12.10 | 491 | 1.92 |
| Madagascar | 15.5 bil RHC (1985) | 7.5 (1986) | 10.6 | | 497 | |
| Malawi | 36.7 mil K (1986) | 6.7 (1986) | 7.4 | 9.35 | 387 | 1.98 |
| Mali | 12.0 bil FCFA (1987) | | 7.6 | 1.61 | 355 | 0.34 |
| Mauritania | 683.4 mil U (1987) | 5.0 (1987) | 1.8 | | 550 | |
| Mauritius | | | 1.0 | 42.06 | 1,869[a] | 0.26 |
| Mozambique | | 3.9 (1988) | 14.2 | | 528 | |
| Namibia | | | | | | |
| Niger | 6.0 bil FCFA (1984) | 7.5 (1984) | 6.6 | | 429 | 0.71 |
| Nigeria | 111.4 mil N (1985) | 1.9 (1988) | 103.1 | | 581[a] | 0.26 |
| Rwanda | 779 mil RWF (1982) | 6.0 (1985) | 6.2 | | 341 | |
| Senegal | 6.7 bil FCFA (1986) | 5.4 (1986) | 6.8 | | 754 | 0.69 |
| Sierra Leone | 29.1 mil LE (1984) | 9.0 (1984) | 3.8 | | 443 | |

22

| Country | MOH Recurrent Budget (currency as indicated) | MOH Recurrent Budget as % of Govt Recurrent Budget | Population Size (mid 1986) (million) | US$ MOH Budget per Capita (PPPR) (1985) | US$ GDP per Capita (PPPR) (1985) | MOH Budget as % of GDP |
|---|---|---|---|---|---|---|
| Somalia | 109.9 mil $ (1982) | 2.7 (1984) | 5.5 | | 348 | 0.25 |
| Sudan | | 4.6 (1986) | 22.6 | | 540 | |
| Swaziland | 10.362 thous E (1984) | 9.9 (1984) | 7 | 44.98 | 1,187[a] | 2.57 |
| Tanzania | 1.838 mil Tsh (1988) | | 23.0 | 6.72 | 355 | 1.51 |
| Togo | 3.3 bil FCFA (1983) | | 3.1 | 8.81 | 389 | 1.41 |
| Uganda | 8.833 mil U sh (1986) | 1.8 (1987) | 15.2 | 5.03 | 347 | 0.27 |
| Zaire | 10.0 mil $ (1986) | 3.0 (1985) | 31.2 | .53 | 210 | 0.27 |
| Zambia | 75.3 mil K (1983) | 8.3 (1983) | 6.9 | | 584 | |
| Zimbabwe | 80.100 thous Z$ (1981) | 8.3 (1981) | 6.9 | 23.89 | 948[a] | 1.96 |

[a]These countries are classified by the World Bank as "lower middle income," with the exception of Gabon, which is classified as "upper middle income."

*Source:* The sources for the column entries for each of the countries are the various World Bank documents and reports listed in the second part of the references section of this volume, Summers and Heston (1988), and the World Bank (1988).

amounts spent per capita in each country, ranging from $0.53 in Zaire to $46.70 in Botswana.[6] A fair percentage of the differences in MOH health expenditure per capita in Column 4 may be attributable to differences in the per capita income of these countries.  Column 5 gives per capita GDP and Column 6 shows the ratio of MOH recurrent health expenditures to GDP.  Analysis of the contents of Table 1-9 thus far indicates that there seem to be differences in both budgetary priorities among the countries and differences in willingness to spend per capita on health as a percentage of GDP per capita.

### Time-Series Data

To begin with, the trends in health expenditures in this section can only be constructed for government (MOH) data.  We only continue to have snapshots of what is happening in the private health-care sector.[7] The U.N. pharmaceutical import data presented in this section of Chapter 1 does, however, contain time-series data for the public and private sectors combined.[8]

Table 1-10 contains data on estimated central government per capita expenditures on health for the years 1975-1985; the expenditure trends were adjusted to real 1980 dollars, and between-country trends were adjusted for purchasing power parity ratios (PPPR).[9]  The contents of Table 1-10 are somewhat striking because they clearly show the large variation in real resources that central governments spend on health on a per capita basis from country to country.[10]  The data for Nigeria only reflect federal expenditures.  Although the average real per capita health expenditure in 1985 was U.S. $11.81, Mauritius and Botswana spent U.S. $40.65 and $37.05 per capita, respectively, while Zaire and Somalia spent only U.S. $0.57 and $0.88.  Examining the least-squares annual growth rates (LSGR), Somalia's real per capita health expenditures had an annual average decline of 15.9 percent, falling from U.S. $5.45 in 1975 to $0.88 in 1985; on the other hand Cameroon experienced an average annual growth rate of 6.9 percent, with real per capita expenditures rising from U.S. $10.96 to $23.91.  The LSGR for the all-country averages in the last row of Table 1-10 indicate that the LSGR between 1975-1979 was 3.16 percent; between 1980-1985, the LSGR fell to 1.87 percent.  Also, for the twenty-two countries in Table 1-10, twelve had real per capita negative LSGR between 1975-1985.  For eleven of the twenty-two countries, World Bank indices of "good" economic performance and "poor" economic

**Table 1-10**

**Central Government Per Capita Expenditures on Health, Sub-Saharan Africa, 1975-1985 (In International 1980 Dollars, PPPR)**

| | 1975 | 1976 | 1977 | 1978 | 1979 | 1980 | 1981 | 1982 | 1983 | 1984 | 1985 | LSGR[a] | |
|---|---|---|---|---|---|---|---|---|---|---|---|---|---|
| Botswana | 19.00 | 20.91 | 25.10 | 23.04 | 19.13 | 27.06 | 34.13 | 29.72 | 31.00 | 32.64 | 37.05 | 6.42 | (G)[b] |
| Burkina Faso | 2.37 | 2.75 | 2.42 | 2.47 | 2.61 | 3.01 | 2.96 | 3.76 | 3.03 | 2.71 | 2.82 | 2.24 | |
| Cameroon | 10.96 | 11.09 | 10.82 | 11.56 | 10.94 | 12.36 | 9.88 | 13.52 | 14.50 | 19.98 | 23.91 | 6.90 | (G) |
| Egypt | 11.60 | 11.97 | 12.95 | 13.42 | 12.42 | 10.53 | 8.64 | 11.72 | 13.39 | 11.76 | 11.14 | -0.73 | |
| Ghana | 9.03 | 8.56 | 6.91 | 6.77 | 4.63 | 3.96 | 3.81 | 3.32 | 1.72 | 4.33 | 6.78 | -8.64 | |
| Kenya | 10.43 | 10.02 | 10.05 | 11.88 | 12.59 | 13.42 | 14.07 | 13.41 | 11.23 | 10.55 | 10.26 | 0.74 | (G) |
| Lesotho | 10.75 | 11.75 | 13.91 | 15.87 | 15.87 | 15.87 | 15.87 | 17.82 | 20.86 | 16.38 | 22.59 | 6.08 | |
| Liberia | 12.33 | 14.31 | 14.52 | 18.38 | 15.33 | 10.91 | 17.06 | 17.10 | 15.67 | 11.35 | 9.44 | -1.87 | (P) |
| Malawi | 5.84 | 5.30 | 4.76 | 6.01 | 7.28 | 8.03 | 6.92 | 5.17 | 7.01 | 8.29 | 7.66 | 3.66 | |
| Mali | 2.15 | 2.26 | 2.04 | 1.73 | 1.65 | 1.36 | 2.13 | 1.39 | 1.22 | 1.15 | 1.17 | -6.56 | |
| Mauritius | 26.06 | 33.11 | 37.46 | 40.54 | 40.95 | 29.96 | 30.46 | 32.74 | 35.35 | 33.86 | 40.65 | 1.29 | (G) |
| Morocco | 11.61 | 13.45 | 13.20 | 13.94 | 12.49 | 14.07 | 14.14 | 13.36 | 11.50 | 11.74 | 11.08 | -1.04 | |
| Niger | 2.76 | 3.02 | 2.51 | 3.00 | 3.24 | 3.35 | 2.60 | 2.21 | 2.56 | 2.83 | 3.03 | -0.52 | (P) |
| Nigeria | 3.45 | 3.90 | 3.71 | 2.72 | 3.67 | 3.79 | 1.85 | 2.19 | 2.07 | 1.42 | 1.49 | -9.63 | |
| Senegal | 8.39 | 8.19 | 8.19 | 8.19 | 8.19 | 7.98 | 8.33 | 8.57 | 10.12 | 6.32 | 5.22 | -2.39 | (P) |
| Somalia | 5.45 | 5.63 | 5.83 | 5.78 | 4.68 | 3.58 | 3.39 | 3.12 | 2.65 | 1.23 | 0.88 | -15.94 | |
| Swaziland | 16.43 | 19.97 | 20.95 | 21.85 | 19.70 | 21.81 | 20.81 | 28.94 | 27.72 | 21.82 | 30.50 | 4.56 | |
| Tanzania | 7.12 | 6.08 | 6.08 | 6.85 | 6.98 | 6.25 | 5.70 | 6.49 | 5.51 | 5.06 | 4.66 | -3.09 | (P) |
| Togo | 12.37 | 12.36 | 12.13 | 12.66 | 11.54 | 10.78 | 10.03 | 10.70 | 9.03 | 9.89 | 6.89 | -4.60 | (P) |
| Uganda | 2.07 | 2.73 | 2.66 | 2.59 | 1.12 | 1.09 | 1.82 | 3.61 | 4.25 | 3.17 | 3.36 | 5.20 | |
| Zaire | 2.20 | 4.74 | 4.15 | 3.17 | 2.19 | 1.75 | 2.25 | 2.56 | 1.99 | 1.41 | 0.57 | -12.11 | (P) |
| Zimbabwe | 16.17 | 16.65 | 15.68 | 16.96 | 16.07 | 16.99 | 20.64 | 23.22 | 19.58 | 20.76 | 18.61 | 2.89 | (G) |
| | | | | | | | | | | | | | |
| AVERAGES | 9.48 | 10.40 | 10.73 | 11.34 | 10.60 | 10.36 | 10.79 | 11.57 | 11.36 | 10.85 | 11.81 | - | |
| AVERAGE LSGR | <------------ | | 3.16 ------------ | | ------------> | <------------ | | | 1.87 ------------ | | ------------> | | |

[a]Least-Squares Growth Rate

[b]The (G) and the (P) refer to "good performance" and "poor performance" countries, based upon various indicators of macroeconomic performance that the World Bank uses.

*Source:* Gallagher (1988).

performance were available (the (G) and the (P) in the last column). In every instance where the indices were available for a country, the "good" performance countries had positive LSGR for per capita health expenditures and the "poor" performance countries had negative LSGR.

Figure 1-5 (drawn from the country averages in the last row in Table 1-10) shows the trend lines for the country averages for 1975-1980 and 1980-1985, and the deviations around each trend line. The deviations around the trend are relatively large, and call for further investigation in the future.

The previous paragraphs indicated that the trends for the countries where the data were available are not always clear-cut, although they do tell us which countries could have used significant help from the outside for, say, the year 1985. Perhaps Ghana is one of the outstanding examples. The data here and in Vogel (1988) show a drastic decline in Ghana in per capita government health expenditures during the early part of the 1980s (1981-1983), and then the attainment in 1985 of a per capita expenditure that was similar to that of the "best" years in Ghana (1975-1978). What the data here do not show is that, as a result of rapidly declining real incomes, the physician stock in Ghana decreased from 1,700 physicians in 1981 to 800 physicians in 1984 (Vogel, 1988). The short, rapid deterioration in the government health-care sector was not unique to the health sector; because of the politically chaotic situation in Ghana during 1981-1983, all sectors suffered, and the cause would seem to have been primarily political. In this case, it is clear that "health welfare" and "other welfare" declined in Ghana, but did it do so in the rest of Sub-Saharan Africa? Although the averages presented in Table 1-10 and in Figure 1-5 tell one type of story, they are also somewhat misleading, because, as averages, each country is given equal weight in the denominator of the calculation of the average. If every country had the same size population, this would not be a cause of concern for interpretation, but these countries do vary enormously in their population sizes. In mid-1986, Nigeria had a population of 103.1 million people, whereas the population of Gambia was .8 million; in other words, the population of Nigeria was 129 times the size of that of Gambia. Unless health expenditure data in both countries were very similar, making an average of the data for the two that was not population-weighted could be to distort the underlying realities as to how much was being spent on how many people. That is to say, the welfare implications of nonweighted averages may be very different from those of population-weighted averages.

**Figure 1-5**
**Per Capita Government Expenditure on Health**
**for Selected African Countries, 1975-1985**

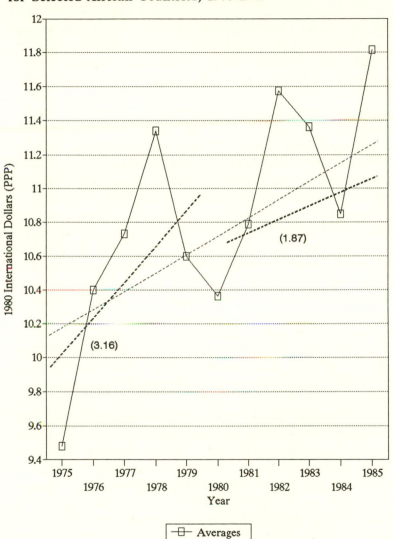

The contents of Table 1-11 make an effort to deal with this problem. As it turns out, how Nigeria is handled in the calculations does affect the outcome. Nigeria presents a problem, not only because of its large population size (the population of Nigeria is little more than one-fifth that of the size of this Sub-Saharan African sample population), but because of its federal government system, with twenty-one fairly autonomous states that each have their own ministry of health, and with extensive Local Government Authority (LGA) involvement in the health sector. The data that are usually presented for Nigeria in international health expenditure comparisons are for the federal government, and can be quite misleading if note is not taken of state and local expenditure activity. A further problem is that until Over and Denton (1988) had made the tentative, pioneering effort to put all of the data together, nobody did know exactly what were the *total* health care expenditures in Nigeria.[11]

In Table 1-11 we attempt to make the total Sub-Saharan African "health care welfare" comparison for three points in time: 1975, 1980, and 1985.[12] Row 1 gives the total sample population size. Row 2 gives the population of Nigeria, Row 3 shows the Nigerian population as a percentage of the total sample population and Row 4 shows total population without Nigeria. Row 5 presents total government health expenditures that include, for Nigeria, *only* federal health expenditures, while Row 6 gives total health expenditures, excluding Nigeria. Row 7 gives an estimate of *total* Nigerian health expenditures, based upon ratios derived from Over and Denton (1988), Row 8 contains total health expenditures for all of the countries, including the adjusted total for Nigeria.

Here, we define Sub-Saharan African health-care welfare in a very limited sense, consisting of levels and changes in the levels of real per capita government health expenditures. The last three rows of Table 1-11 show how important Nigeria weighs in the results. In Row 9, using Row 5 (total government health expenditures, with only Nigerian federal expenditures) as the numerator, and Row 1 as the denominator, one sees that real per capita health expenditures in Sub-Saharan Africa were U.S. $5.16 in 1975, $5.17 in 1980, and $4.70 in 1985. Thus, health welfare was about the same in 1980 as it was in 1975, but declined by about 9 percent between 1980-1985. If we exclude Nigeria from the calculations in Row 10 (Row 6 divided by Row 4), the data tell a different story, i.e., that health welfare declined slightly in 1980, but by 1985 was at the same level as it had been in 1975. Finally, Row 10 shows the health-care welfare measures that

**Table 1-11**
**Sub-Saharan Health Welfare Ratios**

|  | 1975 | 1980 | 1985 |
|---|---|---|---|
| (1) Total Population in Sample (thousands) | 234,052 | 269,148 | 313,923 |
| (2) Population of Nigeria (thousands) | 74,884 | 84,732 | 99,753 |
| (3) Nigeria as Percent of Total | 32.0 | 31.5 | 31.8 |
| (4) Total Population without Nigeria (thousands) | 159,168 | 184,416 | 214,170 |
| (5) Total Government Health Expenditures (millions) | 1,207 | 1,392 | 1,475 |
| (6) Total Government Health Expenditures, excluding Nigeria (millions) | 949 | 1,071 | 1,277 |
| (7) Adjusted Nigerian Health Expenditures (millions) | 490.8 | 963.3 | 802.7 |
| (8) Adjusted Total Government Health Expenditures (millions) | 1,439.8 | 2,034.3 | 2,079.7 |
| (9) Per Capita Expenditures from Unadjusted Total | 5.16 | 5.17 | 4.70 |
| (10) Per Capita Expenditures, excluding Nigeria | 5.96 | 5.81 | 5.96 |
| (11) Per Capita Expenditures, with Nigeria Adjusted | 6.15 | 7.56 | 6.62 |

include the Nigerian data, adjusted for *total* Nigerian health expenditures (Row 8 divided by Row 1). Using this measure, health-care welfare rose from $6.15 in 1975 to $7.56 in 1980, and then declined to $6.62 in 1985 (or a 12.4 percent decline between 1980-1985). What is interesting about these comparisons is the extent to which the decline in oil prices in the early 1980s affected Nigerian revenues, and consequently Nigerian expenditures on health and other government programs (see Over and Denton, 1988); because Nigeria has such a large percentage of the population of Sub-Saharan Africa, relative to any other country, what happens to or in Nigeria has a decisive influence upon the welfare of all of Africa, when welfare is measured, as it has been above. Of course, this per capita measure has many of the same weaknesses as an indicator of health-care welfare on the continent of Africa, as does a per capita measure for a single nation as a whole. For example, even though the real per capita (adjusted) government health expenditure in Sub-Saharan Africa was $6.62 in 1985, the real per capita expenditure in tiny Mauritius (population, 1.020 million) was $40.70 and in larger Zaire (population, 14.695 million) was $0.60. What we do know from the latter statistics is that the average citizen in Mauritius is better off, government health expenditure-wise, than the average citizen in Zaire. But, if the expenditures in Mauritius are badly skewed toward only a few persons, those who *receive* no expenditures in Mauritius could be worse off than all of the citizens in Zaire, *if* the expenditures in Zaire are spread evenly.

Table 1-12 presents United Nations data on pharmaceutical imports. The pharmaceutical imports are shown both in millions of real U.S. dollars (1985 base) and on a per capita basis for each country. These data give some important clues about what has been happening in the whole modern health-care sector in the Sub-Saharan countries, because they are the only time-series data available that pertain to both private and public health-care expenditures, although, for each country it is not possible to know what percentage of the pharmaceutical imports is public and what is private. Unfortunately, there are less data for the late 1980s than for the early 1980s and the 1970s for many of the countries. As with the data for government health expenditures in Table 1-10, the data for real pharmaceutical imports in Table 1-12 show wide variability both across countries and over time. On a per capita basis at the high end, the Seychelles spent $20.40 in 1987 and Mauritius spent $13.15 in 1988; at the low end, Ethiopia spent $0.41 in 1988 and Rwanda spent $0.96 in 1986. Since

## Table 1-12
## Real Pharmaceutical Imports[a]
## (Thousands U.S. $ (1985) and U.S. $ (1985) per Capita)

| Country | 1972 | 1973 | 1974 | 1975 | 1976 | 1977 | 1978 | 1979 | 1980 |
|---|---|---|---|---|---|---|---|---|---|
| Angola | 45547.01 | 55719.58 | 59273.36 | | | | | | 41640.82 |
| | 7.32 | 8.74 | 9.08 | | | | | | 5.49 |
| Benin | 7837.61 | 11079.37 | 9815.42 | 10609.24 | 16317.83 | 5953.57 | | 19836.89 | 5668.03 |
| | 2.80 | 3.86 | 3.33 | 3.50 | 5.25 | 1.87 | | 5.90 | 1.64 |
| Burkina Faso | 4222.22 | 5494.71 | 8119.16 | 10619.75 | 8934.11 | 11430.36 | 10414.31 | 15536.59 | 14208.16 |
| | 0.80 | 1.02 | 1.48 | 1.90 | 1.57 | 1.97 | 1.76 | 2.57 | 2.31 |
| Burundi | 3045.58 | 1825.40 | 2002.34 | 7144.96 | 2418.60 | 3748.21 | 5204.66 | 4015.24 | 5269.39 |
| | 0.89 | 0.51 | 0.55 | 1.92 | 0.64 | 0.97 | 1.32 | 1.00 | 1.28 |
| Cameroon | 19660.97 | 26719.58 | 24455.61 | 27294.12 | 25281.01 | 31862.50 | 41432.61 | 46416.16 | 55933.33 |
| | 2.86 | 3.79 | 3.38 | 3.67 | 3.29 | 4.02 | 5.07 | 5.50 | 6.43 |
| Cent. Af. Repub. | 3088.32 | 3402.12 | 3542.06 | 3901.26 | 4624.03 | 3826.79 | 3134.78 | 4878.05 | 6242.18 |
| | 1.59 | 1.73 | 1.77 | 1.92 | 2.21 | 1.78 | 1.42 | 2.17 | 2.73 |
| Chad | 3905.98 | 4857.14 | 3792.06 | 4304.62 | | | | | |
| | 1.03 | 1.25 | 0.96 | 1.07 | | | | | |
| Congo | 9712.25 | 10478.84 | 7544.39 | 9329.83 | 7736.43 | 15548.21 | 17981.70 | 16272.87 | 25691.16 |
| | 7.63 | 8.02 | 5.63 | 6.78 | 5.45 | 10.63 | 11.92 | 10.46 | 16.01 |
| Cote d'Ivoire | 27669.52 | 37148.15 | 36731.31 | 46115.55 | 44116.28 | 42933.93 | 76036.61 | 71413.11 | |
| | 4.91 | 6.21 | 5.78 | 6.83 | 6.26 | 5.84 | 9.91 | 8.92 | |
| Ethiopia | 14390.31 | 18248.68 | 18509.35 | 22651.26 | 17864.34 | 27212.50 | 3467.55 | 26967.99 | 13010.88 |
| | 0.47 | 0.58 | 0.58 | 0.69 | 0.53 | 0.78 | 0.10 | 0.73 | 0.34 |
| Gabon | 2871.79 | 3761.90 | | 6863.45 | 10271.32 | 17687.50 | 10633.94 | 17346.04 | 20646.26 |
| | 2.96 | 3.83 | | 6.84 | 10.11 | 17.19 | 10.20 | 16.40 | 19.22 |
| Gambia | 1837.61 | 2291.01 | 2042.06 | 2577.73 | 2645.35 | 2137.50 | | | |
| | 3.79 | 4.63 | 3.97 | 4.81 | 4.75 | 3.69 | | | |

Table 1-12 (continued)

| Country | 1981 | 1982 | 1983 | 1984 | 1985 | 1986 | 1987 | 1988 | 1989 |
|---|---|---|---|---|---|---|---|---|---|
| Angola | 75074.07<br>9.65 | | | | | | | | |
| Benin | | 9840.41<br>2.67 | | | | | | | |
| Burkina Faso | | 12485.65<br>1.96 | 10404.58<br>1.61 | | | | | | |
| Burundi | 14818.52<br>2.37 | 3766.93<br>0.87 | 4945.47<br>1.11 | 4553.13<br>0.99 | 5900.00<br>1.25 | 10511.72<br>2.16 | 6308.35<br>1.26 | 6646.79<br>1.29 | 7268.01<br>1.37 |
| Cameroon | 0.87 | 46706.08<br>5.04 | | | | | | | |
| Cent. Af.<br>Repub. | | | | | | | | | |
| Chad | | | | | | | | | |
| Congo | | | 17415.49<br>9.80 | 20392.71<br>11.20 | 21267.00<br>11.32 | 22634.77<br>12.66 | | | |
| Cote d'Ivoire | 70240.74<br>8.06 | 64576.35<br>7.11 | 60379.50<br>6.37 | | 58938.00<br>5.83 | | | | |
| Ethiopia | 28524.69<br>0.74 | 21353.62<br>0.54 | 24441.66<br>0.60 | 25277.08<br>0.60 | 22847.00<br>0.54 | 31703.13<br>0.71 | 2649.91<br>0.62 | 19588.07<br>0.41 | |
| Gabon | 16851.85<br>15.45 | 17601.61<br>15.89 | 13979.28<br>12.40 | | | | | | |
| Gambia | | | | | | | | | |

| Country | 1972 | 1973 | 1974 | 1975 | 1976 | 1977 | 1978 | 1979 | 1980 |
|---|---|---|---|---|---|---|---|---|---|
| Ghana | 14584.05 | 42825.40 | 45546.73 | 39195.38 | 30674.42 | 30925.00 | 26557.40 | 30628.05 | 31111.56 |
| | 1.60 | 4.60 | 4.70 | 3.93 | 2.99 | 2.93 | 2.45 | 2.74 | 2.71 |
| Guinea-Bissau | | | | 1063.03 | 1207.36 | 1460.71 | 708.82 | 1696.65 | 1160.54 |
| | | | | 2.01 | 2.28 | 2.71 | 1.29 | 3.03 | 1.49 |
| Kenya | 28601.14 | 29791.01 | 42824.77 | 37380.25 | 30990.31 | 43958.93 | 56730.45 | 45810.98 | 58416.33 |
| | 2.34 | 2.35 | 3.25 | 2.73 | 2.17 | 2.97 | 3.68 | 2.86 | 3.51 |
| Liberia | 5660.97 | 8878.31 | 9119.16 | 8676.47 | 9007.75 | 12500.00 | 13748.75 | 14980.18 | 11780.95 |
| | 3.91 | 5.95 | 5.94 | 5.48 | 5.51 | 7.39 | 7.86 | 8.28 | 6.30 |
| Madagascar | 18507.12 | 20608.47 | 23997.66 | 24957.98 | 26645.35 | 27223.21 | 30798.67 | 34980.18 | 3191.84 |
| | 2.59 | 2.82 | 3.20 | 3.25 | 3.38 | 3.37 | 3.72 | 4.12 | 0.37 |
| Malawi | 4202.28 | 5026.46 | 7014.02 | 6810.92 | 4457.36 | 4930.36 | 6322.80 | 8408.54 | 11669.39 |
| | 0.88 | 1.02 | 1.38 | 1.31 | 0.83 | 0.89 | 1.10 | 1.42 | 1.91 |
| Mali | 7276.35 | | 7859.81 | 13821.43 | 9011.63 | 8557.14 | 10203.00 | 6615.85 | 7794.56 |
| | 1.34 | | 1.37 | 2.35 | 1.50 | 1.38 | 1.61 | 1.01 | 1.16 |
| Mauritaria | 2381.77 | | | | | | | | |
| | 1.85 | | | | | | | | |
| Mauritius | 6156.70 | 6439.15 | 6850.47 | 9432.77 | 7445.74 | 11330.36 | 10833.61 | | 10953.74 |
| | 7.22 | 7.44 | 7.80 | 10.59 | 8.24 | 12.36 | 11.65 | | 11.45 |
| Mozambique | 23598.29 | 31674.60 | 29563.08 | 20344.54 | | | | | |
| | 2.70 | 3.50 | 3.15 | 2.09 | | | | | |
| Niger | 3413.11 | 3489.42 | 4028.04 | 2638.66 | 3498.06 | | 5570.72 | 9358.23 | 8835.37 |
| | 0.78 | 0.77 | 0.87 | 0.55 | 0.71 | | 1.07 | 1.74 | 1.60 |
| Nigeria | 138076.92 | 158481.48 | 174324.77 | 293193.28 | 331011.63 | 364223.21 | 421925.12 | 336867.38 | |
| | 1.99 | 2.22 | 2.39 | 3.92 | 4.31 | 4.64 | 5.24 | 4.08 | |

**Table 1-12 (continued)**

| Country | 1981 | 1982 | 1983 | 1984 | 1985 | 1986 | 1987 | 1988 | 1989 |
|---|---|---|---|---|---|---|---|---|---|
| Ghana | 14435.80 | 9408.73 | | | | | | | |
| | 1.21 | 0.77 | | | | | | | |
| Guinea-Bissau | | | | | | | | | |
| Kenya | 48838.27 | 37533.87 | 32246.46 | 28816.67 | 28410.00 | 39339.84 | 44042.69 | | |
| | 2.81 | 2.07 | 1.71 | 1.47 | 1.39 | 1.86 | 1.92 | | |
| Liberia | 11058.02 | 5109.07 | 6706.65 | 7138.54 | | | | | |
| | 5.72 | 2.56 | 3.26 | 3.34 | | | | | |
| Madagascar | 18861.73 | 10783.01 | 10403.49 | 9359.38 | 7947.00 | 12456.05 | | | |
| | 2.11 | 1.17 | 1.10 | 0.95 | 0.78 | 1.18 | | | |
| Malawi | 7525.93 | 6786.45 | 7272.63 | 4694.79 | 5344.00 | | | | |
| | 1.19 | 1.04 | 1.08 | 0.68 | 0.75 | | | | |
| Mali | | 12819.75 | | | | | | | |
| | | 1.81 | | | | | | | |
| Mauritania | | | | | | | | | |
| Mauritius | 8143.21 | 8080.37 | 7196.29 | 6203.13 | 6321.00 | 7535.16 | 11201.14 | 14166.97 | |
| | 8.38 | 8.22 | 7.25 | 6.14 | 6.20 | 7.32 | 10.77 | 13.15 | |
| Mozambique | | | | | | | | | |
| Niger | 8238.27 | | | | | | | | |
| | 1.44 | | | | | | | | |
| Nigeria | 767138.27 | 393733.64 | 292768.81 | 166569.79 | 187274.00 | 141200.20 | | | |
| | 8.76 | 4.35 | 3.13 | 1.72 | 1.88 | 1.44 | | | |

| Country | 1972 | 1973 | 1974 | 1975 | 1976 | 1977 | 1978 | 1979 | 1980 |
|---|---|---|---|---|---|---|---|---|---|
| Rwanda | 1965.81 | 1637.57 | 3287.38 | 3079.83 | 3019.38 | 4355.36 | 4805.32 | 3618.90 | 4515.65 |
|  | 0.50 | 0.40 | 0.78 | 0.71 | 0.67 | 0.94 | 1.00 | 0.73 | 0.88 |
| Senegal | 786.32 | 748.68 | 14266.36 | 20605.04 | 17174.42 | 20417.86 | 3357.74 | 4245.43 | 2937.41 |
|  | 0.17 | 0.16 | 2.94 | 4.15 | 3.37 | 3.90 | 0.62 | 0.77 | 0.52 |
| Seychelles |  | 518.52 | 626.17 | 659.66 | 674.42 | 780.36 | 758.74 | 913.11 | 2142.86 |
|  |  | 8.64 | 10.44 | 10.99 | 11.24 | 13.01 | 12.65 | 15.22 | 34.01 |
| Sierra Leone | 8113.96 | 10050.26 | 10369.16 | 7157.56 | 7895.35 |  |  |  |  |
|  | 2.78 | 3.40 | 3.45 | 2.35 | 2.55 |  |  |  |  |
| Somalia | 4760.68 | 15719.58 | 8974.30 | 8426.47 | 8596.90 | 13464.29 | 5289.52 | 8597.56 | 8223.13 |
|  | 1.28 | 4.09 | 2.26 | 2.05 | 2.04 | 3.11 | 1.19 | 1.89 | 1.76 |
| Sudan | 37658.12 | 39214.29 | 34964.95 | 58485.29 | 47968.99 | 55296.43 | 60787.02 | 46082.32 | 51005.44 |
|  | 2.55 | 2.58 | 2.23 | 3.61 | 2.87 | 3.21 | 3.42 | 2.51 | 2.69 |
| Tanzania | 22128.21 | 29735.45 | 35049.07 | 57539.92 | 28182.17 | 29832.14 | 64004.99 | 37996.95 | 42991.84 |
|  | 1.53 | 1.99 | 2.27 | 3.61 | 1.71 | 1.75 | 3.64 | 2.09 | 2.29 |
| Togo | 6569.80 | 7563.49 | 7130.84 | 9995.80 | 8222.87 | 9748.21 | 9203.00 | 11282.01 | 14819.05 |
|  | 3.10 | 3.48 | 3.20 | 4.38 | 3.52 | 4.07 | 3.75 | 4.48 | 5.75 |
| Uganda | 9965.81 | 10634.92 | 14644.86 | 12021.01 | 12422.48 |  |  |  |  |
|  | 0.97 | 1.01 | 1.35 | 1.08 | 1.09 |  |  |  |  |
| Zaire | 54792.02 | 63944.44 | 67282.71 | 47189.08 | 34631.78 | 47387.50 | 34647.25 |  |  |
|  | 2.40 | 2.72 | 2.77 | 1.89 | 1.35 | 1.79 | 1.27 |  |  |
| Zambia | 24584.05 | 21722.22 | 22897.20 | 24810.92 | 20406.98 | 23200.00 | 23054.91 | 28376.52 |  |
|  | 5.56 | 4.76 | 4.87 | 5.12 | 4.08 | 4.50 | 4.34 | 5.18 |  |
| Zimbabwe |  |  |  |  | 20269.38 | 20423.21 | 23585.69 | 26608.23 | 24586.39 |
|  |  |  |  |  | 3.26 | 3.19 | 3.58 | 3.92 | 3.52 |

# Table 1-12 (continued)

| Country | 1981 | 1982 | 1983 | 1984 | 1985 | 1986 | 1987 | 1988 | 1989 |
|---|---|---|---|---|---|---|---|---|---|
| Rwanda | | | 3937.84 | 5341.67 | 4984.00 | 6074.22 | 37004.74 | | |
| | | | 0.69 | 0.91 | 0.83 | 0.96 | 5.35 | | |
| Senegal | 3445.68 | | | | | 26735.35 | | | |
| | 0.59 | | | | | 3.97 | | | |
| Seychelles | 1495.06 | 1060.85 | 912.76 | 778.13 | 1096.00 | 957.03 | 1346.30 | | |
| | 23.36 | 16.58 | 14.26 | 11.97 | 16.86 | 14.50 | 20.40 | | |
| Sierra Leone | | | 2859.32 | 1722.92 | | | | | |
| | | | 0.82 | 0.48 | | | | | |
| Somalia | 4491.36 | | | | | | | | |
| | 0.93 | | | | | | | | |
| Sudan | 47760.49 | 23253.73 | | | | | | | |
| | 2.44 | 1.15 | | | | | | | |
| Tanzania | 31732.10 | | | 27376.04 | 21647.00 | 22251.95 | 25141.37 | | |
| | 1.64 | | | 1.27 | 0.97 | 0.99 | 1.08 | | |
| Togo | 14945.68 | 11257.18 | 8677.21 | 8940.63 | 8800.00 | 16552.73 | 14166.98 | 15597.25 | |
| | 5.62 | 4.10 | 3.06 | 3.04 | 2.90 | 5.42 | 4.50 | 4.73 | |
| Uganda | | | | | | | | | |
| Zaire | | | | | | | | | |
| Zambia | | | | | | | | | |
| Zimbabwe | 28958.02 | 25803.67 | 17446.02 | 14697.92 | 12917.00 | 15495.12 | 15440.23 | | |
| | 3.99 | 3.42 | 2.22 | 1.82 | 1.54 | 1.84 | 1.79 | | |

[a]The deflator used was the IMF Industrial Country Consumer Price Index.
*Sources*: United Nations (various years); SITC Code #541; Summers and Heston (1988).

1981, pharmaceuticals imports into Zimbabwe have shown a somewhat steady decline, but this may simply reflect increased pharmaceutical manufacturing capability there; Nigeria exhibits a U-shaped, concave time-series with a peak of $8.76 per capita in 1981, but only $1.44 in 1986.

Figures 1-6 and 1-7 convey a better time-series feel for these data.[13] In Figure 1-6 the upper line is the simple average for each year for all of the countries for which data were available in the year; a trend line also runs through these data. Because population size varies so much between the countries, the lower line in Figure 1-6 shows a population-weighted time series for each year for all of the countries for which data were available in that year; a trend line also runs through these population-weighted data. What is interesting about Figure 1-6 is how different the simple-average trend is from the population-weighted trend. The population-weighted trend is lower than the simple average trend. Both trends peak in 1979, but the simple-average trend shows only a slight descent to 1986, whereas the population-weighted trend drops very sharply. If pharmaceuticals are as important in the health-care production function, as has often been hypothesized, the population-weighted trend in real pharmaceutical imports in the 1980s is somewhat disturbing.

In Figure 1-7, we have plotted the data for six of the countries for which the more complete time-series data were available (Burundi, Ethiopia, Kenya, Mauritius, Nigeria, and Togo). Examination of the time-series line for Nigeria in Figure 1-7 explains in part why the population-weighted trend line in Figure 1-6 showed such a steep descent in the 1980s; Nigeria has the largest population in Sub-Saharan Africa, and its importation of pharmaceuticals dropped sharply in the 1980s. Three of the other countries in Figure 1-7 (Mauritius, Kenya, and Togo) show declines in pharmaceutical imports. By 1984, pharmaceutical imports in Burundi and Ethiopia showed slight increases up to 1986, and pharmaceutical imports again began to increase in Mauritius in 1985. Without more detailed data on, for example, an increase in internal pharmaceutical manufacturing capacity, it is difficult to generalize beyond saying that it would appear that public and private formal health-care activity somewhat diminished in many countries during the first half of the 1980s.

**Figure 1-6**
**Per Capita Real Pharmaceutical Imports, 1972-1986**
**(U.S. $ 1985)**

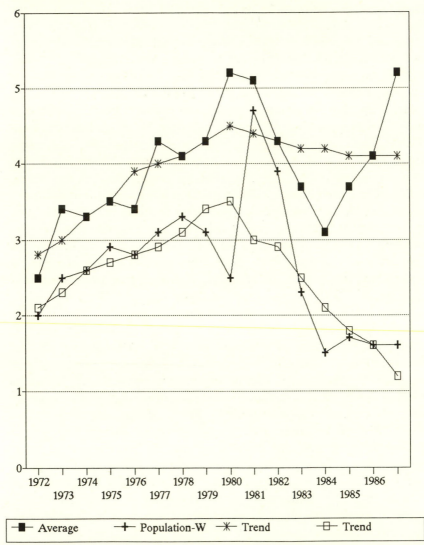

**Figure 1-7**
**Per Capita Real Pharmaceutical Imports, Selected**
**Sub-Saharan Countries, 1972-1986**

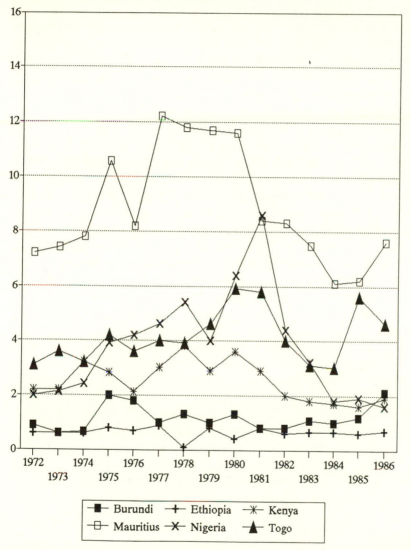

## HEALTH STATUS OUTCOMES OVER TIME

In the previous two sections of this chapter, we showed that, although the majority of countries in Sub-Saharan Africa began the early years of the decade of the 1980s with severe economic problems, the last three or four years of the decade showed a resumption in positive economic growth rates for some of the countries, particularly for countries that were not oil exporters (World Bank and UNDP, 1989).[14]  To the extent that health-care expenditures per capita are a function of GNP per capita (Parkin, McGuire, and Yule, 1987), and to the extent that health status is a function of health expenditures per capita, we would expect to be able to document changes in health status that mirror changes in GNP and health expenditures per capita during the 1980s.

Table 1-13 contains data on infant and child mortality rates for Sub-Saharan Africa.  The first two columns of Table 1-13 show infant mortality rates (IMR) for forty of the countries for the periods 1980-1985, and 1985-1990.  Although there is a wide variation in the IMR between countries, ranging from 23 infant deaths per 1,000 live births in Mauritius in 1985-1990 to 169 in Mali, what is striking about the first two columns of Table 1-13 is that for every country for which the data are available for both time periods, the trend in the IMR is downward.

UNICEF (1992) considers the under-five mortality rate (U5MR) to be the better measure of "human as well as economic progress."[15]  Accordingly, Columns 3 and 4 in Table 1-13 contain data on the under-five mortality rate for the years 1980 and 1990.  Again, the U5MR data show wide variation.  For Angola and Mozambique there was an increase in the U5MR between 1980 and 1990.  For the thirty-eight countries for which the data were available, fifteen had U5MR above 200 and Angola and Mozambique were close to 300.  Only three countries (Botswana, Mauritius, and Zimbabwe) had U5MR that were below 100.  The most important aspect of Columns 3 and 4, though, is that for thirty-six of the thirty-eight countries, the U5MR declined between the two years.

Finally, Column 5 of Table 1-13 shows the maternal mortality rate per 100,000 live births for the period 1980-1990.  We could find no data for showing trends.  The rate ranged from 2,000 in Mali to 99 in Mauritius.  By way of comparison, the rate was three in Australia and five in Sweden.  Herz and Measham (1987) contains good insight into this problem.

**Table 1-13**
**Infant Mortality Rates, 1980-1985 and 1985-1990; Child Mortality Rates, 1980 and 1990; and Maternal Mortality Rates, 1980-1990**

| Country | Infant Mortality Rate 1980-1985 | Infant Mortality Rate 1985-1990 | Under 5 Mortality Rate 1980 | Under 5 Mortality Rate 1990 | Maternal Mortality Rate 1980-1990 |
|---|---|---|---|---|---|
| Angola | 149 | 137 | 261 | 292 | N/A |
| Benin | 120 | 116 | 176 | 147 | 160 |
| Botswana | 50 | 42 | 110 | 85 | 200 |
| Burkina Faso | 149 | 138 | 266 | 228 | 810 |
| Burundi | 103 | 75 | 225 | 192 | N/A |
| Cameroon | 103 | 94 | 175 | 148 | 430 |
| Cent. Af. Repub. | 114 | 104 | 213 | 169 | 600 |
| Chad | 143 | 132 | 254 | 216 | 960 |
| Congo | 124 | 119 | 132 | 110 | 900 |
| Cote D'Ivoire | 105 | 96 | 167 | 136 | N/A |
| Ethiopia | 159 | 137 | 260 | 220 | N/A |
| Gabon | 112 | 103 | 194 | 164 | 190 |
| Gambia | 154 | 143 | N/A | 238 | N/A |
| Ghana | 98 | 90 | 166 | 140 | 1000 |
| Guinea | 157 | 145 | 275 | 237 | 800 |
| Guinea-Bissau | 159 | 145 | 290 | 246 | 700 |
| Kenya | 80 | 72 | 133 | 108 | 170 |
| Lesotho | 111 | 100 | 161 | 129 | N/A |
| Liberia | 145 | 132 | 245 | 205 | N/A |
| Madagascar | 130 | 120 | 216 | 176 | 570 |
| Malawi | 163 | 150 | 299 | 253 | 170 |
| Mali | 179 | 169 | 325 | 284 | 2000 |
| Mauritania | 137 | 127 | 249 | 214 | N/A |
| Mauritius | 28 | 23 | 42 | 28 | 99 |
| Mozambique | 153 | 141 | 269 | 297 | 300 |
| Namibia | 116 | 106 | 202 | 167 | 370 |
| Niger | 146 | 135 | 259 | 221 | 700 |
| Nigeria | 114 | 105 | 198 | 167 | 800 |
| Rwanda | 132 | 122 | 231 | 198 | 210 |
| Senegal | 87 | 80 | 232 | 185 | 600 |
| Sierra Leone | 166 | 154 | 300 | 257 | 450 |
| Somalia | 143 | 132 | 247 | 215 | 1100 |
| Sudan | 118 | 108 | 210 | 172 | 550 |
| Swaziland | 129 | 118 | N/A | 167 | N/A |
| Tanzania | N/A | 115 | 202 | 170 | 340 |
| Togo | 105 | 94 | 184 | 147 | 420 |
| Uganda | 112 | 103 | 186 | 164 | 300 |
| Zaire | 107 | 98 | 163 | 130 | 800 |
| Zambia | 142 | 127 | 146 | 122 | 150 |
| Zimbabwe | N/A | 77 | 116 | 87 | N/A |

*Sources*:  Infant Mortality Rates, Stephens, Box, Vu & Bulatao (1991); Under 5 Mortality Rates and Maternal Mortality Rates, UNICEF (1992).

How can the trends in infant and child mortality be explained? Diop, Hill, and Sirageldin (1991) examined the effects of economic crisis and structural adjustment upon infant and child mortality in Sub-Saharan Africa during the 1980s. They had data on ten countries[16] from the Demographic and Health Surveys (DHS) Program, and more detailed data on the Cote d'Ivoire from the World Bank's Living Standards Measurement Survey (LSMS). In linear regressions for the ten countries, the authors used the following dependent variables: (a) the probability of dying by age five; (b) the probability of dying by age one; and (c) the probability of dying between ages one and five. Regression coefficients for the time-period dummy variables for 1980-1984 and 1985-1989 (relative to the omitted period 1975-1979) showed that the declines in the three probabilities above are similar in size in both periods. Because the time-period regression coefficients on the probability of dying between ages one and five are about 50 percent larger than the time-period coefficients on the probability on dying by age one, the authors hypothesize that, "perhaps . . . child survival interventions expected to have their largest effects in post-infancy have been successful." The authors then disaggregate the data and regress the probability of dying by age five on the same time-period dummy variables and on preadjustment and postadjustment dummies for the following socioeconomic categories: total, urban, rural, no education, primary education, secondary education, rural–no education, and urban–no education. Their ten country results indicate that neither economic difficulties nor resulting adjustment policies had the effect of increasing child mortality at the national level relative to countries not undergoing adjustment, but not necessarily avoiding economic difficulties; the results were, however, consistent with differential effects across socioeconomic groups, such as an increase in child mortality for the urban poor, relative to rural nonpoor children. Using the more detailed data for the Cote d'Ivoire for the mid-1980s, the authors arrive at very similar results of little net effect of structural adjustment upon infant and child mortality at the national level. However, in the Cote d'Ivoire, urban, middle-class children were adversely affected relative to rural children.

Returning to the evidence shown in World Bank and UNDP (1989), these results are not completely surprising. First, during the period of roughly 1984-1988 the Food and Agriculture Organizations (FAO) index for agricultural production in Sub-Saharan Africa has been well above the trend line for the period 1970-88. Second, net disbursements of official development assistance to Sub-Saharan Africa increased substantially during the 1980s; part of this assistance came in the form of the WHO-sponsored, expanded program of immunization (EPI) that was targeted to rural areas.  Third, as explained by Diop, Hill, and Sirageldin (1991) and Vogel (1989), rural people are not much affected by the formal economic sector and by the pattern of subsidies (including formal health care) that exist in most of the Sub-Saharan countries.  If world food prices decline, but weather is good, rural people continue to grow their own food and eat it; their children grow stronger.   If WHO and donors bypass the local national health-care bureaucracy and disburse vaccines in rural areas, more rural children survive.  On the other hand, the urban poor and middle class are much more dependent upon the formal economy and subsidies (see Vogel 1990c for the example of subsidized health insurance for the middle class).  If a structural adjustment program necessitates the abolition of most of the subsidies, the *real* income of urban people falls at an even greater rate than the rate of decline of the formal economy during periods of economic distress, as in the early 1980s.

Diop, Hill, and Sirageldin (1991) hypothesized that the EPI may have contributed to the continuing upward trend in child survival in the 1980s.  Table 1-14 presents data on the percentage of one-year-old children fully immunized against tuberculosis, diphtheria, polio, and measles for 1981 and 1990, and for pregnant women immunized against tetanus for the same two years.  As in Table 1-13, there is a wide variability in EPI for one-year-old children among the countries.  For countries for which data on both years are available, there is only one country (Liberia) where more than one of the immunization rates have actually gone down (three of four); The Congo, Mauritania, Mozambique, and Nigeria each had one of the four decline.  In other countries, immunization rates were 80 percent or better by 1990.  In four countries (Central African Republic, Mauritius, Rwanda, and Tanzania) immunizations against all four diseases were 80 percent or better, and in four other countries (Botswana, Burundi, Malawi, and Sierra Leone) three of the four had 80 percent or better immunization coverage.   In many of the countries, coverage rates approached 80 percent.   By 1990 the rate of immunization coverage for TB was particularly high in many of the countries; eighteen countries had TB immunization coverage that was 90 percent or higher.   In some countries, coverage rates increased dramatically between the two years; Sudan's coverage rate increased from between 1 and 3 percent to better than 55 percent for the four infant indicators.  The data on the immunization of pregnant women against tetanus is difficult to compare

**Table 1-14**

**Percentage of One-Year-Old Children Fully Immunized against Four Diseases and Percentage of Pregnant Women Immunized against Tetanus, 1981 and 1990**

| Country | TB 1981 | TB 1990 | DPT 1981 | DPT 1990 | Polio 1981 | Polio 1990 | Measles 1981 | Measles 1990 | Pregnant Women against Tetnus 1981 | Pregnant Women against Tetnus 1990 |
|---|---|---|---|---|---|---|---|---|---|---|
| Angola | NA | 47 | NA | 23 | NA | 23 | NA | 38 | NA | 26 |
| Benin | NA | 92 | NA | 67 | NA | 67 | NA | 70 | NA | 83 |
| Botswana | 80 | 92 | 64 | 86 | 71 | 82 | 68 | 78 | 32 | 62 |
| Burkina Faso | 16 | 84 | 2 | 37 | 2 | 37 | 23 | 42 | 11 | 76 |
| Burundi | 65 | 97 | 38 | 86 | 6 | 86 | 30 | 75 | 25 | 56 |
| Cameroon | 8 | 76 | 5 | 56 | 5 | 54 | 16 | 56 | NA | 63 |
| Cent. Af. Repub. | 26 | 96 | 12 | 82 | 12 | 82 | 16 | 82 | NA | 87 |
| Chad | NA | 59 | NA | 20 | NA | 20 | NA | 32 | NA | 42 |
| Congo | 92 | 90 | 42 | 79 | 42 | 79 | 49 | 75 | NA | 60 |
| Cote D'Ivoire | 70 | 63 | 42 | 48 | 34 | 48 | 28 | 42 | 25 | 63 |
| Ethiopia | 10 | 57 | 6 | 44 | 7 | 44 | 7 | 37 | NA | 43 |
| Gabon | NA | 96 | NA | 78 | NA | 78 | NA | 76 | NA | 86 |
| Gambia | NA | NA | NA | NA | NA | NA | NA | NA | NA | NA |
| Ghana | 67 | 81 | 22 | 57 | 25 | 56 | 23 | 60 | 11 | 33 |
| Guinea | 4 | 53 | NA | 17 | NA | 17 | 15 | 18 | 5 | 10 |
| Guinea-Bissau | NA | 90 | NA | 38 | NA | 38 | NA | 42 | NA | 44 |
| Kenya | NA | 80 | NA | 74 | NA | 71 | NA | 59 | NA | 37 |
| Lesotho | 81 | 97 | 56 | 76 | 54 | 75 | 49 | 76 | NA | NA |
| Liberia | 87 | 62 | 39 | 28 | 26 | 28 | 99 | 55 | 60 | 20 |
| Madagascar | 25 | 67 | 40 | 46 | NA | 46 | NA | 33 | NA | 60 |
| Malawi | 86 | 97 | 66 | 81 | 68 | 79 | 65 | 80 | NA | 82 |
| Mali | 19 | 82 | NA | 42 | NA | 42 | NA | 43 | 1 | 31 |
| Mauritania | 57 | 75 | 18 | 28 | 18 | 28 | 45 | 33 | 1 | 40 |
| Mauritius | 87 | 94 | 82 | 90 | 82 | 90 | NA | 84 | 1 | 94 |
| Mozambique | 46 | 59 | 56 | 46 | 32 | 46 | 32 | 58 | NA | 25 |
| Namibia | NA | 85 | NA | 53 | NA | 53 | NA | 41 | NA | 50 |
| Niger | 28 | 50 | 6 | 13 | 6 | 13 | 19 | 21 | 3 | 44 |
| Nigeria | 23 | 96 | 24 | 57 | 24 | 57 | 55 | 54 | 11 | 58 |
| Rwanda | 51 | 92 | 17 | 84 | 15 | 83 | 42 | 83 | 5 | 87 |
| Senegal | NA | 92 | NA | 60 | NA | 66 | NA | 59 | NA | 45 |
| Sierra Leone | 35 | 98 | 15 | 83 | 13 | 83 | 28 | 75 | 10 | 77 |
| Somalia | 3 | 31 | 2 | 18 | 2 | 18 | 3 | 30 | 5 | 5 |
| Sudan | 3 | 73 | 1 | 62 | 1 | 62 | 1 | 57 | 1 | 14 |
| Swaziland | NA | NA | NA | NA | NA | NA | NA | NA | NA | NA |
| Tanzania | 78 | 93 | 58 | 85 | 49 | 82 | 76 | 83 | 36 | 42 |
| Togo | 44 | 94 | 9 | 61 | 9 | 61 | 47 | 57 | 57 | 81 |
| Uganda | 18 | 99 | 9 | 77 | 8 | 77 | 22 | 74 | 20 | 31 |
| Zaire | 34 | 65 | 18 | 32 | 18 | 31 | 23 | 31 | NA | 29 |
| Zambia | 72 | 97 | 44 | 79 | 77 | 78 | 21 | 76 | NA | 68 |
| Zimbabwe | 64 | 71 | 39 | 73 | 38 | 72 | 56 | 69 | NA | 60 |

*Source*:  UNICEF (1992).

for the two years, because data for 1981 are missing for twenty-two of the countries, but the data that do exist for the two years, again, mostly show large increases in immunization rates for pregnant women.

In order to test the causal connection between changes in child and infant mortality rates,[17] and changes in immunization prevalence, we first ran two regressions for the countries for which all of the necessary data were available. The specification of a relative change model was as follows:

$$\Delta p_1 = a + b\Delta I_1$$

$$\Delta p_5 = a + b\Delta I_1$$

where

$\Delta p_1$ = the average annual downward change in the infant mortality rate between the two periods 1980-1985 and 1985-1990,

$\Delta p_5$ = the average annual downward change in the under-five mortality rate between 1980-1990,

$\Delta I_1$ = the average annual change in the one-year old child immunization rate between 1981-1990.[18]

We would expect the coefficient on $\Delta I_1$ to be negative, or, the higher the average annual rate of change in the immunization index, the higher the average annual rate of downward change in the $p_1$ and $p_5$.

Another specification of the model could be an absolute levels model:

$$p_{1t} = a + bI_{1t}$$

$$p_{5t} = a + bI_{1t}$$

In this case, we double the number of observations for each country, where $p_{11}$ is 1980-1985 and $p_{12}$ is 1985-1990, $p_{51}$ is 1980 and $p_{52}$ is 1990, and $I_{11}$ is 1981 and $I_{12}$ is 1990.[19] We would expect the coefficient on $I_{1t}$ to be negative, or, the higher the immunization index, the lower would be $p_{1t}$ and $p_{5t}$.

Table 1-15 summarizes the regression results.  The eight models in Table 1-15 were run in the double-log form so that elasticities of the IMR and the U5MR with respect to the immunization rate index (IRI) could be directly calculated.[20]  In equations 1 and 2, the two relative change models explain very little about changes in the IMR and the U5MR with respect to changes in the IRI.  In equation 1, the coefficient does not have the expected sign, nor is it statistically significant; in equation 2, the coefficient has the expected sign, but is not statistically significant.  The absolute-levels models in equations 3 through 8 show more interesting results.  In equations 3 and 4, where the data for the two time periods are pooled, the coefficients have the expected sign and are statistically significant.  Equation 3 indicates that a 10 percent increase in the IRI would cause a 1.2 percent decrease in the IMR; equation 4 indicates that a 10 percent increase in the IRI would cause a 1.8 percent decrease in the U5MR.  When the data are broken down by time period in equations 5 through 8, the coefficients all have the expected sign, but are only statistically significant for 1985-1990 for the IMR (equation 6) and for 1990 for the U5MR (equation 8).  Equation 6 indicates that a 10 percent increase in the IRI would cause a 4.1 percent decrease in the IMR, while equation 8 shows that a 10 percent increase in the IRI would cause a 5.1 percent decrease in the U5MR.  Table 1-14 showed the sometimes dramatic increases in one-year-old immunization rates between 1981 and 1990 (e.g., Sudan, Burkina Faso, Cameroon).  Perhaps the meaning of the regression results in equations 6 and 8 is that the higher immunization saturation rates reached in the last half of the 1980s are now having an appreciable effect upon the IMR and the U5MR.

While these changes in the infant mortality rate and the under-five mortality rate over time do indicate progress in health status outcomes for Sub-Saharan Africa, what other indicators of progress or lack of progress can be found?  The contents of Tables 1-16 and 1-17 shed some light on the question.  In Table 1-16, trends of various measures are given for all of the Sub-Saharan countries combined.  Thus, life expectancy at birth in Sub-Saharan Africa increased from 40.0 years in 1960 to 51.8 years in 1991, or a 29.5 percent gain over the thirty-one-year-period.  The average under-five mortality rate fell from 284 to 179 per thousand live births between 1960-1989, or a 37.0 percent decline.  The percentage of the population with access to safe water increased from 27 percent in 1975-1980 to 40 percent in 1988, for a 48.1 percentage increase.  Daily calorie supply declined slightly from 92 percent of daily requirements to 91 percent, for a 1.1 percent

# Table 1-15
## Regression Results: Infant and Child Mortality Rates and Immunization Coverage

| Equation | Constant[a] | Coefficient[a] | $R^2$ | N |
|---|---|---|---|---|
| (1) Log change in IMR 1980-85 and 1985-1990 = constant + Log change in IRI 1981 and 1990 | -.2407 + 01 (.1936 + 02) | .6270 - 02 (.1197-00) | 0[b] | 23 |
| (2) Log change in U5MR 1980-1990 = constant + Log Change in IRI 1981-1990 | .5103 - 00 (.7493 + 01) | -.4273 - 01 (.1497 +01) | .051 | 24 |
| (3) Log IMR 1980-85 and 1985-1990 = constant + Log IRI 1981 and 1990 | .5351 + 01 (.2091 + 02) | -.1238 - 00 (.2498 + 01) | .079 | 62 |
| (4) Log U5MR 1980 and 1990 = constant + Log IRI 1981 and 1990 | .6086 + 01 (.2110 + 02) | -.1753 - 00 (.3143 + 01) | .1235 | 64 |
| (5) Log IMR 1980-1985 = constant + Log IRI 1981 | .5017 + 01 (.2062 + 02) | -.4772 - 01 (.9086 - 00) | 0[b] | 24 |
| (6) Log IMR 1985-1990 = constant + Log IRI 1990 | .6900 - 00 (.8639 + 01) | -.4089 - 00 (.2801 + 01) | .156 | 38 |
| (7) Log U5MR 1980 = constant + Log IRI 1981 | .5706 + 01 (.2256 + 02) | -.8899 - 01 (.1653 + 01) | .065 | 26 |
| (8) Log U5MR 1990 = constant + Log IRI 1990 | .7880 + 01 (.8518 + 01) | -.5060 - 00 (.2992 + 01) | .177 | 38 |

[a]Numbers in parentheses are T values.
[b]0 when adjusted for degrees of freedom.

**Table 1-16**
**Health Status Trends:  Sub-Saharan Africa**

| Category | Years | Measure | Percent Change |
|---|---|---|---|
| Life expectancy at birth | 1960 | 40.0 years | |
| | 1991 | 51.8 years | +29.5 |
| Under-five mortality rate | 1960 | 284/1,000 | |
| | 1989 | 179/1,000 | -37.0 |
| Population with access to safe water | 1975-80 | 27% | |
| | 1988 | 40% | +48.1 |
| Daily calorie supply | 1965 | 92% | |
| | 1985 | 91% | -1.1 |
| Adult literacy rate | 1970 | 27% | |
| | 1985 | 45% | +66.7 |
| Combined primary and secondary enrollment ratio | 1970 | 26% | |
| | 1987 | 45% | +73.1 |
| Real GDP per capita | 1960 | $ 640 | |
| | 1988 | $1,180 | +84.4 |
| One-year-olds immunized | 1981 | 30% | |
| | 1989 | 54% | +80.0 |
| Food import dependency ratio | 1971 | 13.1% | |
| | 1988 | 10.0% | -23.7 |

*Source*:  UNDP (1991).

**Table 1-17**
**Trends in Basic Human Gaps:  North versus Sub-Saharan Africa**[a]

| Category | Years | Measure | Percent Change |
|---|---|---|---|
| Life expectancy at | | | |
| birth | 1960 | 58 | |
| | 1990 | 70 | +20.7 |
| Under-five mortality | | | |
| rate | 1960 | 16 | |
| | 1989 | 11 | -31.3 |
| Daily calorie supply | 1966 | 74 | |
| | 1986 | 69 | -6.8 |
| Combined primary and | | | |
| secondary enrolment | | | |
| ratio | 1970 | 30 | |
| | 1988 | 47 | +56.7 |
| Real GDP per capita | 1960 | 14 | |
| | 1987 | 8 | -42.9 |

[a]The measures in the Table are expressed in relation to the North average, which is indexed to equal 100.  The smaller the measure, the larger the gap between the North and Sub-Saharan Africa.
*Source*:  UNDP (1991).

decrease between 1965 and 1985.  The adult literacy rate increased from 27 percent in 1970 to 45 percent in 1985, or, a 66.7 percent increase.  The combined primary and secondary enrollment ratio increased from 26 percent to 45 percent between 1970 and 1987, for a 73.1 percent increase.  Real GDP per capita changed from $640 to $1,180 between 1960-1988, or an 84.4 percent increase.  The percentage of one-year-olds immunized increased from 30 percent to 54 percent between 1981 and 1989, for a percentage increase of 80.0 percent in only eight years.  Finally, the food import dependency ratio dropped from 13.1 percent of food produced locally to 10 percent in 1988, for a 23.7 percent decline.  Therefore, with the exception of the daily calorie supply measure, which is worrisome because of the very real problem of childhood malnutrition and learning disabilities (see Selowsky and Taylor, 1973), all of the trend indicators in Table 1-16 are highly encouraging. Two caveats remain, however.  The one is the fallacy of the average which was discussed in the preceding section of this chapter with respect to population weights.  The second caveat comes in the form of a question:  are these rates of progress rapid enough?  The contents of Table 1-17 help to partially resolve the question.

In Table 1-17, Sub-Saharan Africa is compared to the countries of the North, the industrialized, higher income countries.  The measure used is an index number, which is expressed in relation to the North average, which is set at 100.  The smaller the measure in Table 1-17, the larger the gap between the North and Sub-Saharan Africa.  This then is one comparative measure of the rapidity of the rate of progress for health status in Sub-Saharan Africa, and the results are mixed.  In 1960, life expectancy at birth in the Sub-Sahara was only 58 percent of what it was in the North.  By 1990, it had reached 70 percent, for a 20.7 percent gain.  Even though the under-five mortality rate has improved in Sub-Saharan Africa, it has not done so as rapidly as in the North between 1960-1989.  In 1960, the rate was 16 percent of the North; by 1989 it fell to 11 percent (or a 31.3 percent decline).  Relative daily calorie supply has also fallen relative to the North; in 1966, it was 74 percent and in 1986 only 69 percent, for a 6.8 percent decline.  The largest relative increase was for the combined primary and secondary enrollment ratio that went from 30 percent to 47 percent between 1970-1988, or a 56.7 percent increase.  Finally the gap in real GNP per capita widened between 1960-1987; the index stood at 14 in 1960 and declined to 8 by 1987, for a 42.9 percent decrease.

## CONCLUSION

While the contents of this chapter give cause for concern, they also give cause for optimism for Sub-Saharan Africa. In general, GNP per capita grew more slowly in the 1980s than it did in the two previous postindependence decades. While some countries experienced a great deal of difficulty in this respect, others did not. Likewise, the various measures of government health expenditures and total pharmaceutical imports used in this chapter show a downward trend on a real per capita basis for some of the countries, but not for all of them. The analysis for Table 1-11 vividly shows how welfare interpretations for Sub-Saharan Africa as a whole can change if one extremely large-in-population country, such as Nigeria, is included or withheld from the data set. Making comparisons among countries is somewhat analogous to making interpersonal comparisons of utility or welfare among different families. If the country or the family is the unit of comparison, the comparison ignores population size among countries or among families. From a policy perspective, the resource requirements for aid, or the welfare implications, can be quite different, depending upon the size of the country, or the size of the family. On the population-weighted basis, Table 1-11 shows that health-care welfare in Sub-Saharan Africa was lower in 1985 than it was in 1980, but higher than it was in 1975, *if* indeed government health expenditures per capita are the appropriate measure of health-care welfare. Real per capita pharmaceutical imports also seem to have declined in the 1980s, so that one might reasonably infer that private-sector health-care activity has also diminished. Obviously, increases in GDP growth, or in the case of Nigeria, increase in oil prices which would cause GDP to grow, would solve this dilemma. But what can be said about the other major policy variables, such as population growth and efficiency within the health-care sector itself?

Population in Sub-Saharan Africa has continued to grow at a fairly high, constant rate during the 1970s and the 1980s, even though more and more of these countries have become interested in population programs during the late 1980s. As these population programs take hold and begin to mature, and as the education of women continues to make progress, we should expect to see a slow diminution in the rate of population growth. However, because one of the major causes of population growth is attitudinal among males, and because attitudes only change slowly over time, there should not be much decrease in the rate of national population growth during the rest of the twentieth century and on into the early part of the twenty-first century.

One consequence of rapid population growth, when the growth of GDP and health expenditures does not keep pace, is to dilute the amount of funds spent on health care. The data show a decrease in the rate of growth of per capita government health-care expenditures for some countries in the 1980s, when country averages are studied. This trend in government health expenditures would not cause concern (1) if the reduction were caused by greater efficiencies;[21] and/or (2) if private-sector health care were being substituted for public-sector care, especially in rural areas, and/or (3) if health-care expenditures did not have much effect on health status or on productivity, because they are an inefficient kind of health expenditure, given the prevailing epidemiology. On the first score, there is evidence that more and more countries in Africa are adopting essential drug programs (WHO, 1988), but Akin, Birdsall, and De Ferranti (1987) show that many inefficiencies continue to persist in these countries. With regard to the second possibility, the private health-care sector plays an important role in many of these countries,[22] but not in rural or poor areas (except for missions and traditional care), and the data on pharmaceutical imports reported herein do not show much evidence that substitution has taken place during the recent economic downturn, if indeed, total pharmaceutical imports are a sufficient proxy for total health-sector activity.[23] With respect to the third possibility, Gwatkin (1983) was hard-pressed to find any direct evidence of the relationship between health expenditures and productivity in the large number of empirical studies that he reviewed; however, he did find evidence that *better nutrition* did seem to increase productivity, and recommended "an examination of the long-range interactions between health improvements and other factors of production in producing further output." If past and present government and for-profit private health expenditures in these countries have been mainly directed at the few, in urban hospital settings and for curative care, then a fall in these kinds of expenditures should not have much effect upon the health of the population as a whole. Patel (1989) notes that social indicators (for health and education) have shown much greater improvement in the developing countries than have the economic indicators (GDP, GDP per capita, etc.), but does not readily find an explanation. Experienced observers and analysts of the health-status situation in Africa have anecdotally concluded that, perhaps, health indicators have improved because of better nutrition in the 1970s and 1980s, and also, possibly because of the large expansion of immunization programs during the latter part of the 1980s.  Better sanitation and water supply may have played a secondary role with curative health care, per se, playing a distinct third or fourth-level role.  If this is all true, then it becomes much more important to ascertain what has happened to nutrition and immunization expenditures during the 1980s.

As has been shown in this chapter, there has been a remarkable increase in the percentage of children immunized against the four major epidemiological killers in the majority of these countries, as well as a large increase in the percentage of pregnant women immunized against tetanus.  There has also been a large increase (48.1 percent) in the percentage of the population with access to safe water.  On the other hand, the gap between North and Sub-Saharan Africa in daily calorie supply has widened, and the daily calorie supply in 1985 was still only 91 percent of the required.  Nevertheless, for all of the countries, the infant mortality rate, the under-five mortality rate, and life expectancy at birth continue to improve.  To the extent that nutrition expenditures have nothing to do with health-care expenditures, but are simply a function of greater food availability and quality, which themselves are functions of the growth of GDP, we should not really be concerned with short-term downturns in health expenditures that are often "wasted" on curative care for the few (in a cost-efficient sense), but we should be concerned with downturns in the GDP, on the causes of these downturns, and on the distribution of GDP.  And yet, even this conclusion could be tempered, because Hill and Pebley (1988) "find little basis to conclude that there has been a general slowdown in the pace of [child] mortality decline in the early-1980s as a consequence of economic conditions or other circumstance."[24]

If, on the other hand, the greater percentage of these per capita health expenditure downturns fall on that part of the health budget that is already technically disproportionately small, or on that part of the population that was already underserved (using some definition of equity) in the past, then the marginal health and well-being effect of these expenditure downturns could be large for some segments of the population.  As an example of the former, a U.S. $1 million downturn, directed at a pharmaceutical budget that was already only 7 percent of a U.S. $50 million total health budget, would probably have more negative health consequences (from a technical efficiency point of view) than the same U.S. $1 million downturn directed at the other 93 percent of the total health budget.  Likewise, a U.S. $1 million downturn directed at the 11 percent rural primary health-care portion of a total U.S. $50 million health budget should have a greater effect on health-care technical efficiency, at the margin, than if the downturn were directed at the 50 to 70 percent of the total health budget that urban hospital care receives.

Obviously, in order to have the wherewithal to finance better nutrition, more immunizations, and more appropriate health care, these countries desperately need greater economic growth per capita, in the long run.  In the short run, more donor assistance or loans would act as a substitute for an immediate spurt in economic growth, but over the intermediate run, donor forbearance may be a function of seeing some promise of economic growth per capita, as may be the willingness of lenders to lend.  De Ferranti (1985) shows that, if anything, donor assistance to the health sector has declined in recent years, and he sees no reason to be optimistic on that account for the next five to ten years.  We shall return to this point again in a later chapter.

What this means, then, is that the countries in Sub-Saharan Africa will have to make greater efforts to create financial and managerial efficiencies in the health-care and related sectors.  We now turn our attention to a more in-depth analysis of some of the inefficiencies that presently exist, and ways of creating greater efficiencies in the health-care sector.

## NOTES

1.  In the jargon of welfare economics, if human pain is additive, a famine in Nigeria would cause more human suffering than a famine in Burundi.

2.  Gross Domestic Product (GDP) measures the total value of production originating within the geographic boundaries of the country, regardless of whether the factors of production are owned by residents or nonresidents.  Gross National Product (GNP) measures income received by resident factors of production, regardless of where the production takes place.  In this section, we use some GNP comparisons in order to keep the data consistent with the earlier work of Dunlop (1983), and some GDP comparisons in order to be able to use the more recent data of the World Bank and UNDP (1989).

3.  Later in this study, when ODA for health care is analyzed in Chapter 3, a similar lack-of-pattern emerges.  One might expect that the countries with the worst health status, or with the lowest per capita incomes, would receive the most ODA per capita for health care, but they do not (Orivel and Tchicaya, 1988).

4.  The data in Table 1-9 show an MOH percentage of only 1.9 for Nigeria, but this is because *only* Nigerian federal health expenditures are included.  As will be shown shortly, when estimated State and Local Government Authority expenditures are included for Nigeria, total government spending rises appreciably.

5.  This statement assumes that health care expenditures enhance human welfare, either in producing better health (curing) or in producing caring.  See Newhouse (1987) for the distinction between curing and caring.  This type of welfare comparison will be more specifically and empirically treated in the discussion of Table 1-11, "Sub-Saharan Health Welfare Ratios."

6.  These data tell nothing about the distribution of these expenditures within the country, for which some indicatory data will be presented in Chapter 2.

7.  This information will be analyzed in Chapter 3.

8.  The U.N. data (U.N., various years) do not distinguish between public and private imports, but only give totals for each country over time.

9.  While the PPPR adjustment is probably the closest that one can get to the "true real value" of expenditures between countries for comparative purposes, the PPPR has one potential major shortcoming with respect to health expenditures.  The purpose of the PPPR is primarily to reflect the differences in the cost, or value, of labor between countries.  To the extent that health care is labor intensive, the PPPR should make this adjustment rather well.  However, the percentage of the health budget spent on pharmaceuticals varies by country.  Most of these pharmaceuticals are bought on international markets, where the medium of exchange is the U.S. dollar, and where the value of the pharmaceuticals is partially determined by the cost of labor in the developed country of manufacture.  To the extent that the developing country budget contains the value of pharmaceuticals purchased abroad, to that extent does the PPPR adjustment convert foreign-labor (developed country) value-added into local-labor value-added in the developing country health budget.

10.   However, even these data must be read with caution.   For example, the data on Nigeria are misleading with respect to amounts spent by State and Local Government Authority governments.   Because of its federal governmental system, many states in Nigeria spend even more on a per capita basis than does the Nigerian federal government. Subsequent pages (and see Table 1-11) will make an effort to deal with this very real problem that the Nigerian data pose for making welfare judgments for Sub-Saharan Africa.

11.   Even though the work of Over and Denton represents a good start, it is not even clear that Nigeria should be considered as a "country" for international African comparisons.   Some of the states in Nigeria have larger populations than many of the countries of Africa. There is a wide variation in state and LGA funding capacity and effort. Therefore, for example, a family living in Imo State in Nigeria may have more total government funds for health spent on it than a family living in Senegal, but the family living in Senegal may have more spent on it than a family living in Anambra State in Nigeria.

12.   The data that form most of the basis of these comparisons may be found in Appendix 1.

13.   We only show the data up to 1986, because, for later years, there were too few observations.

14.   This is just one more reason why it is so difficult to make generalizations about Sub-Saharan Africa.   Low worldwide oil prices hurt countries such as Nigeria and Gabon, but benefit the oil-importing countries of the Sub-Sahara such as Ethiopia and Senegal.   Even though Cameroon is an oil exporting country, it had an average annual per capita GNP growth rate of 3.0 percent during the period 1980-1988.

15.   Also, if a person can manage to survive beyond the age of five years, the range of life expectancies between all countries narrows relative to the range of life expectancies at birth.   See Appendix 2.

16.   These were:  Botswana, Ghana, Kenya, Liberia, Mauritania, Senegal, Sudan, Togo, Uganda, and Zaire.   Five of the countries (Botswana, Ghana, Kenya, Senegal, and Togo) are in the process of structural adjustment; the other five countries are not.

17.   The mortality rate, whether infant or age five is the probability of dying between birth and age one or age five.

18.   This is calculated using an unweighted index.   For example, in 1981, Botswana had coverage rates of 80 (TB) + 64 (DPT) + 71 (polio) + 68 (measles) = 283; and in 1990, 92 (TB) + 86 (DPT) + 82 (polio) + 78 (measles) = 338.  The percentage change from 283 to 338

is 19.4 percent, which is an average annual rate of change of 1.9 percent. Likewise, the IMR dropped from 50 to 42 per thousand live births, or 16.0 percent which is an average annual rate of change of 3.2 percent between 1980-85 and 1985-90, with 1982½ and 1987½ as the midpoints.

19. For example, for Botswana, $p_{11} = 50$ and $p_{12} = 42$; $p_{51} = 110$ and $p_{52} = 85$; $I_{11} = 283$ and $I_{12} = 338$.

20. There is no a priori evidence to indicate that a linear or semilog form would be superior to the double-log form.

21. For example, the adoption of a well-managed and essential drugs program could diminish *total* pharmaceutical expenditures, if *quantity* of pharmaceuticals is held constant.

22. Chapter 3 of this study contains a more complete analysis of the role of the private sector.

23. Substitution between public and private health care may be taking place, but it may be masked in the totals data. For example, efficient private-sector purchase and use may be replacing inefficient public-sector purchase and use, causing total expenditures but not total therapeutic power to fall.

24. Hill and Pebley also found, though, that child mortality has declined more slowly in Africa than elsewhere in the developing world in the early 1980s. Gwatkin (1980) comes to a somewhat similar conclusion for the 1970s.

# 2

# Health Resource Efficiency

## INSUFFICIENT SPENDING UPON COST-EFFECTIVE PROGRAMS

The epidemiology of Sub-Saharan Africa is much different than that in developed countries, and yet the pattern of health-care spending in the countries of the Sub-Sahara is very similar to the pattern of health-care spending in developed countries. Table 2-1 shows the percentage distribution of deaths by cause in a "model" developing country, in a "model" developed country, and the average in Organization for Economic Cooperation and Development (OECD) countries. In the model developing country, the overwhelming majority of deaths (43.7 percent) are caused by infectious, parasitic, and respiratory diseases (versus only 10.8 percent in a model developed country and 8.4 percent in the OECD countries). Because life expectancy at birth is lower in developing countries, due to the large percentage of deaths at an early age caused by infectious, parasitic, and respiratory diseases, a larger percentage of the people born do not live long enough to acquire the diseases of middle and older age. That is why cancer and diseases of the circulatory system only account for 18.5 percent of the deaths in the model developing country, whereas they account for 47.4 percent of the deaths in the model developed country, and 69.3 percent of deaths in the OECD countries. Deaths due to traumatic injury are only 3.5 percent of the total in the model developing country, compared to 6.8 percent in the model developed country; the difference of almost 100 percent probably reflects differences in automobile ownership and use. The residual category, "All Causes," accounts for almost the same percentage of deaths in both model types of country.

Table 2-2 shows the pattern of health-care spending in the typical developing country, compared to the pattern of health-care spending in the U.S.[1]

**Table 2-1**
**Percentage Distribution of Deaths by Cause in Three Selected Models**

| Cause of Death | Model Developing Country | Model Developed Country | OECD Countries (Average) |
|---|---|---|---|
| Infectious, parasitic, and respiratory diseases | 43.7 | 10.8 | 8.4 |
| Cancer | 3.7 | 15.2 | 23.1 |
| Diseases of the circulatory system | 14.8 | 32.2 | 46.2 |
| Traumatic injury | 3.5 | 6.8 | 5.2 |
| Other causes | 34.3 | 35.0 | 17.1 |
| All causes | 100.0 | 100.0 | 100.0 |

*Sources*:  Golladay (1980), as constructed from *Population Bulletin of the United Nations*, No. 6 (New York:  United Nations, 1963, pp. 111-112, particularly Table V, 33, and also pp. 106-110 for a description of methods used in constructing these and other models);  Organization for Economic Cooperation and Development (OECD) (1987), Table 15.  The OECD reports injury and poisoning as a single category.  We simply assumed that .75 of injury and   poisoning was traumatic injury for purposes of assembling Table 2-1.

**Table 2-2**
**Composition of Health Spending:  Developing Countries and
United States**

| Services | Percent of Total Expenditure on Health, Developing Countries | Percent of Total Expenditure on Health, U.S., 1988 |
|---|---|---|
| Curative Care | 70 to 87 | 84 |
| 1.  Personal services (care of patients) by health facilities and independent providers, including traditional practitioners. | | |
| 2.  Purchases of medicines. | | |
| Preventive Services:  Patient Related | 10 to 20 | 11 |
| 1.  Maternal and child health clinics, at health facilities. | | |
| 2.  Community health programs (e.g., home visiting). | | |
| Preventive Services:  Other | 3 to 10 | 5 |
| 1.  Disease control programs. | | |
| 2.  Sanitation. | | |
| 3.  Education and promotion of health and hygiene. | | |
| 4.  Control of pests and zoonotic diseases. | | |
| 5.  Monitoring disease patterns. | | |
| Total | 100 | 100 |

*Sources*:    De Ferranti (1985); U.S. Department of Health and Human
Services (1991).

What is striking is how roughly similar these expenditure patterns are, given the great disparity in causes of death between the model developing country and the model developed country, and/or the average for the OECD countries.[2]  Curative care garners the largest share of total health-care expenditures, ranging from 70 to 87 percent in developing countries, while preventive care and public health only receive 13 to 30 percent in developing countries; in the United States, the respective percentages are 84 and 16 percent.  Because of the disparity in mortality patterns in Table 2-1 and the similarity of expenditure patterns in Table 2-2, legitimate questions can be raised about which (of any) expenditure  pattern is more efficient and what does efficiency mean within this context.  These two questions cannot be answered without a more explicit discussion of governmental objectives for the health of the population.

Most Sub-Saharan national health plans are remarkably vague about national objectives for health.  Many of these plans are quite thick in volume of pages, but quantified concrete goals or objectives are rarely, if ever, placed upon paper and ranked by order of national priority.  While no one would deny that health for all is a desirable objective, this objective lacks operational content within the economic context of the existence of scarcity, and the consequent necessity of making choices, at the margin, among equally desirable objectives in producing other consumption and investment goods besides health care.  The ministry of health (MOH), or some higher government body, must decide how it will spend its necessarily limited budget, or increments to that limited budget.  The total spending will be a function of the objectives that are chosen, as will be the components of that spending.  For example, in the United States, one rather vague policy objective has been to "conquer" cancer.  This policy objective has resulted in the expenditure of hundreds of millions of dollars upon cancer centers, which, in turn, has increased the demand for cancer researchers, most of whom have medical degrees and, in addition, usually have a Ph.D. in one of the biological sciences.  At the same time, there are a number of rural counties in the U.S. that do not even have a physician in residence, and black infant mortality rates are twice as high as infant mortality rates for whites.  Had less emphasis and budgetary funds been placed upon training cancer research specialists and providing research laboratories for them, and more emphasis placed upon training primary care physicians, these rural counties would probably have had physicians in residence and/or more nurses and nurse practitioners, while urban areas would have had more prenatal care available.

Infant mortality rates vary widely by region in all of the countries in Sub-Saharan Africa. Suppose that the MOH in hypothetical Sub-Saharan Country A were to give the highest priority to the reduction of infant mortality. Then the MOH might state its objectives and consequent policies somewhat along the lines shown in Table 2-3. In Table 2-3 the stated Objective 1 is to push the infant mortality rate in the fifteen health regions of Country A down to the average national infant mortality rate of about 100 per 1,000 live births. In order to efficiently attain this short-run objective, the budgetary (and policy making) process must deal with two different concepts of efficiency. The first of these efficiency concepts is that of *technical efficiency*, which refers to input mixes that are appropriate for achieving the objectives. Thus, all health personnel, all health-care facilities, all medicines and drugs, and all pregnant women would appear to be feasible inputs for attaining the stated Objective 1; the use of airline pilots and flight crews would be an egregious example of infeasible inputs for the reduction of infant mortality. However, under the heading, "Technically Efficient Method" in Table 2-3 we see that the research literature reveals that one of the more feasible sets, including health-care personnel and facilities, for reducing infant mortality is the identification and selection of the group of pregnant women who are at high risk for having nonviable babies, namely, the so-called "too" group (i.e., women who are either too young or too old, women who have already had too many children, and/or women who have too little spacing between children).

The second efficiency concept is that of *economic efficiency*. Economic efficiency refers to the least-cost mix of the technically efficient combination of inputs for reducing infant mortality. Again, as a somewhat egregious example of the application of the concepts of technical and economic efficiency, training more surgeons and placing them in the regions with infant mortality rates that are higher than the national average would meet technical efficiency criteria (surgeons can act as primary-care physicians as well as do surgery), but they are simply too expensive to train *and* pay to meet the criterion of economic efficiency in the reduction of infant mortality. Therefore, under the heading, "Economically Efficient Method" in Table 2-3 we see that relatively inexpensively trained *and* paid nurses' aides meet the economic efficiency criterion for the objective of reducing infant mortality in each health region down to the national average of about

**Table 2-3**
**MOH in Sub-Saharan Country A:  Example of Setting Objectives and then Budgeting for Efficiency in Production of Health Care**

---

Objective 1:    Push infant mortality rate in the fifteen regions down to the average national infant mortality rate of 100/1,000 live births.

Technically     Research literature (WHO and others) indicate that special and
Efficient       specific monitoring of pregnant women in three categories be done:
Method:
        1.  Too young or too old—less than 18 or more than 45 years of age.
        2.  Too many children—more than 3.
        3.  Too little spacing—less than 2 years.

Economically    Use inexpensive nurses' aides to seek out these women regularly
Efficient       and examine them, and/or use community presentations to alert
Method:         these women that their pregnancies are at great risk, and that they
should be regularly examined by nurses' aides.  Among this subset of pregnant women, refer the subset of this subset to higher-level health-care facilities when it is obvious (medically) that they will have difficulties with their pregnancies.   Also, emphasize family planning for women in groups 1-3 above.

Objective 2:    Within three years, reduce the average national infant mortality rate to 85/1,000 live births.

Technically     Same as for Objective 1 above, and improve maternal and child
Efficient       nutrition.
Method:

Economically    Same as for Objective 1 above, and provide vitamin supplements.
Efficient
Method:

Other Budget Implications of
Fulfilling Objectives 1 and 2 Above

1.  Reduce budgetary resources going to national hospitals and to specialty hospitals by 5 percent.
2.  Reduce number of physicians being produced by medical schools and increase number of nurses' aides.
3.  Reallocate MOH personnel (especially nurses' aides) to regions with infant mortality rates that are higher than the national average.

---

100 per 1,000 live births.    Implicit in the reasoning for meeting
Objective 1 would be that some nurses' aides would be transferred
from regions such as hypothetical Region 15, where the infant mortality
rate is a relatively low 35 per 1,000 live births, to regions such as
hypothetical Region 9, where the infant mortality rate is a relatively
high 140 per 1,000 live births.    Again, supposing that the reduction of
infant mortality were to be given a continuing high priority, Objective
2 in Table 2-3 might be stated as, "Within 3 years, reduce the average
national infant mortality rate to 85 per 1,000 live births."    The pursuit
of Objective 1 is now well on its way and there is little variation among
regions in the infant mortality rate.    A side effect of this equalization
of infant mortality rates among regions would probably be a further
drop in the average national infant mortality rate.    As with the pursuit
of Objective 1, the pursuit of Objective 2 uses the same technically and
economically efficient methods, but adds maternal and child nutrition
as an additional input.

Finally, the bottom third of Table 2-3 lists, as examples, some of
the other possible budgetary implications of pursuing or fulfilling
Objectives 1 and 2.    One possible outcome of the explicit setting of
quantifiable and measurable objectives for infant mortality may well be
that the so-called "high tech" diseases treated at national and specialty
hospitals may end up being much further down on the list of explicit
budgetary priorities.    In that case, the more intensified pursuit of
Objectives 1 and 2 implies that these two types of hospitals would
receive lower budgetary allocations.    Likewise, as shown in Table 2-3,
the present budgetary example also has longer-run manpower
implications.    Given the stated priorities in Objectives 1 and 2 and
given the efficiency criteria used, it now becomes apparent that the
health-care system has been producing too many physicians and not
enough nurses' aides, which indicates that manpower policies and
budgets must be changed.    Finally, financial incentives may have to be
used in order to induce nurses' aides who live and work in low infant
mortality regions to live and work in regions with high infant mortality
rates.

The essential efficiency lesson to be learned from the foregoing
discussion of the contents of Table 2-3 is that it is highly useful to
state explicitly and rank health-care objectives and priorities.    Such an
exercise enables the policy maker to systematically evaluate the
resource requirements, using technical and economic efficiency criteria,
for the achievement of the objectives, as ranked by level of national
importance.    Such an exercise also makes it possible to examine and

even quantify the budgetary "fall out" (e.g., the reduction in hospital budgets) that will occur as the result of pursuing, say, an infant mortality reduction policy as a primary objective.

Another way of thinking about this allocation problem is in terms of cost effectiveness. Unlike cost/benefit analysis, where the benefits from an intervention, whether for health or for other sectors of the economy, are often difficult to measure, cost-effectiveness analysis simply poses the question in terms of what is the least costly way of achieving a given result. Assume that the result sought is a child death averted. We use Table 2-4 as a framework of discussion for the health sector. Depending upon the type of intervention in Table 2-4, the annual cost of a child death averted can range from a low of $100 for home-distributed, oral-rehydration therapy to a high of $41,000 for medical services. If one examines the first five interventions in Table 2-4, what one sees is that the primary economic characteristics of these interventions is that they are either relatively inexpensive on a per capita basis and/or are relatively more effective in terms of number of deaths averted per 100,000 population than the last six interventions. For example, both "DDT spraying against malaria" and "Non-DDT spraying against malaria" cause 800 deaths per 100,000 population to be averted, but the former intervention costs "$2.00 per capita, while the latter costs $15.00 per capita."[3] That is why the annual cost per death averted is $250 for the former intervention and $1,875 for the latter. Intervention two, "Expanded program of immunization" is the least costly on a per capita basis ($0.05), but is less effective in the number of deaths averted per 100,000 (thirty-five deaths averted) than the slightly more expensive, on a per capita basis, "home-distributed, oral-rehydration therapy" ($0.07). The oral-hydration therapy is almost twice as effective in number of deaths averted per 100,000 (sixty-nine versus thirty-five).

Although the exact size of the numerical values in Table 2-4 is subject to some debate because the application of cost-effectiveness analysis to health care is so tentative and new,[4] the general economic principle that it illustrates is clear: if the epidemiology of a country produces many illness cases that need "medical care" in order to avert deaths, either the total medical expenditure will have to be high, or, if total medical expenditures are to be kept low because of budgetary constraints, fewer deaths will be averted. Alternatively, if the epidemiology of the country produces many illness cases that need the first five interventions in Table 2-4, many deaths can be averted at a

**Table 2-4**
**Cost Effectiveness of Selected Health Interventions in Developing Countries (U.S. $)**

| Intervention and Country | Cost per Capita | Number of Deaths Averted per 100,000 | Annual Cost per Death Averted |
|---|---|---|---|
| Home-distributed, oral-rehydration therapy (Egypt) | 0.07 | 69 | 100 |
| Expanded program of immunization (Indonesia) | 0.05 | 35 | 130 |
| Oral-rehydration program (Zaire) | 0.09 | 48 | 186 |
| DDT spraying against malaria | 2.00 | 800 | 250 |
| Measles vaccination (Cote d'Ivoire) | 0.30 | 63 | 479 |
| Pilot projects in primary health care | 4.00 | 303 | 1,320 |
| Non-DDT spraying against malaria | 15.00 | 800 | 1,875 |
| Community water and sanitation (Sub-Saharan Africa) | 2.70 | 98 | 2,750 |
| Nutrition supplementation (Narrangwal, India) | 1.75 | 58 | 3,000 |
| Nutrition surveillance medical services (Imesi, Nigeria) | 1.50 | 48 | 3,500 |
| Medical services (Etimesgut, Turkey) | 7.00 | 17 | 41,000 |

*Source:*   Over (1991). This Table is Mead Over's synthesis of the work of a number of researchers; the detailed references to their work may be found in the source document.

much lower cost per capita and per death averted, and at a much lower total cost.

Table 2-1 showed how dramatically different the epidemiology is in the model developing country compared to that in the model developed country or in OECD countries. The predominant cause of deaths there (43.7 percent) could be inexpensively averted by the first five interventions in Table 2-4. The contents of Table 2-2 showed average expenditure patterns of health spending in developing countries versus the U.S. Had a reader seen only Table 2-2 and not both Tables 2-1 *and* 2-2, he/she would have been logically forced to conclude that the epidemiology in developing countries (and in Sub-Saharan Africa) was similar to that in the United States! These kinds of comparison (for Tables 2-1, 2-2, and 2-4) vividly illustrate just how insufficient is spending upon cost-effective health programs in Sub-Saharan Africa.


## INEFFICIENT GOVERNMENT PROGRAMS

The word "inefficient" only has meaning with reference to some notion of what is "efficient." On the macro level, we assume that the parliamentary process or the ministry of finance process of allocating a budget to the MOH has used a calculus that allocates the given level of general tax revenues to those budgetary areas where the highest marginal social returns were available, until marginal benefits were equal across the budgetary areas, such as health, education, defense, etc. If that process did occur in that way, then we can judge it to be efficient in both a political sense and in a welfare economics sense.[5] At its level, the MOH faces a similar allocation problem: it seeks to equalize marginal benefits among programs as measured by some objective output (for example, equalizing the infant mortality rate among the various regions of the country, or lowering the total infant mortality rate for the whole country). Once the MOH has set its objectives, it can be judged to be operating inefficiently if it does not spend its given budget in a manner that will best achieve those objectives. The major determinant of those objectives would be the epidemiology of the country.[6] The major determinant of the choice among the various means (or inputs) for achieving the objective, or objectives, would be the relative unit costs of each of the inputs. In the previous section of this chapter, we showed how cost-effectiveness analysis can aid the policy maker in the choice of inputs.

In this section, we turn our attention to the notion of an ideal (efficient) public health-care system, and then try to ascertain the extent to which government health-care programs in the Sub-Sahara deviate from the ideal. As will be shortly seen, the ideal system can be difficult or not difficult to construct, depending upon the value judgments that one is willing to make. Table 2-5 frames the discussion. In Table 2-5, the columns show the different levels of medical sophistication of the public health-care system, with university hospitals at one extreme of sophistication and health posts at the other extreme. In Row 1 of the table, the annual cost per death averted is shown for each kind of facility; some of these values have been taken from Table 2-4. In Row 2, an MOH budget of $100 million is hypothesized, and, as one moves across the row, one sees how many deaths could be averted if the entire MOH budget were spent *only* at one particular kind of health-care facility, solely for purposes of illustration. Thus, if the entire budget were spent only at university hospitals, 10,000 deaths could be averted; if the entire budget were spent only at health posts, 1,000,000 deaths could be averted. Row 3 shows the present expenditure pattern that is prevalent in many Sub-Saharan countries, with about 75 percent of the MOH budget spent on hospitals, 15 percent spent on health centers and 10 percent on health posts. Given such an expenditure pattern and an MOH budget of $100 million, Row 4 shows the amounts of money that each kind of health-care entity would receive. Thus, university hospitals would receive $35 million, provincial hospitals, $23 million, and so on. With these budgets, and given the annual cost per death averted in Row 1, Row 5 shows the number of deaths that could be averted by each of these health-care entities. University hospitals would avert 3,500 deaths; health centers would avert 75,000 deaths, and Health Posts would avert 100,000 deaths. All of the health-care entities together would avert 185,186 deaths at an average cost per death averted of $541.

Row 6 (the epidemiological target) assumes a different MOH expenditure pattern than that shown in Row 3; the percentages in Row 6 roughly match the epidemiology of the model developing country in Table 2-1. In Table 2-5, 22 percent of the causes of mortality (cancer, diseases of the circulatory system, and traumatic injury) from Table 2-1 are assigned to the three levels of hospital, and 78 percent of the causes of mortality (infectious, parasitic, and respiratory diseases, and "other") are assigned to the health centers and health posts.[7] If the same MOH budget of $100 million is now allocated to the health-care entities, using these epidemiological target

**Table 2-5**
**The Allocation of the MOH Budget and Deaths Averted**

|  | University Hospitals | Provincial Hospitals | District Hospitals | Health Centers | Health Posts |
|---|---|---|---|---|---|
| (1) Annual Cost per Death Averted | $10,000 | $7,000 | $5,000 | $200 | $100 |
| (2) Number of Deaths Averted, MOH Budget of $100,000,000[a] | 10,000 | 14,286 | 20,000 | 500,000 | 1,000,000 |
| (3) Present Expenditure Pattern (%) | 35.0 | 23.0 | 17.0 | 15.0 | 10.0 |
| (4) Amount of Budget Received | $35,000,000 | $23,000,000 | $17,000,000 | $15,000,000 | $10,000,000 |
| (5) Number of Deaths Averted (4)/(1)[b] | 3,500 | 3,286 | 3,400 | 75,000 | 100,000 |
| (6) Epidemiological Target (%) | 2.0 | 5.0 | 15.0 | 26.0 | 52.0 |
| (7) Amount of Budget Received | $ 2,000,000 | $ 5,000,000 | $15,000,000 | $26,000,000 | $52,000,000 |
| (8) Number of Deaths Averted (7)/(1)[c] | 200 | 714 | 3,000 | 130,000 | 520,000 |

[a]Assumes that all budgetary funds are only spent on a single kind of provider, for example, if the entire budget were spent only at university hospitals, 10,000 deaths would be averted; if the entire budget were spent only at provincial hospitals, 14,286 deaths would be averted, etc.
[b]Total deaths averted = 185,186, and average cost per death averted = $541.
[c]Total deaths averted = 653,914, and average cost per death averted = $153.

percentages, then university hospitals would only receive $2 million instead of the previous $35 million; provincial hospitals would receive $5 million, instead of $23 million.   District hospitals would receive almost as much as before, $15 million versus $17 million.  But the bulk of the budget would go to health centers and health posts.  Given the new allocation of the MOH budget and given the annual cost per death averted in Row 1, university hospitals would now only avert 200 deaths, but health centers and health posts would avert 130,000 deaths and 520,000 deaths respectively.   Total deaths averted would be 653,914 deaths, at an average cost per death averted of $153.  Thus, depending upon the direction of the MOH budgetary allocation, either 185,186 or 653,914 deaths could be averted.

Because the epidemiological target expenditure pattern is more cost effective than the prevailing expenditure pattern, it can be viewed as an efficient government program, while any government program that deviates from it can be considered inefficient.[8] Table 2-6 contains some indicatory data for the individual countries.   The data are incomplete and fragmentary, and are for varying years, but they do give a rough idea of the pattern of health expenditures and programs in the Sub-Sahara, by country.   The first column in Table 2-6 gives the percent of the MOH budget that is spent upon hospitals.   At the bottom of the column, we show the OECD-country, public-sector average of 54.2 percent of MOH budgetary expenditures for hospitals (OECD, 1987) as a point of reference, not necessarily because the OECD countries should be considered to have more efficient public health-care systems, but simply because, as shown before, the epidemiology in the OECD countries should make their health-care systems more hospital-intensive than in developing countries. Therefore, if a Sub-Saharan country in Table 2-6 spends a larger percentage of its MOH budget on hospitals than the OECD average, it should possibly reexamine its health-expenditure priorities.  The data show that hospital expenditures range from a low of 36.0 percent of the MOH budget in Mauritius in 1988 to a high of 81.0 percent in Malawi; the country average, for the eighteen countries for which firm data were available, was 60.9 percent of the MOH budget for hospitals, as opposed to the OECD average of 54.2 percent.   Eight of the eighteen Sub-Saharan countries had hospital expenditures as a percent of the MOH budget that were 70 percent or higher.   It would be interesting to know what dynamic induced Mauritius to spend less than half of the percentage of its MOH budget than did Malawi (36.0 percent versus 81.0 percent).   Barnum and Kutzin (1990) show how

**Table 2-6**
**Percent of the MOH Budget Spent on Hospitals, Personnel,**
**and Pharmaceuticals in Sub-Saharan Africa**

| Country | % MOH Budget Spent on Hospitals | % MOH Budget Spent on Personnel | % MOH Budget Spent on Pharmaceuticals |
|---|---|---|---|
| Angola | | | |
| Benin | | 84.2 (1987) | |
| Botswana | 48.8 (1984) | | |
| Burkina Faso | | 80.0 (1982) | 15.8 (1982) |
| Burundi | 80.0 (1987) | 61.0 (1982) | 29.0 (1982) |
| Cameroon | 66.0 (1983) | 85.0 (1982) | 11.9 (1980) |
| Central Africa Republic | 71.5 (1988) | 81.0 (1988) | 19.3 (1988) |
| Chad | | | |
| Congo | | | |
| Cote d'Ivoire | 46.0 (1984) | 72.4 (1987) | 7.0 (1987) |
| Ethiopa | 50.0 (1982) | | |
| Gabon | | | |
| Gambia | 45.0 (1986) | | 7.4 (1986) |
| Ghana | | 46.0 (1985) | |
| Guinea | | 52.0 (1983) | 29.0 (1983) |
| Guinea-Bissau | | | |
| Kenya | 73.0 (1986) | 56.5 (1985) | |
| Lesotho | 70.0 (1986) | 45.0 (1986) | 21.8 (1986) |
| Liberia | | | |
| Madagascar | | 69.4 (1986) | 8.0 (1985) |
| Malawi | 81.0 (1986) | 38.4 (1986) | 16.3 (1986) |
| Mali | 28.0 (1987) | 63.0 (1985) | |
| Mauritania | | 70.2 (1987) | 16.3 (1985) |
| Mauritius | | | |
| Mozambique | 36.0 (1988) | | |
| Namibia | | | |
| Niger | | 52.0 (1985) | 19.0 (1984) |
| Nigeria | 70.0 (1985) | 68.0 (1985) | 30.0 (1981) |
| Rwanda | | 57.0 (1985) | 13.0 (1985) |
| Senegal | 50.0 (1982) | 67.4 (1986) | |
| Sierra Leone | | 60.0 (1984) | |
| Somalia | 70.0 (1989) | | |
| Sudan | | | |
| Swaziland | 52.0 (1984) | 33.3 (1984) | 23.4 (1985) |
| Tanzania | 63.7 (1988) | 45.0 (1988) | |
| Togo | | 85.0 (1983) | |
| Uganda | 43.0 (1988) | | |
| Zaire | | 84.0 (1986) | 1.0 (1986) |
| Zambia | 29.0 (1982)[a] | 50.4 (1981) | |
| Zimbabwe | 80.0 (1987) | 66.6 (1989) | |
| OECD Mean | 54.0 (1980s) | | |

[a]Four tertiary hospitals.

*Source*:   Unpublished World Bank documents listed in second section of
references for this study; OECD (1987).

MOH budgetary allocations for hospitals change over time, roughly from the 1970s to the 1980s; they have data for seven Sub-Saharan countries (Botswana, Gambia, Kenya, Lesotho, Malawi, Swaziland, and Zambia). The data show relatively wide variability in direction and magnitude of change. Four of the seven countries have increased the hospital share (Botswana, from 42 to 49 percent; Kenya, from 66 to 73 percent; Lesotho, from 64 to 71 percent; and Malawi, from 73 to 81 percent). In contrast, Gambia went from 67 to 45 percent; Swaziland, from 69 to 52 percent, and Zambia, from 33 to 30 percent.

In his analysis of OECD countries (OECD, 1987) Schieber found that part of the variability in hospital indicators there was due to differences in the definition of "hospital," particularly with respect to short-term acute care and long-term chronic care. It would be important to know if some of the variability in hospitals/MOH budgets in the Sub-Sahara arises from similar differences in definition. Another extremely important source of explanation for these differences in the amount of hospital absorption of the MOH budget, and the changes over time, could possibly be knowledge of the hospitals' rate of acquisition of western medical technologies that are encouraged by the form of "health insurance" (see Chapter 3)[9] and that are not particularly cost effective (Weisbrod, 1991). The answers to both of these speculations call for more in-depth study of individual country health economies.

The second column in Table 2-6 shows the percentage of the MOH budget spent on personnel. The donor community has been somewhat critical of the percent of budgets spent upon personnel in the Sub-Sahara (see Ozgediz, 1983, and Lindauer, Meesook, and Suebsaeng, 1986). Because health care is much more labor intensive than many other forms of government activity, one would expect the personnel component to be a larger percentage of the MOH budget than personnel would be of, say the ministry of public works budget. But the question remains about how much larger it would, or should, be. Economic theory indicates that the percentage would vary, by country, depending upon the relative country costs of the other inputs into the health-production function, such as capital, medical supplies, and drugs. However, because most of the countries in the Sub-Sahara must import the same capital, medical supplies, and drugs that are priced in foreign exchange in internationally competitive markets, one would not expect the nominal prices of these items to vary appreciably for differing Sub-Saharan countries. On the other hand, the shadow price of foreign exchange for the purchase of these items may vary appreciably by Sub-Saharan country, particularly for the non-FCFA[10] countries. The government wage bill in each ministry is a function of both hiring practices and salary policy; hiring practices and salary policies may be exogenous to the MOH in some countries. Nonetheless, research has shown that in many African countries the size of the civil service is too large, and the structure and level of government salaries does *not* reflect skill shortages (Lindauer, Meesook, and Suebsaeng, 1986). Therefore, even if hiring practices and salary policy are exogenous to the MOH, someone in each government ought to be scrutinizing the personnel component of the MOH budget.

In Table 2-6, the personnel percentage ranges from a low of 33.3 percent in Swaziland, to a high of 85.0 percent in Cameroon. The average personnel percentage of the MOH for the twenty-five countries where the data were available was 62.9 percent. Seven of the countries (Benin, Burkina Faso, Cameroon, Central African Republic, Togo, and Zaire) had personnel percentages that were equal to or greater than 80.0 percent. Barnum and Kutzin (1990) cite a 1985 unpublished study by van Lemmen and van Avelsvoort of twenty-three church-mission hospitals. For these hospitals the average percentage of the budget spent on personnel was 47 percent. While church-mission hospitals tend to be located in rural areas in Sub-Saharan Africa, and are smaller than the very large tertiary hospitals run by government (such as Muhimbili Hospital in Tanzania, Jomo Kenyatta Hospital in Kenya, or Parirenyatwa Hospital in Zimbabwe), church-mission hospitals are usually regarded by expert observers as being unusually well-run and efficient, because of their need to meet the bottom line in their budgets. Although no absolute measures of efficiency have yet been developed in this regard, private sector (for-profit) and church-mission sector expenditures for personnel have ranged in the area of 45 to 55 percent of their respective health-care budgets in Ghana, the Cote d'Ivoire, and Senegal (Vogel, 1988).

Column 3 in Table 2-6 shows the percentage of the MOH budget spent on pharmaceuticals. The complaint most often heard about government health-care facilities in Sub-Saharan Africa is that they lack, or have a limited supply of pharmaceuticals, and this is directly linked to peoples' perception of quality in government health-care facilities. Waddington and Enyimayew (1989) conducted a number of consumer focus groups in the Ashanti-Akin District of Ghana. In the responses that pertained to the question of quality, they report the following rankings: the availability of drugs and pharmaceuticals in lower-level health-care facilities (which was, by far, the most important); the availability of medical supplies (bandages, ointments, etc.); and the lack of rudeness on the part of health-care workers. In a questionnaire distributed as part of the interview process with government officials, church-mission officials, private-sector managers, and government and church-mission health-care workers in Cote d'Ivoire, Ghana, Mali, and Senegal, Vogel (1988) found that the most often mentioned indicator of quality in the health sector was the availability of pharmaceuticals and drugs and medical supplies. In their demand analysis for Ogun State in Nigeria, Akin et al. (1991) used three different quality variables in their econometric work: an index of the physical condition of government health-care facilities; government health-care expenditures per person served in the service area; and the percentage of time that pharmaceuticals were available in government health-care facilities. They found that the demand for health care in government facilities was particularly sensitive and responsive to the third quality variable, the percentage of time that pharmaceuticals were available in government facilities. The results of the three studies above confirm the importance of adequate government spending on pharmaceuticals and supplies in Sub-Saharan Africa.

In Table 2-6, the range of percentage of the MOH budget spent on pharmaceuticals for the sixteen countries for which the data are available is at a low of 1.0 percent in Zaire and at a high of 30.0 percent in Nigeria; the sixteen-country average is 16.8 percent. The average for the public sector in the OECD countries in the 1980s was 9.9 percent of total public-sector spending on health care (OECD, 1987), but the mix of public/private expenditures for pharmaceuticals may be different between the Sub-Saharan countries and the OECD countries; for example, in the United States, only a very small percentage of pharmaceuticals is bought by the government.

By way of summary to this section of this chapter, the problem of inefficient government programs exists on both the demand side and supply side. Demand side problems are caused by the quality differences of services, inadequate referral practices, and an inappropriate structure of fees for the services rendered, if such fees exist at all. When fees are used, they are usually imposed at lower-level facilities. Inadequate referral practices cause the pattern of demand to shift toward higher-level facilities which generally offer better care at no or relatively low fees. Crowded higher-level facilities are then expanded, and a vicious circle of investment at inappropriate tertiary sites occurs.

On the supply side, recurrent costs are nearly entirely absorbed by personnel expenditures, resulting in gross underfunding for drugs, maintenance, and vehicles.    In addition, overcentralization of management makes the health system cumbersome and unresponsive, and creates logistical problems.  These management inadequacies lead to a perception on the part of the clientele that health services in the public sector are of low quality.  Problems on the demand and supply side are essentially related to management and pricing issues.  The next chapter of this study deals with resource mobilization, and will analyze the broader pricing problem both on the demand and supply side of service provision.[11]

## INEQUITABLE DISTRIBUTION OF BENEFITS

Among African governments, the prevailing ideology since independence has been one of providing free health care to all.  While this goal would be attainable if substantial resources were available, it cannot be achieved with extremely limited resources.   The effort to provide free care, or provide care at a minimal cost in some instances, given the severe resource constraint, has led to an equity problem that was unforeseen and unintended by governments.   Given the curative and hospital-based biases of Africa's health-care systems, about 70 percent or more of governments' spending on health is used for urban hospital-based care.   Yet, the majority of Africa's population lives in rural areas.  Moreover, when families have significantly higher incomes and life expectancy and suffer from diseases requiring hospitalization in older ages, they tend to benefit from the prevailing public expenditure pattern.   Thus, "free health care for all" translates into a relative neglect of the poorer rural population, to the benefit of older, upper-income urban residents.   This pattern of expenditure is particularly detrimental to primary and preventive health care for mothers and children, who constitute an important percentage of the most vulnerable population in Africa.   Therefore, the inequitable distribution of benefits carries a number of dimensions:  across income groups, across geographic location, across sex and age, and across disease categories.

In order to gain insight into *intracountry* differences in health status, Table 2-7 presents data on intergroup differences in mortality for four Sub-Saharan countries (Kenya, Sudan, Burundi, and Senegal) and for South Africa.  For Kenya and Sudan, the comparison groups

**Table 2-7**

**Intergroup Differences in Mortality: Four Sub-Saharan Countries and South Africa**

| (1) Place and Time — Country | (2) Year | Highest Mortality Group | | | Lowest Mortality Group | | | |
| --- | --- | --- | --- | --- | --- | --- | --- | --- |
| | | (3) Defining Characteristic of Group | (4) % of Total Population Represented by Group | (5) Infant Mortality Rate | (6) Life Expectancy (Years) | (7) Defining Characteristic of Group | (8) % of Total Population Represented by Group | (9) Infant Mortality Rate | (10) Life Expectancy (Years) |
| Kenya | 1974 | Residents of Coast & Nyanga Province | 26.1 | 140.3 | 46.7 | Residents of Central Province | 15.3 | 58.0 | 62.9 |
| Sudan | 1973 | Residents of Bahr El Ghazal Province | 9.4 | 227.5 | 34.2 | Residents of Khartoum Province | 7.8 | 107.6 | 52.5 |
| Burundi | 1981-1987 | Children of women with secondary or higher education | 80.2 | 90.0 | 55.8 | Children of women with secondary or higher education | 2.2 | 32.0 | 69.2 |
| Senegal | 1981-1988 | Children of women with no education | 77.2 | 96.0 | 54.7 | Children of women with higher education | 9.3 | 50.0 | 64.7 |
| South Africa | 1981-1985 | Blacks | 68.0 | 94.0-124.0 | 49.4-55.1 | Whites | 18.2 | 12.3 | 75.3 |

**Table 2-7 (continued)**

| (1) | (2) | (11) | (12) | (13) | (14) |
|---|---|---|---|---|---|
| Place and Time | | Differences between Groups | | | |
| | | Infant Mortality | | Life Expectancy | |
| Country | Year | Absolute Col 5-Col 9 | Relative Col 5/Col 9 | Absolute Col 10-Col 6 | Relative Col 10/Col 6 |
| Kenya | 1974 | 82.3 | 2.42 | 16.2 | 1.35 |
| Sudan | 1973 | 119.9 | 2.11 | 18.3 | 1.54 |
| Burundi | 1981-1987 | 58.0 | 2.81 | 13.4 | 1.24 |
| Senegal | 1981-1988 | 46.0 | 1.92 | 10.0 | 1.18 |
| South Africa | 1981-1985 | 81.7-111.7 | 7.64-10.08 | 20.2-25.9 | 1.37-1.52 |

*Source:* Gwatkin (1992).

are rural versus urban groups.    For Burundi and Senegal, the comparison groups are the children of women with no education versus the children of women with secondary or higher education (Burundi) or with higher education (Senegal).  For South Africa the comparison groups are blacks versus whites.[12]    Columns 4 and 8 show the percentage of the total population that each comparison group represents in each country.  Columns 5 and 9 give the infant mortality rate for each group, and Columns 6 and 10 give life expectancies at birth for each group.  In Columns 11 through 14, the absolute and relative differences in infant mortality and life expectancy between the two groups in each country are shown.  Column 11 shows that the difference in infant mortality between the two groups ranges from 46 infant deaths in Senegal to a 119.9 infant deaths in Sudan.  In Column 12, the difference in infant mortality ranges from a factor of 1.92 in Senegal to a midpoint factor of 8.9 in South Africa.  For the four Sub-Saharan countries, the mean factor is 2.31.[13]  In Column 13 the range in the difference in the absolute level in life expectancies at birth goes from 10.0 years in Senegal to a midpoint value of 23.1 years in South Africa.  Column 14 shows relative life expectancy between the two groups in each country; this measure of inequality ranged from a factor of 1.18 in Senegal to 1.54 in Sudan.  Thus, for the four Sub-Saharan countries, the relative measure of inequality in infant mortality between the two groups in each country is worse than the relative measure of inequality in life expectancies.  Having examined these data on within-country inequalities in health status, which, experience indicates, probably hold for the other countries in Sub-Saharan Africa as well, we now turn to an examination of the data that are available on the in-country distribution of health expenditures.

Table 2-8 shows the percentage of the population living in urban areas and the percentage of the MOH budget that is spent in urban areas for the countries in the Sub-Sahara.  It was difficult to obtain many observations on the percent of the MOH budget spent in urban areas, but it seems reasonable to assume that, where this datum is lacking for a country, the percent of the MOH budget that is spent on hospitals would be a reasonable bottom-line proxy; accordingly the entries that are *not* underlined in Table 2-8 for the percent of the MOH budget spent in urban areas are the percent of the MOH budget that is spent on hospitals (from Table 2-6).  The discrepancies between percent urban and percent MOH are large. For example, even though only 20 percent of the population of Guinea Bissau lives in urban areas, 84 percent of the MOH budget is spent there (a factor of 4.2);

**Table 2-8**
**Percent of Population in Urban Areas and Percent of MOH**
**Budget Spent in Urban Areas in Sub-Saharan Africa**

| Country | % Population in Urban Areas (1985) | % MOH Budget Spent in Urban Areas |
|---|---|---|
| Angola | 85.0 | |
| Benin | 35.0 | |
| Botswana | 20.0 | 42.9 (1970) |
| Burkina Faso | 8.0 | |
| Burundi | 2.0 | 80.0 (1987) |
| Cameroon | 42.0 | 66.0 (1985) |
| Central Africa Republic | 45.0 | 71.5 (1988) |
| Chad | 27.0 | |
| Congo | 40.0 | |
| Cote d'Ivoire | 45.0 | 89.0 (1984) |
| Ethiopa | 15.0 | 50.0 (1982) |
| Gabon | 12.0 | |
| Gambia | | 45.0 (1986) |
| Ghana | 32.0 | 80.0 (1984) |
| Guinea | 22.0 | |
| Guinea-Bissau | | |
| Kenya | 20.0 | 84.0 (1984) |
| Lesotho | 17.0 | 70.0 (1986) |
| Liberia | 37.0 | |
| Madagascar | 21.0 | |
| Malawi | 19.0 | 81.0 (1986) |
| Mali | 20.0 | 28.0 (1987) |
| Mauritania | 31.0 | |
| Mauritius | 54.0 | |
| Mozambique | 19.0 | 36.0 (1988) |
| Namibia | | |
| Niger | 15.0 | |
| Nigeria | 30.0 | 70.0 (1985) |
| Rwanda | 5.0 | |
| Senegal | 36.0 | 50.0 (1982) |
| Sierra Leone | 25.0 | 75.0 (1984) |
| Somalia | 34.0 | 70.0 (1988) |
| Sudan | 21.0 | |
| Swaziland | | 52.0 (1984) |
| Tanzania | 14.0 | 63.7 (1988) |
| Togo | 23.0 | |
| Uganda | 7.0 | 43.0 (1988) |
| Zaire | 39.0 | |
| Zambia | 48.0 | 29.0 (1982)[a] |
| Zimbabwe | 27.0 | 80.0 (1987) |

[a]Four tertiary hospitals

*Source*:　Unpublished World Bank documents listed in second section of references for this study.

in Sierra Leone 25 percent of the population lives in urban areas, and 75 percent of the MOH budget is spent there (a factor of 3.0). Government health spending by income class is not directly attainable for any of these countries, but it is generally recognized that urban areas are the hub of government and commerce in most countries of the world, and the countries in Sub-Saharan Africa are no exception to this rule; if anything, more modern activity is even more highly centralized in urban areas in Sub-Saharan Africa than in other parts of the world.[14] Therefore, not only do MOH budgetary expenditures benefit urban areas, but they also benefit middle-class and upper-class merchants and civil servants in urban areas, in addition to benefiting the urban poor.[15] In Chapter 3, we will show that most private-sector, for-profit health-care and pharmaceutical activity is also based in urban areas, although the church missions tend to concentrate their activities in rural areas. Thus, depending upon the country and upon the extent of church-mission health-care activities there, the *total* amount of health-care activity may be even more biased toward urban areas than even the MOH percentages in Column 2 of Table 2-8 would seem to indicate.

Data on the distribution of MOH expenditures by region of the country are rarely found, but a recent study done in Zimbabwe sheds some light on the matter (Hecht, ed., 1992). These data for Zimbabwe are also indicative of what could be expected to be worse for other countries in the Sub-Sahara, because the members of the team that did the Zimbabwe study generally agreed that Zimbabwe had made great progress with respect to equity, relative to the other Sub-Saharan countries in which some of the team members had worked.[16] In Table 2-9, the national average per capita government expenditure in Zimbabwe in 1987 was Z $22, but it ranged from Z $11 in Masvingo Province to Z $38 in Mashonaland East and Z $26 in Matabeleland North Provinces, where the four central hospitals are located; as noted in the table, the data have been adjusted to take into account referrals from other provinces.[17] Even though the expenditure data are somewhat unevenly distributed, the distribution of health-care facilities is somewhat more even, as measured by the number of hospital beds per 1,000 population and the number of clinics per 10,000 population. Hospital admissions per 1,000 population vary between sixty-four in Manicaland Province to eighty in Matabeleland Province, and outpatient hospital attendance per capita varies from 0.6 to 1.3. It is interesting to note that Masvingo Province, with the lowest per capita expenditure (Z $11) also had the highest outpatient hospital attendance per capita (1.3), and that Mashonaland East, where the large Parirenyatwa referral hospital is located, had the highest per capita expenditure (Z $38), but the lowest outpatient hospital attendance per capita (0.6). The data in Table 2-7 lead one to suspect that one would not find data for most of the other Sub-Saharan countries that would be as equally distributed geographically, as is the case for Zimbabwe in Table 2-9.

Data on the distribution of health-care expenditures by sex in the Sub-Sahara are difficult to find. As Barnum and Kutzin (1990) point out, given male dominance in other sectors, such as education, one might expect to find more government health-care funds spent upon males than upon females. On the other hand, the rate of population growth in Sub-Saharan Africa is the highest in the world, and it is women who give birth to the babies. Barnum and Kutzin give data on

**Table 2-9**
**Zimbabwe:  Health Services by Province, 1987**

| Province | Health Expenditure per Capita (Z $)[a] | Hospital Beds per 1,000 Population[a] | Number of Clinics per 10,000 Population | Hospital Admissions per 1,000 Population[a] | Outpatient Hospital Attendance per Capita |
|---|---|---|---|---|---|
| Manicaland | 18 | 2.1 | 1.5 | 64 | 0.9 |
| Mash Central | 16 | 1.5 | 1.2 | 67 | 0.7 |
| Mash East | 38 | 1.8 | 1.0 | 71 | 0.6 |
| Mash West | 14 | 1.4 | 1.0 | 67 | 0.9 |
| Masvingo | 11 | 2.2 | 0.9 | 70 | 1.3 |
| Mat North | 26 | 2.9 | 1.3 | 80 | 0.7 |
| Mat South | 14 | 2.4 | 1.3 | 74 | 0.9 |
| Midlands | 19 | 2.3 | 1.6 | 67 | 0.9 |
| Nat. Average | 22 | 2.1 | 1.2 | 70 | 0.8 |

[a]Adjusted to take referrals into account.
*Source*:   Hecht, ed. (1992).

hospital admissions by sex for four countries: China (one province), Jamaica (all acute-care hospitals), Korea (insured persons), and Malawi (six district hospitals).  For Malawi, female admissions accounted for 71 percent of all admissions, and males 29 percent.  Once obstetrical admissions were removed from the data, females had 52 percent, and males 48 percent.  The total admissions data pattern was similar for the other three countries.  Data on nonobstetric admissions were only available for Jamaica and Malawi; Jamaica's experience was similar to that of Malawi, 51 percent female and 49 percent male.  Thus, at least in Malawi, the sexes seem to be treated equally for hospital admissions in Sub-Saharan Africa.

Again, data on the distribution of health expenditures by age are difficult to find.  Barnum and Kutzin (1990) contains hospital admission data by age for three Sub-Saharan countries, and these data are shown in Table 2-10.  The data on admissions by age are remarkably similar in Malawi, Niger, and Uganda.  In all three countries, adults have about 70 percent of the admissions, and children, about 30 percent.

**Table 2-10**
**Percentage of Admissions and Patient-Days to Pediatric and Nonpediatric Wards**

| Country | Admissions | | Patient Days | | Pediatric Admission Age Break |
| --- | --- | --- | --- | --- | --- |
| | Pediatric | Adult | Pediatric | Adult | |
| Malawi (six district hospitals) | 29 | 71 | 20 | 80 | < 12 |
| Niger (Niamey Hospital) | 29 | 71 | 17 | 83 | < 12 |
| Uganda (Keluva Hospital) | 30 | 70 | N/A | N/A | < 15 |

*Source*:   Barnum and Kutzin (1990).

Likewise, for patient days, the data for Malawi and Niger are roughly similar, with adults having about 80 percent of the patient-days and children, about 20 percent.  These results are difficult to judge.  Even though the population pattern in the Sub-Sahara is one where almost half of the population in each country is below the age of 15, children do not ordinarily contract the kinds of expensive diseases that require hospitalization, like cancer, that adults do.  Therefore, one would expect adults to use the hospital in a greater proportion than their proportion in the population.  On the other hand, the considerations that were made about cost effectiveness at the beginning of this chapter dictate that less resources be spent on hospitals.  Perhaps this would mean, then, that adults would consume an even greater share of hospital admissions and patient-days, but in a downgraded hospital system; the 30 percent share that children now have of admissions would be lessened because they would have more primary and preventive care.  The end result would be that more children would live and more adults would die, and, in a major sense, this is what a redistribution of health-care resources implies.

Table 2-11 shows data on hospital admissions by type of disease for Malawi and Nigeria; these data come from Barnum and Kutzin

**Table 2-11**
**Percentage Distribution of Causes of Hospital Admissions**

| Causes of Admission | Malawi | Nigeria |
| --- | --- | --- |
| Pregnancy and Perinatal | 31 | 23 |
| Communicable | 36 | 41 |
| Chronic/Noncommunicable | 26 | 22 |
| Accidents/Injuries | 5 | 5 |
| Others | 3 | 8 |

*Source*:   Barnum and Kutzin (1990).

(1990).    The data for the two countries are roughly similar.    The question that the contents of the table raises, however, is why nearly two-thirds of the admissions are for the two categories of "pregnancy and perinatal" and "communicable." What it may indicate is that too many births are occurring in the hospitals in these two countries, when they could occur in more cost-effective birthing centers or health centers.    Secondly, if more resources were spent on primary and preventive care, communicable diseases would occur much less frequently, or would not reach the stage where hospitalization was required, thus requiring less hospital resources.  The nearly 40 percent of hospital admissions for communicable diseases in these two countries points to a breakdown in the primary-care system.

**NOTES**

1.  This comparison does *not* mean to imply that the health-care sector in developed countries is efficient or even equitable.  Numerous studies on the U.S. health-care system, for example, have shown just how inefficient and inequitable that system is (see Feldstein [1988] and Pauly [1986] for summaries of this literature).  The most important difference between the opportunity costs of these inefficiencies in developed and developing countries is that people in developed countries may have to make do with fewer tennis racquets, for example; in developing countries, people may have to make do with less food or with less of the other basic necessities of life.  In other words, there is much more subsistence-slack in a richer economy.

2.  One working hypothesis for explaining the rough similarities in the expenditure patterns could be that all health-care systems (no matter what country—also see Griffin, 1990) are dominated by physicians who have similar priorities and professional points of view that are biased toward the use of technology and the handling of "interesting" medical cases (see Fuchs, 1982).

3.  It is not clear whether the authors of the DDT study took into account the monetary costs to the environment caused by DDT.

4.  Ironically, in view of the subject matter of this study, cost-effectiveness analysis was first developed at the U.S. Department of Defense during the early years of the Cold War for the analysis of alternative military strategies (i.e., what is the most cost-effective way to kill the enemy).

5.  Pareto optimality has been achieved because it is not possible to reallocate the budget in any other way among the various ministries and still maximize social welfare.

6.  Of course, this would only be true in a completely egalitarian society, where every life had the same value.  If another criterion were used, such as clan status, then clan status would determine how health expenditures were used.

7.  The reader may believe that these assumptions are too drastic or cavalier.  Less drastic assumptions could be made, but the general principle that we are attempting to illustrate would still prove to be true.

8.  Again, the reader is reminded that the previous reasoning assumed that every life saved, young or old, rich or poor, educated or uneducated, has equal value.  Not everyone may be willing to make such an assumption.  For a more in-depth treatment of the difficult logical, ethical, and practical considerations involved, see Menzel (1983).

9.  In Chapter 3, we define "health insurance" in a somewhat broad and unconventional sense, but nevertheless, in an economically true sense.

10.  The FCFA is the African Franc (Franc de la Communaute Financiere Africaine), and is usually denoted as FCFA, or CFA; it is pegged to the French Franc (FF) at 50 FCFA = 1 FF.

11.  The same kind of reasoning used in the last two paragraphs can also be applied to another input into the health-status production function, namely water and sanitation.  Appendix 3, "Improvement in In-Country Water and Sanitation Efficiency" contains a short discussion on this subject.

12.  Even though South Africa is not usually considered a part of Sub-Saharan Africa, the South African data are presented as a proxy comparison for the other Sub-Saharan countries that have a sizeable white expatriate community, such as Senegal or the Cote d'Ivoire.

13.  In the United States, the black infant mortality rate was 17.6 in 1988 and the white infant mortality rate was 8.5, or a factor of 2.07 (USDHHS, 1991).

14.  In Chapter 3, we will devote additional analysis to this problem.

15.  Of course in countries and cities where the private, for-profit health sector is relatively well developed, such as in Senegal with the Hopital Principal in Dakar and in the Cote d'Ivoire with the Policlinique Internationale Sainte Anne Marie in Abidjan, many of the

upper class bypass the public system entirely.  In countries such as Mali and Guinea-Bissau, where the private sector scarcely exists, public-sector bypass is not possible.

16.    The author was a member of the team that wrote the Zimbabwe health-finance report, and made three separate trips there during the course of that study.

17.    20 percent of the referral hospitals budgets were distributed to the other provinces on a population-weighted basis.

# 3

# Resource Mobilization

## COST RECOVERY AND PRICING

The objectives of cost recovery can be viewed as revenue generating for the MOH and/or as establishing a set of price signals that induce efficiencies in the production and consumption of health-care services, but *not* necessarily in that order (Ellis, 1987, Jimenez, 1987, and Mwabu, 1990). In order to preserve equity objectives, it is absolutely essential to establish administrative mechanisms to protect the poor from having to pay any user fees that result from a cost-recovery policy. In very poor countries, it is doubtful that cost recovery will raise a large proportion of revenue, expressed as a percentage of the MOH budget; but cost recovery may become a powerful tool for reinforcing and encouraging referral systems that, up to now, only exist on paper in national health plans. One of the major reasons such a large percentage of MOH budgets is spent upon hospitals is that, under systems of free care for all, patients have very little financial incentive to go first to a health post or to a health center, if there is a hospital within a reasonable traveling distance. Demand for free care at hospitals is great, because it is more likely that there will be drugs and higher level health-care personnel at the hospitals. But, the whole incentive system needs to be drastically altered. In practice, free care for all means free care for the urban middle class (mainly civil servants) and for some of the poor. The hospitals end up garnering a large percentage of MOH resources, with the result that a disproportionately small percentage residual of MOH funds remains for spending on the proportionately larger poor rural population. Because the hospitals have a such a large percentage of the resources, a large amount of inappropriate care is given there.[1] This produces inefficiencies and the waste of scarce resources. A more efficient approach would be to charge fees to those who use the hospitals *if* they had not been referred up to the hospitals through lower levels of the health-care system. Even then, those who could afford to pay would be charged to use the hospital for care, although at a lower rate than if they had not been referred upward. The logic of this argument is that, at the hospital level, hospitals would then have additional financial resources for cost recovery, which ought then to allow the MOH to spend a larger percentage of its budget on lower-level facilities in rural areas. The system of prices thus gives signals that even out demand for health care and enable the redistribution of resources among the health-care facilities.

Some countries in Sub-Saharan Africa have already begun cost-recovery programs, although they have had varying success with it (Vogel, 1988 and 1991). Table 3-1 shows cost-recovery revenues as a percent of the MOH recurrent budget for the countries for which the data could be found.[2] The cost-recovery ratios range from a low of 0.5 percent in Burkina Faso in 1981 to a high of 12.1 percent in Ghana in 1987. Also, Ethiopia (1982) and Mauritania (1986) had cost-recovery ratios of 12.0 percent. The sixteen country average was 5.2 percent. There appears to be no systematic, positive relationship between these ratios and GDP per capita. Botswana, with a GDP per capita of $2,040 in 1990 was at the low end of the cost-recovery range; Ethiopia, with a GDP per capita of $120 was at the high end of the range. But then, Zimbabwe, with a relatively high per capita income had a low ratio and so did Burkina Faso, which is poor. Perhaps countries with low per capita incomes feel a greater pressure to mobilize more resources for the health-care sector; on the other hand, the revenue that they could hope to generate would be small, given the general poverty of the population. No ready explanation arises for the between-country differences.

It would seem that the subject of cost recovery requires consideration within a broader context than that of simple GDP comparisons (Vogel and Frant, 1992). Figure 3-1 shows the economic context in which health care is delivered in any country where the public sector plays a large role in the financing and delivery of health care. On the right-hand side of Figure 3-1, the population has a choice of using either private health-care facilities, including church-mission facilities, or public health-care facilities. The population's effective demand for health care in government health-care facilities is a function of a number of socioeconomic variables, empirically the most important of which have been listed in Figure 3-1 (Akin et al., 1991):

**Table 3-1**
**Government Revenue from User Charges as a Percent of Recurrent Government Expenditures on Health Services:  Sub-Saharan Africa**

| Country | Percent of Recurrent Expenditure |
|---|---|
| Botswana, 1979 | 1.3 |
| Burkina Faso, 1981 | 0.5 |
| Burundi, 1982 | 4.0 |
| Cote d'Ivoire, 1986 | 3.1 |
| Ethiopia, 1982 | 12.0 |
| Ghana, 1987 | 12.1 |
| Kenya, 1984 | 2.0 |
| Lesotho, 1984 | 5.7 |
| Malawi, 1983 | 3.3 |
| Mali, 1986 | 2.7 |
| Mauritania, 1986 | 12.0 |
| Mozambique, 1985 | 8.0 |
| Rwanda, 1984 | 7.0 |
| Senegal, 1986 | 4.7 |
| Swaziland, 1984 | 2.1 |
| Zimbabwe, 1986 | 2.2 |

*Source*:  Vogel (1988 and 1989).

# Figure 3-1
## The Financing and Consumption of Health Care: A Prototypical Sub-Saharan Country

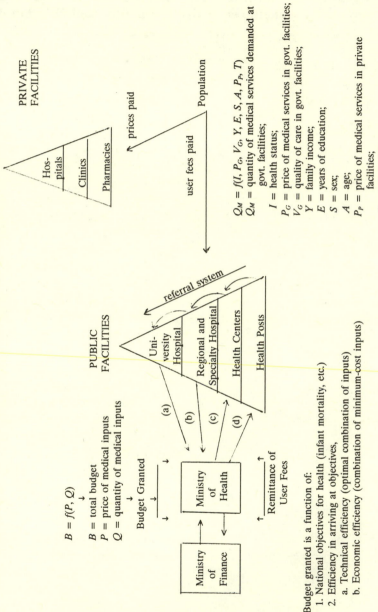

$B = f(P, Q)$

$B$ = total budget
$P$ = price of medical inputs
$Q$ = quantity of medical inputs

Budget granted is a function of:
1. National objectives for health (infant mortality, etc.)
2. Efficiency in arriving at objectives,
   a. Technical efficiency (optimal combination of inputs)
   b. Economic efficiency (combination of minimum-cost inputs)

$Q_M = f(I, P_G, V_G, Y, E, S, A, P_P, T)$
$Q_M$ = quantity of medical services demanded at govt. facilities;
$I$ = health status;
$P_G$ = price of medical services in govt. facilities;
$V_G$ = quality of care in govt. facilities;
$Y$ = family income;
$E$ = years of education;
$S$ = sex;
$A$ = age;
$P_P$ = price of medical services in private facilities;
$T$ = value of time.

(1) the person's physical or mental state of illness or well-being; (2) the price of medical care in government facilities; (3) the quality of care in government facilities; (4) family income; (5) the education level of the person; (6) the sex of the person; (7) the age of the person; (8) the price of medical care in private health-care facilities; and (9) the time and distance traveled to obtain medical care in government facilities.  As shown at the center of Figure 3-1, the ideal (most efficient) public health-care system would be pyramidal in shape, with less expensive health-care posts at the bottom of the pyramid, rendering health services to the daily aches and pains of ordinary existence.  Slightly more serious health problems would be treated at health centers, and so on, up the referral system.  Hospitals, particularly tertiary and quartenary hospitals such as university hospitals, are extremely resource intensive, and hence, expensive to operate on a per patient basis.  If patients do not voluntarily adhere, or are not forced to adhere to a referral system, then a well-known pattern of patient behavior and government response slowly evolves into a larger use of and misallocation of economic resources toward hospitals at the upper level of the pyramid.  Typically, patients bypass lower levels of the health-care pyramid, particularly in large cities, and present cases of minor illness to hospitals; these forms of illness could just as well have been treated at health posts or at health centers.  The next step along the way is that hospitals begin working over capacity, while health posts and health centers work under capacity.  Such a situation then sends the wrong investment signals to government, and government invests in further hospital capacity to the relative detriment of investment in health post and health center capacity.  Furthermore, recurrent budgetary allocations tend to follow capital budgetary allocations, and an inefficient, vicious budgetary cycle emerges.  Setting a well-designed and balanced structure of user fees is seen as one way of avoiding this kind of budgetary and resource allocation dilemma.  For example, if hospitals charge fairly high fees to any person who comes to the hospital (even if the person is indigent) without a referral from the lower-level health center, except in the case of a valid emergency, then there is a strong economic incentive to go first to a health center for treatment and for a referral upwards.  Likewise, if the health center also charges fees to those who do not have a referral from a health post, then there also exists an economic incentive to go first to a health post rather than to a health center.  In this way, the health-care system allocates health-care resources toward a more appropriate use of health care, with respect to the gravity of the illness,

protects hospitals from overuse, and makes it less likely that investment and recurrent expenditure decisions will be skewed towards the hospital sector.

On the left-hand side of Figure 3-1, the ministry of finance allocates a budget to the ministry of health and the ministry of health allocates budgets to the hospitals, centers, and posts. But, also, once a cost-recovery system has been put in place, the MOF and/or the MOH may wish to lay a claim upon the cost-recovery revenues of the hospitals. This could be done either in the form of direct remittances from the hospitals to the MOF and/or to the MOH, or in the form of smaller budgets to the hospitals than had been previously granted. For example, since 1985 in Ghana the formula for the allocation of cost-recovery revenues has been that the MOF receives 50 percent of all cost-recovery revenues from the health-care units, the MOH receives 25 percent and the collecting entity retains only 25 percent. In Senegal, hospitals must remit 100 percent of any revenues collected from certain classes of patient to the MOF. Economic theoreticians in public finance argue persuasively that any revenues collected by any government entity (such as a hospital that is run by the government) should be returned to the MOF. The underlying argument is that beginning-of-year budgets are allocated by the MOF to each ministry on the basis of the MOF's estimation of the marginal social benefits that each ministry provides to the public. Therefore, any revenues collected by any ministry should not accrue to that ministry itself alone, but should be remitted to the MOF, in order that the MOF might disburse these additional revenues, using the same marginal social benefit principles as it did when it disbursed the original beginning-of-year budgets. While such an argument makes sense when applied to the economic nexus between the theory of taxation and the theory of public expenditure, it is not particularly applicable to public revenues that come from charging prices or user fees for services rendered, rather than from taxation (Birdsall, 1987; Akin, Birdsall, and De Ferranti, 1987). Moreover, once it is recognized that the remission of user-fee revenue to the MOF carries the same incentive effects for collectors of user fees as does the taxation of income, careful thought must be given to the whole notion of the remittance of user fees to the MOF. Although the economic reasoning is somewhat complex, having to do with so-called income and substitution effects that different forms of taxation cause for those who have to pay the taxes, the economic work that has been done on the subject indicates the following as the best practice in the matter.

1. On marginal social benefit grounds, it *is* desirable that a portion of the user-fee revenue be remitted to the MOF, or by the collecting entity to its own proper ministry, and then on the to the MOF (Musgrave and Musgrave, 1980).
2. The best "tax" for collecting this user-fee revenue from the entity that charges the user fees is on a lump-sum basis, rather than on a proportional or progressive basis.  "Best" is here defined as that form of "taxation" that *least* attenuates the incentives of the collector of user fees to actually collect the user fees (Vogel and Frant, 1992).

The discussion in the previous paragraph was necessarily somewhat abstract.  Here we apply the reasoning above to the health-care sector in Sub-Saharan Africa, and use Senegal as an example.  If the hospitals must remit 100 percent of their user-fee revenue to the MOF, in effect, the hospitals face the equivalent of a 100 percent tax on income.  Such a tax should have some of the analogous effects as that of expecting a person to continue to work even though that person knew that 100 percent of his/her additional income would be taxed away.  In fact, the hospitals in Senegal collect very little in user-fee revenue; this should come as no surprise, given the incentive system that they face.  It should be clear that higher-level health-care facilities should be provided with positive economic incentives to collect user fees.  Otherwise, they may not consider the additional effort required to collect the fees to be worth the effort.  As a general rule, from an incentive point of view, the most desirable form of remittance to the MOF/MOH should be in a lump-sum; the least desirable would be any progressive form of remittance.  In order to illustrate this last, important point, consider three ways that the MOF/MOH could "tax" user-fee revenue from hospitals:

1. With a *progressive tax*, the MOF/MOH would tax the first 33 percent of revenues at a 50 percent rate, the next 33 percent at a 60 percent rate, and the final 33 percent at a 70 percent rate.  Here, there is a stronger and stronger incentive for the hospital not to collect each additional 33 percent of user-fee revenue.
2. With a *proportional tax*, the MOF/MOH would tax all user-fee revenue at a rate of 50 percent.  There is a stronger incentive to collect additional user-fee revenue than in (1), but because only 50 percent of the user-fee revenue can be kept by the hospital, the hospital has less of an incentive to collect the user

fees than if it did not have to remit any user-fee revenue to the MOF/MOH.

3.  With a *lump-sum tax*, the MOF/MOH would tax the first FCFA 10 million (or whatever amount) the hospital collects at the rate of 100 percent, and then the hospital can keep whatever it collects over and above that amount. Here, the hospital has much stronger incentives to collect user fees than in (1) and (2) because it retains 100 percent of the user-fee revenues that it collects after it has paid the lump-sum tax to the MOF/MOH.

Another important dimension of the left-hand side of Figure 3-1 is what is done with the proceeds of the lump-sum tax on hospital user-fee revenue. Earlier in this chapter, we discussed the importance of the user-fee pricing structure as an enforcer of the discipline of the referral system. The second reason for adopting user fees is in order to mobilize more resources for the neglected components of the health-care system. Thus, while the hospitals must be allowed to retain some of their cost-recovery revenue, in order to give them incentives to collect it vigorously, the MOF must have sufficient additional revenue from the (mostly) urban hospitals, in order to redistribute resources to lower-level health-care facilities. These resource flows are depicted in Figure 3-1 as (a), (b), (c), and (d). For (a) and (b), the university, provincial, and district hospitals pay a lump-sum tax on their user-fee revenues to the MOH in the form of cash. The MOH in turn pays a portion of this revenue to the MOF as a tax.[3] The portion that the MOH retains is then disbursed to health centers and health posts, not in the form of cash, but in the form of medical supplies, drugs, and pharmaceuticals, which can be more economically purchased and distributed from the central level (Vogel and Frant, 1992).

Finally, on the left-hand side and center of Figure 3-1, we assume that all of the resource efficiencies discussed in Chapter 2 are being vigorously pursued by the MOH and the health-care institutions. We now return to the right-hand side of Figure 3-1.

On the right-hand side, patients have the option of choosing either the private sector or the public sector for health care. This option will vary by country. For example, in Mali, until very recently, the private practice of medicine was forbidden, and few church-mission facilities existed. In Tanzania, church-mission facilities provide much of the rural health care. In the Cote d'Ivoire and in Zimbabwe, the private practice of medicine flourishes in their respective capitals. Given the health objectives that the MOH has established, it must create the incentives that will induce the population to use the "right" types and amounts of health care.  The three policy instruments that the MOH can control are pricing policy ($P_G$ in the equation in Figure 3-1), quality-of-care policy ($V_G$), and a policy for the exemption of the poor from having to pay any fees.  The use of the first two instruments depends basically upon empirical questions about the nature of the demand for health care in government health-care facilities.

Only a handful of empirical economic studies have been conducted in the Sub-Saharan region that address the demand for health care, and these studies cover only three countries:  the Cote d'Ivoire, Kenya, and Ogun State in Nigeria (Dor, Gertler, and van der Gaag, 1989, Mwabu and Mwangi, 1986, and Akin et al., 1991).  Evidence from other developing countries indicates that the demand for health care is price inelastic (Bitran, 1988).[4]  However, evidence from the Sub-Saharan studies brings considerably more detail into light.   In the econometric study done on the Cote d'Ivoire, the authors discovered that price elasticities among five different income groups varied considerably, and concluded that while cost recovery may be an effective tool in the Cote d'Ivoire, equitable charges could only be achieved through varying price schedules for the poor.

The econometric study conducted in Kenya used estimation of visit-demand functions for two income groups, higher- and lower-income households, for private and public hospitals and clinics.  The authors conclude that societal welfare could be improved by increasing levels of quality at these health-care sites, and by charging fees to hospitals used frequently by the higher-income households.  The lower-income households would be protected from these fees through referral waivers; clinics in poorer areas would continue to be free of user fees, and lower income persons referred to hospitals which charge fees would receive full or partial fee waivers.

The econometric study of health-care demand in Ogun State in Nigeria involved estimating demand and cost functions from surveys of households and health-care facilities.  Using the parameters from the demand and cost functions, it was possible to estimate several cost-recovery scenarios, giving policy makers a chance to explore possible outcomes of governmental changes, such as price and/or quality changes.   The econometric results for Ogun State concurred with studies done in other developing countries that indicate that the own-price elasticity of demand is less than minus 1.  The Nigerian study also suggests that the elasticity of demand with respect to quality variations is positive, and outweighs the negative price elasticity.

There are three important lessons to be learned from the empirical studies in these three Sub-Saharan countries. The first is that the poor are sensitive to the level of prices, and because one of the primary objectives of health-care reform is to improve the health of the poor, they should not have to pay any fees. The second is that the not-so-poor are willing and able to pay fees in government health-care facilities, if they perceive a change in quality, particularly with respect to the drug supply.[5] The third is that government can indeed mobilize additional resources for health care by pursuing cost-recovery options, if the cost-recovery mechanism is well designed.

The basic elements for a cost-recovery policy that is supportive of government's health outcome objectives are implicitly contained in the structure of the health-provider pyramid in the center of Figure 3-1. Vogel (1991) provides a prototypical matrix of prices, by level of service (health post to university hospital), and by type of service (inpatient drugs to registration fee per illness). The *level* of fees in that matrix, set for a prototypical country with a GNP per capita of $350, is not as important from the point of view of reforming the referral system, as the *structure* of the fees.[6] The structure of fees would be set so as to create patient incentives to use the referral system (see Chapter 2 for resource efficiencies) and to promote equity (i.e., fees would be nonexistent or relatively low at the base of the pyramid in Figure 3-1, and relatively high at the top of the pyramid, except for means-tested patients who have arrived at the top of the pyramid by means of the referral system). A stop-loss provision is also built into the fee structure, whereby payment of fees for hospital services ceases after five days of hospitalization; five days is seen as the financially catastrophic threshold for the average family. With relatively higher prices at the top of the pyramid, government hospitals, such as university hospitals, would become less competitive with the private sector, if the hospitals did not improve the quality of care. However, as the result of cost recovery and increased internal resource efficiencies, government hospitals would now have the financial means for improving the quality of care. The creation of this kind of pricing system in government hospitals would also increase the demand for health insurance on the right-hand side of Figure 3-1; the government must then be careful that the form of health insurance that does evolve channels provider and consumer incentives for making efficient choices in the production and consumption of health care. The prices in the health-care system would be pegged to the consumer price index, or to some other index of price inflation, so as not to erode the value of the prices for the strengthening of the referral system and for the mobilization of resources.    Means-testing devices, such as those suggested by Griffin (1989), would be put into place and periodically evaluated for their fairness.   Hospital billing and collection procedures would be strengthened and improved.

Some have argued that, to date, cost recovery has harmed rather than ameliorated access to health care for the poor (Waddington and Enyimayew, 1989; Creese, 1990; Mwabu, Wang'ombe, and Kimani, 1992).    With respect to these arguments, three observations are in order.   First, not everyone agrees that all of the empirical evidence on this subject has been resolved by adequate experience in the countries and by consequent research.   Second, the empirical evidence that does presently exist may simply indicate that administrative mechanisms for distinguishing the poor from the nonpoor for the purposes of payment need greater strengthening and more experience in the process.   The empirical evidence, particularly from Ghana, may also simply indicate that the systemic national price schedule in use needs further refinement with respect to the poor; for example, perhaps it would further the cause of equity in Ghana if *no* fees for care and drugs were charged at lower-level health-care facilities, such as health posts and centers.    Finally, at least in Africa, there is a large body of descriptive evidence that the church missions do charge for health care, that they do *not* charge the poor, that they cover anywhere from 30-50 percent of recurrent costs with user fees, that they have a reputation for quality care, and that the church-mission facilities are usually filled to capacity with patients.   Often, government facilities nearby, that do not charge, have far fewer patients.[7]   Much more systematic empirical research work needs to be done on fee schedules and administrative processes at these church-mission facilities, so that governments can learn equitable cost recovery from them.

## HEALTH INSURANCE AND RISK-SHARING MECHANISMS

Health insurance is one in a portfolio of options that are available to augment government budgetary resources for health-care spending (Saunders, 1989; Akin, 1989; Borch, 1990).   Yet little comparative information is available on the kinds of health insurance that are presently extant in Sub-Saharan Africa.   The purpose of this section is to fill that gap in knowledge.   This section first attempts to define "health insurance."   Then, the following three ideas will be discussed:

the prevalence of health insurance; the contribution of health insurance to health finance; and the characteristics of the health insurance. Next will be an analysis of these schemes with respect to insurance criteria developed in the research literature on health insurance. And finally there will be a summary of what has been learned and the conclusions that can be drawn.

### What Constitutes Health Insurance?

Health insurance might be defined in various ways. For example, at some level of abstraction, a government health-care system, financed through general tax revenues and provided without charge to the population, could be considered to be a form of national health insurance, albeit an implicit or informal one. Likewise, throughout Sub-Saharan Africa, many firms provide free health care to their employees and to their families, either in the form of company-run clinics or through contracts with private physicians and clinics. In some countries (e.g., Zaire), this kind of coverage is mandated by government. At another level of abstraction, this too could be considered health insurance, because, in effect, the employer is required to maintain a pool of funds for health care (analogous to a sinking fund for the depreciation of physical capital), and, depending upon elasticities of the demand for and supply of labor, much of the "premium" may be shifted onto labor. In other countries (e.g., Zimbabwe), employers voluntarily provide company clinics or pay for health care for their employees and their families through contracts. Human capital theory would allow this practice to be considered to be providing health insurance, particularly for skilled and not-easily-replaced employees; in effect, the employer is self-insuring against the loss of skilled labor, particularly where the skilled labor is highly specialized, and hence, scarce.

Table 3-2 provides a typology for thinking about the nature of the conceptual problem in defining health insurance. Health-care risk-spreading mechanisms (health insurance) can either be mandated by government, or government and the private sector can offer risk-spreading plans that are voluntary. Because one of the major objectives of many government health insurance arrangements is usually to pool risk (or to redistribute the paying for the pooling of risk), participation in government arrangements is almost always compulsory. As shown in Table 3-2, government implicit and explicit health

**Table 3-2**
**Typology of the Forms of "Health Insurance" in Sub-Saharan Africa**

I.   Government: Mandated or Voluntary

   A. Free health care for all citizens (Tanzania).[a]

   B. Free health care for the poor, and cost recovery for those who can afford to pay (Ghana).

   C. Social security, or national health insurance (Senegal).[b]

   D. Government employees health insurance fund (Sudan).

   E. Discount for government employees (Ethiopia).

   F. Other public insurance (Kenya).

   G. Mandated employer coverage of employees, either by directly providing health care or contracting for it (Zaire).

II.  Private Sector: Voluntary

   A. Private insurance policies bought from insurance companies (Zimbabwe).

   B. Voluntary (self-insuring) risk pools (Rwanda).

   C. Employer-provided medical care directly in clinics (Zambia), or through contract (Nigeria).

[a]Countries in brackets are examples of where this form of "insurance" exists.
[b]Senegal has Social Security (the Prevoyance Sociale); no country in Sub-Saharan Africa presently has national health insurance (NHI), as it exists, say, in Great Britain, although forms of NHI that would cover fairly large segments of the formalized work force are under various phases of discussion in Ghana, Nigeria, and Zimbabwe.
*Source*:  Unpublished World Bank documents listed in second section of the references for this study.

insurance arrangements in Sub-Saharan Africa can be broadly characterized as taking these forms: free health care provided and financed for all citizens (e.g., Tanzania); health care provided by government and financed through the general tax fund and through cost recovery (e.g., Ghana); compulsory social security for the entire formal labor market (e.g., Senegal); a special health insurance fund for government employees (e.g., Sudan); a discount at health-care facilities for government employees (e.g., Ethiopia); other public "insurance," such as government employees' entitlement to private medical care as a fringe benefit (e.g., Kenya); and mandated employer coverage of health care for employees (e.g., Zaire). Likewise, in the private sector, one observes private insurance policies bought from insurance companies (e.g., Zimbabwe); small, local, voluntary risk pools (e.g., Rwanda); and employers voluntarily providing medical care directly (e.g., Zambia) or providing medical care on contract with private health-care providers (e.g., Nigeria). Each one of these arrangements spreads risk in varying degrees. The incidence of the payment for the spreading of the risk also varies, depending upon elasticities of supply and demand for labor, and the progressivity of the tax system used to finance the governmental arrangements.

Having considered these conceptual problems, some operational definitions have to be made. Therefore, for purposes of this section, "health insurance" is defined as a formal pool of funds, held by a third party (or by the provider, in the case of a Health Maintenance Organization, which relies on prepayment by its insurees), that pays for the health-care costs of the membership of the pool. This third party can be a governmental social security or other public insurance fund-pool, or any private fund-pool. Given this conservative definition of formal health insurance, employer-provided health care is not considered "health insurance."[8] Nonetheless, it must also be pointed out that, to the extent that these employer arrangements exist, they do free resources for MOH expenditures for the rest of the population.

### The Prevalence of Health Insurance

Table 3-3 summarizes the extent of explicit, or formal, health insurance coverage relative to population size in the twenty-three countries for which some data were available. As might be expected, there is a wide variation in the percentage of the population covered. Many countries simply have no formal health insurance arrangements.

# Table 3-3
## Coverage of Health Insurance in Sub-Saharan Africa[a]

| Country | Year | Population Size (Millions) (mid-1986) | Population Covered by | | | Total[b] | Percent of Population Insured (Including Family Members) |
|---|---|---|---|---|---|---|---|
| | | | Social Security | Other Public Insurance | Private Insurance | | |
| Burkina Faso | 1981 | 6.7 (1982) | Caisse Nationale de la Securite Sociale (CNSS) covers 60,000 workers in private sector and government employment, but no number of government employees is given for the government employees covered. | -- | -- | -- | -- |
| Burundi | 1986 | 4.9 (1986) | -- | .070[e] | -- | .070 | 1.4% |
| Cameroon | 1984 | 9.3 (1982) | d | -- | -- | -- | -- |
| Cote d'Ivoire | 1985 | 10.2 (1985) | Data not available on numbers of people insured, but a small private health insurance sector exists. | | | | |
| Ethiopia | 1986 | 43.5 | c | f | .060 | .060 | .14% |
| Ghana | 1987 | 13.2 | g | -- | -- | -- | -- |

# Table 3-3 (continued)

| Country | Year | Population Size (Millions) (mid-1986) | Population Covered by | | | Total[b] | Percent of Population Insured (Including Family Members) |
| --- | --- | --- | --- | --- | --- | --- | --- |
| | | | Social Security | Other Public Insurance | Private Insurance | | |
| Guinea | 1985 | 6.1 (1985) | Government employees are exempt from hospital admission charges. | | | -- | -- |
| Kenya | 1985 | 21.2 | 2.1[b] | .251[i] | .060 | 2.4[j] | 11.4% |
| Lesotho | 1986 | 1.6 | No insurance because of (a) large migratory labor force to South Africa where employers usually provide health care, and (b) enterprise coverage of local workers with health care provided. | | | | -- |
| Madagascar | 1985 | 10.3 (1985) | Apparently no formal insurance. | | | | |
| Malawi | 1985 | 7.2 | -- | | [k] | -- | -- |
| Mali | 1986 | 7.6 | .250 | 1 | -- | .250[m] | 3.3% |
| Mozambique | 1986 | 14.2 | -- | -- | -- | -- | -- |
| Niger | 1984 | 6.1 | -- | -- | -- | -- | -- |
| Nigeria | 1986 | 103.1 | -- | [n] | .426 | .426 | .04% |
| Senegal | 1987 | 6.8 | [o] | -- | -- | -- | -- |

| Country | Year | Population Size (Millions) (mid-1986) | Population Covered by | | | Total[b] | Percent of Population Insured (Including Family Members) |
| --- | --- | --- | --- | --- | --- | --- | --- |
| | | | Social Security | Other Public Insurance | Private Insurance | | |
| Sudan | 1986 | 22.6 | p | -- | -- | -- | -- |
| Swaziland | 1984 | .721 | -- | -- | Private insurance exists, but data not available from source. | -- | -- |
| Tanzania | 1987 | 23.0 | -- | -- | -- | -- | -- |
| Uganda | 1987 | 15.2 | -- | -- | -- | -- | -- |
| Zaire | 1986 | 32.2 | -- | -- | -- | -- | -- |
| Zambia | 1981 | 5.6 (1980) | -- | .342 | -- | .342 | 6.1% |
| Zimbabwe | 1987 | 8.7 | -- | -- | .400 | .400 | 4.6%[q] |

[a]The sources for the information contained in Tables 3-3, 3-4, and 3-5 are given for each country as the last entry for each country heading, in Table 3-5.

**Table 3-3 Notes (continued)**

[b]As explained in the text, in some countries (e.g., Zaire) private companies may be required to furnish health care or pay for health care for their employees. At some level of abstraction, this may be considered to be "health insurance." Here, for purposes of consistency of treatment, health insurance means *formal* health insurance, where contributions (either voluntary or by law) are placed into an insurance pool, and then withdrawn to pay medical bills. What the law in Zaire does, in effect, is force employers to self insure for its employees' health care. Because of space limitations in the Tables, numbers of people are always given in the millions. Thus, for example, the total population of Burundi is 4.9 million, and the total number of people insured is .070 million (or 70,000).

[c]Mutuelle de la Fonction Publique. 3% of salary paid by employee and 4.5% paid by government. Covers government employees and their families.

[d]Report (see sources) has an entry for "National Social Insurance Fund," data "not available."

[e]Social security and pension fund not involved in health care. Long range plan to adopt ILO guidelines for health insurance in social security plan.

[f]Government employees receive 50% discount at government facilities.

[g]Government has been studying the possibility of national health insurance (NHI) (mandated contributory) since 1985.

[h]Equivalent to more than half the urban population (NHIF-National Hospital Insurance Fund).

[i]Public service employees entitled to private medical care as a fringe benefit. Coverage is funded through MOH budget. Cost to MOH budget was Ksh 34.7 million in 1985-1986, or 2.2% of *total* MOH recurrent expenditure.

[j]Does not include workers in private sector who receive medical care from employer or have employer pay for medical care directly: see Table 3-4.

[k]Public fee schedule distinguishes between those with and without insurance, but no information on health insurance available.

[l]Each government ministry is expected to pay 80% of health care costs for its employees.

[m]Social security and other public insurance are not additive because public employees belong to both.

[n]Government employees and their families receive free government health care; but because cost recovery is so low, most of the rest of the population also receives free health care.

106

[o]Senegal has a social security system, the Institutions de Prevoyance Maladie (IPM). No data are available on the number of members. Every firm with 100 or more employees is required to form an "Institution" that will pay most of the costs of outpatient medical care and pharmaceuticals and, generally, all of the costs of hospitalization, including deliveries of children. Firms with less than 100 employees can join together to form an "Institution." This actuarial construction violates most insurance principles, because it ignores the law of large numbers, which protects against adverse selection (see Vogel, 1988).

[p]Government employees receive small monthly deduction from paycheck (1% for "regular" employees) in return for free health care at government facilities.

[q]Does not include workers in industry, mines, and commercial farms; see Table 3-4.

For the seven countries with formal health insurance (as defined above), the percentage of the total population insured ranges from a high of 11.4 percent in Kenya to .001 percent in Ethiopia. Table 3-3 shows that government employees are always given preferential treatment within public forms of health insurance. In Ethiopia, for example, government employees receive a 50 percent discount at government facilities, whereas the rest of the population, except for the very poor, does not receive the discount. As another example of this kind of preferential treatment, civil service employees in Kenya are entitled to private medical care as a fringe benefit; this fringe benefit is paid from funds in the MOH budget and cost 2.2 percent of the total MOH budget in 1986. Government employees are exempt from hospital admission charges in Guinea. In Mali, each ministry is expected to pay for 80 percent of its employees' health-care costs. Also, there is wide variation in the use of the social security system as a vehicle for health insurance.

The prevalence of private, formal health insurance in Sub-Saharan Africa is extremely small, as evidenced by the low percentage of the population covered. Private insurance has a foothold in only six countries: Cote d'Ivoire, Ethiopia, Kenya, Nigeria, Swaziland, and Zimbabwe. Even in Zimbabwe, where private insurance is comparatively well-developed, it only covers 4.6 percent of the total population. In Kenya, about 60,000 persons are covered by private health insurance plans, although the private insurance market for hospital care, at least, seems to have been preempted by the National Hospital Insurance Fund (NHIF), established in 1967, which is similar to social security in other Sub-Saharan countries, and which covers 2.1 million persons in Kenya.[9] Insurance schemes seem to cover the upper-income classes in the countries for which such information is available. As was alluded to earlier, many private companies directly provide free health care to their employees or contract for it. In this respect, Lesotho is a curious case, because many of its workers obtain employer health coverage in South Africa, into and out of which they migrate for work; their wives and children who remain in Lesotho depend upon the government of Lesotho for health care.

Finally, in studying the contents of Table 3-3, particularly for a country like Kenya, one wonders how many resources could be freed for the use of the poor, if expanded insurance coverage were provided to any more groups. In Kenya, at least, there already appears to be fairly widespread insurance coverage of the middle and upper classes, such that it would seem to be politically possible to devote more MOH resources to the poor.    However, the Kenyan health-care system remains urban and hospital intensive, even though the large majority of the population lives in rural areas.

### The Contribution of Insurance to Health Finance

Table 3-4 shows the contribution of health insurance to health-care finance.    Total recurrent expenditures are divided between the public and private sector, and between public and private insurance sources; out-of-pocket expenditures are also included.    However, the definition of out-of-pocket expenditures does pose some conceptual difficulties, depending upon whether the patient goes to a modern or traditional healer.    For example, some governments practice cost recovery.    If a person goes to a government health-care facility, he/she may pay for 20 percent of the cost of the care.    This is clearly an out-of-pocket payment.    If the same person goes to a traditional healer, and the cost of the treatment there is only one-fifth that in a government facility and the person pays 100 percent of this cost, he/she has paid the same total amount as at the government facility.    The basic problem here is directly related to the definition of total health expenditures in a country.    The truth of the matter is that estimates of expenditures for traditional care vary widely from country to country (Vogel, 1989) and from analyst to analyst.[10]    These traditional health expenditure estimates make up part of the "total" for each country in Vogel (1989), but they appear unreliable.    To the extent that they cannot be used in the base for health-insurance ratio comparisons, the percent of health expenditures that is insured becomes distorted.    For the share (ratio) comparisons in the last three columns of Table 3-4, traditional health care expenditures are excluded from both the category "out-of-pocket" and from the base, simply because they appear to be too variable and unreliable (Brunet-Jailly, 1988).

Estimates on the percentage share of out-of-pocket expenditures, including user fees and private expenditures, in the total range from 7.3 and 7.4 percent in Malawi and Mozambique, respectively, to 70.1 and 72.1 percent in Uganda and Mali.[11]    Part of this variability may be due to imprecision in the measurement of the total-expenditure base of the ratio.    Although every effort was made to include only those foreign aid expenditures in the total that were clearly for recurrent expenditures, some investment expenditures may have slipped into the estimates in the reports for each country that were used as sources.

## Table 3-4
## Contribution of Health Insurance to Health Finance

| Country | Year | Currency | Recurrent Health Expenditure, by Source* | | | | | | Total | Share of Out-of-Pocket in Total | Share of Private Insurance in Total | Share of Formal Public Insurance in Total |
| | | | Public | | | Private | | | | | | |
| | | | MOH Budget | Social Security Budget | Other Public Budget | Out-of-Pocket | Private Insurance | Other Private | | | | |
|---|---|---|---|---|---|---|---|---|---|---|---|---|
| Burkina Faso | 1981 | FCFA (millions) | 3,086 | 203a | 3,607b | 2,352c | -- | -- | 9,248 | 25.4% | -- | 0.220% |
| Burundi | 1986 | FBu (millions) | 1,267a | 489b | 1,076c | 628d | -- | -- | 2,984 | 21.0% | -- | 16.4% |
| Cameroon | 1983 | FCFA (millions) | 22,140 | -- | 331a | -- | -- | 6,100b | 28,571 | -- | -- | -- |

Burkina Faso
a Amount only available for government employees.
b Includes: (i) Other ministries, 1,068; (ii) Foreign aid, 2,349; (iii) Local government, 190.
c Includes: (i) Drug purchases, 2,298; (ii) Payment of hospital fees, 54.

Burundi
a Includes: (i) MOH 1,077; (ii) MOE 181; (iii) MSA 9.
b Includes: (i) Mutuelle de la Fonction Publique, 476; and (ii) social security, 13.
c Foreign aid.
d Includes missions (210 FBu), which are almost totally financed by out-of-pocket (210 FBu of 215 FBu).

Cameroon
a Foreign assistance for recurrent costs.
b No information on private sector available for Cameroon, except for the NGOs that spent the 6,100 million.

Recurrent Health Expenditure, by Source*

| Country | Year | Currency | Public | | | Private | | | Total | Share of Out-of-Pocket in Total | Share of Private Insurance in Total | Share of Formal Public Insurance in Total |
|---|---|---|---|---|---|---|---|---|---|---|---|---|
| | | | MOH Budget | Social Security Budget | Other Public Budget | Out-of-Pocket | Private Insurance | Other Private | | | | |
| Cote d'Ivoire | 1985 | FCFA (millions) | 29,085 | 300[a] | --[b] | 39,585[c] | 562 | -- | 69,532 | 56.9% | .081% | .043% |
| Ethiopia | 1986 | BIRR (millions) | 79.0[a] | -- | 20.0 | 196.5 | 0.6 | 5.7 | 301.8 | 65.0% | .02% | -- |
| Ghana | 1987 | Cedi (billions) | 5.5 | -- | --[a] | 11.0 | -- | 2.5 | 19.0 | 57.9% | -- | -- |
| Guinea | 1983 | Sylis (thousands) | 518,240 | -- | 35,000 | 236,000 | -- | -- | 789,240 | 29.9% | -- | -- |

[a]CNPS (Caisse Nationale de Prevoyance Sociale).
[b]Mutuelle Generale de Fonctionnaires and contained in MOH budget.
[c]Of this amount, 32,641 for drugs.

[a]Government employees receive 50% discount at government facilities.

[a]MOH employees and trainees receive all care free and 40% of all drugs issued at a sample of hospitals studied in 1988.

# Table 3-4 (continued)

| Country | Year | Currency | Public | | | Private | | | Total | Share of Out-of-Pocket in Total | Share of Private Insurance in Total | Share of Formal Public Insurance in Total |
|---|---|---|---|---|---|---|---|---|---|---|---|---|
| | | | MOH Budget | Social Security Budget | Other Public Budget | Out-of-Pocket | Private Insurance | Other Private | | | | |
| Kenya | 1984 | Kenyan Shilling (millions) | 1,232.2 | 109.0[a] | 227.3[b] | 1,175.6 | 35.3 | 96.6[c] | 2,876 | 40.9% | 1.23% | 3.8% |
| Lesotho | 1986 | Maloti (thousands) | 20,938 | -- | 3,122 | 10,726 | 432 | 26,519[a] | 61,737 | 17.4% | .07% | -- |
| Madagascar | 1985 | FMG (millions) | 13,693 | -- | 8,051[a] | 13,921 | -- | 4,753[b] | 40,418 | 34.4% | -- | -- |
| Malawi | 1986 | Malawi Kwacha (K) | 36,753 | -- | 8,600[a] | 3,578[b] | -- | -- | 48,931 | 7.3% | -- | -- |

*Recurrent Health Expenditure, by Source*

**Kenya**

[a]NHIF (National Hospital Insurance Fund).
[b]Includes: (i) Appropriations in aid to MOH, 3.7; (ii) Municipalities, 152.6; (iii) International donations, 71.0.
[c]Includes: (i) Missions, 29.3; (ii) Other NGOs, 13.4; (iii) Private companies, 53.9.

**Lesotho**

[a]Includes: (i) Foreign industry, 20,460; (ii) Foreign private aid, 1,174; (iii) Local voluntary bodies, 1,024; (iv) Missions, 3,861.

**Madagascar**

[a]Includes: (i) Other ministries, 3,599; (ii) Foreign aid, 4,452.
[b]Includes: (i) Collectivities, 399; (ii) NGOs, 934; (iii) Private enterprise, 3,420.

**Malawi**

[a]Includes: (i) Value of drugs in foreign assistance, 6,000; (ii) Foreign medical personnel in technical assistance, 2,600.
[b]Includes: (i) Fees at MOH facilities, 1,048; (ii) Fees at PHAM facilities, 2,530 (estimated).

| | | | Recurrent Health Expenditure, by Source* | | | | | | | Share of Out-of-Pocket in Total | Share of Private Insurance in Total | Share of Formal Public Insurance in Total |
| | | | Public | | | Private | | | | | | |
| Country | Year | Currency | MOH Budget | Social Security Budget | Other Public Budget | Out-of-Pocket | Private Insurance | Other Private | Total | | | |
|---|---|---|---|---|---|---|---|---|---|---|---|---|
| Mali | 1986 | FCFA (millions) | 4,025 | 380[a] | 640[b] | 13,036 | -- | -- | 18,081 | 72.1% | -- | 2.1% |

[a]About 50% of these funds go for administrative expenses.
[b]Includes: (i) Other Ministries, 98; (ii) Foreign aid, 542.

| Mozambique | 1985 | Metical (millions) | 698.8 | -- | --[a] | 55.9[b] | -- | -- | 754.7 | 7.4% | -- | -- |

[a]According to source, donor contributions have been substantial in recent years; amount not known.
[b]Cost-recovery revenues. In 1987, in the face of growing financial difficulties, a new, more comprehensive cost-recovery scheme was introduced, consisting of (i) a flat, one-time fee for outpatient consultations, (ii) payment for outpatient drugs, and (iii) a daily inpatient fee in urban hospitals.

| Niger | 1984 | FCFA (millions) | 4,455 | -- | 4,045[a] | 3,000[b] | -- | -- | 11,500 | 35.2% | -- | -- |

[a]Includes: (i) External assistance, 2,500; (ii) Ministry of Higher Education, 350; (iii) Ministry of Finance, 1,090 (of which 800 for foreign evacuations); (iv) Others, 105.
[b]Includes: (i) Drugs, 2,800; (ii) Other, 200.

| Nigeria | 1985 | Naira (millions) | 177.2 | -- | 592.1[a] | 698.9[b] | -- | 74.9[c] | 1,543.1 | 45.3 | -- | -- |

[a]Includes: (i) State expenditures, 436.6; (ii) Local government authorities, 155.5.
[b]Estimated from Over and Denton (1988), para. 5.14 and Table 5.3; 103.1 x .16 x 42.37 (population x %ill x average expenditure).
[c]Assumes that only the respondents to MOH questionnaire provide care; see "Comments" column in Table 3-5.

113

# Table 3-4 (continued)

| Country | Year | Currency | Recurrent Health Expenditure, by Source* | | | | | | Total | Share of Out-of-Pocket in Total | Share of Private Insurance in Total | Share of Formal Public Insurance in Total |
| --- | --- | --- | --- | --- | --- | --- | --- | --- | --- | --- | --- | --- |
| | | | Public | | | Private | | | | | | |
| | | | MOH Budget | Social Security Budget | Other Public Budget | Out-of-Pocket | Private Insurance | Other Private | | | | |
| Senegal | 1981 | FCFA (millions) | 6,890.4 | 175.7 | 9,479.9ᵃ | 6,919.9ᵇ | 4,156.8ᶜ | -- | 27,622.4 | 25.1% | 15.0% | .06% |
| Sudan | 1986 | LS (millions) | 131.0ᵃ | -- | -- | 479.1ᵇ | -- | 7.5ᶜ | 617.6 | 77.6% | -- | .09%ᵈ |
| Swaziland | 1984 | E (thousands) | 9,745 | -- | 3,500ᵃ | 3,600 | 1,200 | 3,100ᵇ | 21,145 | 17.0% | 5.7% | -- |

Senegal:
ᵃIncludes: (i) Special budget for civil servants, 1,201.2; (ii) External contributors, 4,530.9; (iii) Parastatal expenditures, 1,525.1; (iv) Local government expenditure, 1,179.1.
ᵇIncludes: (i) Community participation, 425.0; (ii) Import of pharmaceuticals, 6,494.9.
ᶜIncludes: (i) Hopital Principal, 2,294.0; (ii) Private doctors, 562.8; (iii) Private clinics, 1,300.0.

Sudan:
ᵃIncludes LS5.9 from deductions from monthly pay of government employees.
ᵇAverage of high and low estimate.
ᶜExpenditure by private firms.
ᵈ5.9/617.6, where 5.9 is deducted from government employees—see ᵃ.

Swaziland:
ᵃIncludes: (i) Other ministries, 600; (ii) Foreign assistance, 2,900.
ᵇIncludes: (i) Missions, 800; (ii) Voluntary organizations, 300; (iii) Industry and mines, 2,000.

**Recurrent Health Expenditure, by Source***

| Country | Year | Currency | Public | | | Private | | | Total | Share of Out-of-Pocket in Total | Share of Private Insurance in Total | Share of Formal Public Insurance in Total |
|---|---|---|---|---|---|---|---|---|---|---|---|---|
| | | | MOH Budget | Social Security Budget | Other Public Budget | Out-of-Pocket | Private Insurance | Other Private | | | | |
| Tanzania | 1987 | Tanzania Shilling (millions) | 1,838 | -- | 3,376[a] | --[b] | -- | -- | 5,214 | -- | -- | -- |
| Uganda | 1988 | Uganda Shilling (millions) | 62,417 | -- | 43,090[a] | 290,000 | -- | 14,861[b] | 410,368[c] | 70.1% | -- | -- |
| Zaire | 1986 | US$ (millions) | 10.0[a] | -- | -- | 41.0 | -- | 154[b] | 205.0 | 20.0% | -- | -- |

Tanzania:
[a]Includes: (i) Ministry of Local Government and Cooperation, 1,358; (ii) Office of the Prime Minister, 1,112; (iii) Donations of Drugs by Danida, 770; (iv) District and Urban Development Levy, 136.
[b]All health care at government facilities is officially free. Users of some mission facilities pay government-regulated fees. Many of the fees are for the drugs donated by Danida, but only at mission facilities. The expenditure amounts are unknown.

Uganda:
[a]Includes: (i) Mulago Hospital and Complex, 35,093; (ii) Ministry of Local Government, 7,997.
[b]NGOs.
[c]"Old" Shillings.

Zaire:
[a]Also covers health care of government employees.
[b]Includes: (i) Private-sector firms, 144.0; (ii) Donors and NGOs, separate breakdown not available, 10.0.

# Table 3-4 (continued)

| Country | Year | Currency | Recurrent Health Expenditure, by Source* | | | | | | | Share of Out-of-Pocket in Total | Share of Private Insurance in Total | Share of Formal Public Insurance in Total |
| --- | --- | --- | --- | --- | --- | --- | --- | --- | --- | --- | --- | --- |
| | | | Public | | | Private | | | | | | |
| | | | MOH Budget | Social Security Budget | Other Public Budget | Out-of-Pocket | Private Insurance | Other Private | Total | | | |
| Zambia | 1981 | Kwacha (millions) | 72.9 | -- | 30.9[a] | 19.9 | -- | 4.5 | 128.2 | 15.5% | -- | 24.1% |
| Zimbabwe | 1987 | Z$ (millions) | 310.18[a] | -- | 99.32[b] | 63.90 | 105.00 | 57.81[c] | 636.21 | 10.04% | 16.51% | -- |

[a]Zambian Consolidated Copper Mines (ZCCM), the state mining corporation.

[a]Central government.
[b]Includes: (i) Municipalities, 25.00; (ii) Foreign assistance 74.32.
[c]Includes: (i) Church missions, 2.56; (ii) Industries, mines, commercial farms, 50.75; (iii) Voluntary organizations, 4.50.

*Includes only recurrent expenditures and excludes expenditures on traditional medicine for reasons given in text.

One pattern that seems to emerge with respect to out-of-pocket costs is that in countries where there are large mining and enterprise interests, such as in Swaziland, Zaire, Zambia, and Zimbabwe, the percentages of out-of-pocket expenditures (at least for *formal* care) seem to be lower than in countries where such activity does not exist. What makes all of these estimates difficult though is the paucity and unreliability of the existing data on expenditures upon traditional care. For example, the out-of-pocket share for Burkina Faso, an extremely poor country, is 25.4 percent and in Guinea it is 29.9 percent which seem low relative to the 56.9 percent in the Cote d'Ivoire. However, these percentages may simply reflect the fact that the Cote d'Ivoire has been a relatively large importer of pharmaceuticals (see Vogel, 1989), for which people willingly pay cash at the many private pharmacies located around the country, but principally in the more affluent cities. Because of a lower per capita economic base, lower rate of economic growth, and consequent lack of foreign exchange, people in Burkina Faso and in Guinea do not have the pharmaceuticals available for purchase, and therefore turn to traditional healers; these people may be spending as high a share out-of-pocket, or even higher, than the people in the  Cote d'Ivoire, but this will not be reflected in the kind of data in Table 3-4.

The share of private insurance in the total ranges from zero in sixteen of the twenty-three countries to 15.0 and 16.5 percent in Senegal and Zimbabwe.   The estimate on private insurance expenditures in Zimbabwe is fairly firm, because the National Association of Medical Aid Societies (NAMAS, the approximate equivalent of the Blue Cross/Blue Shield Association in the U.S.) keeps good statistics.  The large share of private insurance for Senegal (15 percent) may simply be an artifact of the large expatriate community (mostly French) living in Senegal.[12] The expatriates are usually insured by sources outside of Senegal, such as the French Prevoyance Sociale, that pay expatriate health-care bills in Senegal.  As a case in point, the private Hopital Principal in Dakar is totally supported by insurance payments and out-of-pocket expenditures by its clientele, which is largely expatriate.  The annual budget of the Hopital Principal is about one-third the size of the Senegalese MOH budget (Vogel, 1987a).

The interpretation of the share of formal public insurance in the total is also subject to some ambiguity.  For example, in Burundi (16.4 percent), public insurance is dominated by the Mutuelle de la Fonction Publique which is for civil servants.   On the other hand, Table 3-4 shows no public health insurance in Nigeria, yet some thirty million (out of a total population of some 103 million) government employees and their families receive free health care from government facilities. Likewise, in Zambia public insurance finances 24.1 percent of recurrent health expenditure.    This figure results from the fact that the government owned Zambian Consolidated Copper Mines (ZCCM) has established a formal health insurance pool for the employees of the enterprise.

### The Characteristics of the Health Insurance

Table 3-5 presents the characteristics of the health insurance presently available in Sub-Saharan Africa.    It shows type of management, services covered, and whether there are deductibles and/or coinsurance.    Table 3-5 somewhat relaxes the definition of health insurance that has been previously used in this section, in order to give an idea of the variety of the types of health insurance coverage in Sub-Saharan Africa.  For example, in Nigeria, five large government owned businesses provide extremely comprehensive care for their employees and their families, either through their own health-care facilities or through contracts, and the 2,751 registered private employers (out of a total of 8,794 registered employers), who responded to a ministry of health questionnaire, provided similar combinations of coverage for their employees and families (Nigeria, Federal Ministry of Health, 1988).  The chief complaint from those employers who provided care for their employees either directly or on contract was the cost of the health care provided; it averaged about 6 percent of payroll for those employers who responded to the questionnaire.    Also, many of the employers who used contracts thought that many of their employees were abusing their health-care privileges by too-frequent use.  In general, these Nigerian plans cover both inpatient and outpatient treatment, and drugs.

In Kenya, an estimated 2.1 million employees and their families participate in the National Hospital Insurance Fund (NHIF) that was established by a parliamentary act in 1967.  Persons with a taxable income of Ksh 1,000 or more per month are required to contribute 20 shillings a month to the fund.  This amount has remained constant since 1967, with the result that while only 40,000 persons qualified in 1967, inflation in wages and salaries had driven the number to 90,000 by 1988.  Benefits include a fixed daily payment to the hospital of Ksh 200 with an upper limit of 180 days per year.  There is no deductible,

# Table 3-5
## Characteristics of Health Insurance in Sub-Saharan Africa

| Country | Plan | Year | Group(s) Covered | Type of Management | Enrolled | | Services Covered | | | |
|---|---|---|---|---|---|---|---|---|---|---|
| | | | | | Number | Percent Population | Inpatient Care | Outpatient Care | Preventive Care | Drugs |
| Burkina Faso | Caisse Nationale de la Securite Sociale | 1982 | Private workers in formal sector and government workers. | Public | 60,000 workers in private sector; number in public sector not known. No data on families. | .070 | Limited to medical expenditures and disabilities due to occupational injuries, and to the provision of MCH services for beneficiary families in towns. | | | |
| Burundi | Mutuelle de la Fonction Publique. | 1986 | Civil Servants and families. | Public | | 1.4% | Yes | Yes | Yes | Yes |
| Cameroon | There is no health insurance in Cameroon, except for the National Social Insurance Fund for which no data were available. | | | | | | | | | |

**Table 3-5 (continued)**

| Country | Unit of Enrollment | Annual Premium | Uniform Premium | Copayment | Deductible | Total Budget | Comments and Sources of Data |
|---|---|---|---|---|---|---|---|
| Burkina Faso ......... | Employee. | Deduction of 2.5% of salaries paid. | Varies with salary. | Not available. | Not available. | 203 million CFA | In 1984, Medecine du Travail was introduced (contributory system) but no further information is given on this. SAR, May, 1985. *Sources:* *Upper Volta: Health and Nutrition Sector Review*, November, 1982; *Staff Appraisal Report, Burkina Health Services Development Project*, May, 1985. |
| Burundi ......... | Person employed. | 3% of salary. | Varies with salary. | Yes—20%. | None. | 489 million FBU | The Mutuelle was begun in 1980 for civil servants and their families and (as of 1987) will be gradually extended to include employees of parastatals and commercial firms. *The insurance is currently financially viable.* State currently spending US$ 27 per capita on civil servants and US$ 2 on remaining population. *Source:* *Staff Appraisal Report, Burundi Population and Health Project*, November, 1987. |
| Cameroon ......... | -- | -- | -- | -- | -- | -- | *Source:* Cameroon: *Population, Health and Nutrition Sector Review*, October, 1984. |

120

# Table 3-5 (continued)

| Country | Plan | Year | Group(s) Covered | Type of Management | Enrolled | | Services Covered | | | |
|---|---|---|---|---|---|---|---|---|---|---|
| | | | | | Number | Percent Population | Inpatient Care | Outpatient Care | Preventive Care | Drugs |
| Cote d'Ivoire | (1) Caisse Nationale de Prevoyance Sociale. | -- | -- | Public | -- | -- | No information available on services covered for these three types of plan. | | | |
| | (2) Mutuelle Generale de Fonctionnaires. | -- | -- | Public | -- | -- | -- | -- | -- | -- |
| | (3) Numerous private insurance plans, including: | | | | | | | | | |
| | (a) group policies—for professional groups. | -- | -- | Private | -- | -- | -- | -- | -- | -- |
| | (b) individual policies. | -- | -- | Private | -- | -- | -- | -- | -- | -- |
| Ethiopia | Ethiopian Insurance Company | 1986 | Private persons. | Private | -- | -- | Yes | Yes | Yes | Yes |

121

# Table 3-5 (continued)

| Country | Unit of Enrollment | Annual Premium | Uniform Premium | Copayment | Deductible | Total Budget | Comments and Sources of Data |
|---|---|---|---|---|---|---|---|
| Cote d'Ivoire ........ | -- | -- | -- | -- | -- | -- | -- |
| ........ | -- | -- | -- | -- | -- | -- | -- |
| ........ | Person and family. | 156,000 per annum. | Apparently. | -- | -- | -- | *Sources:* F. Decaillet et G. Desrochers, Analyse du Systeme de Sante et Financement de Son Fonctionnement, Rapport de Mission en Cote d'Ivoire, aout, 1988 (2 ieme Partie); R. Vogel, *Cost Recovery in the Health Care Sector: Selected Country Studies in West Africa,* May, 1988. |
| ........ | Person and family. | 250,000-300,000 per annum. | Apparently. | -- | -- | -- | |
| Ethiopia ........ | Family. | 230 Birr. | -- | Upper limits on Birr per visit and number of visits per year. | | 0.6 million Birr | When economic conditions improve, Ethiopia plans to implement health insurance benefits within its social security and pension fund. The Ethiopian Insurance Company now has acquired valuable administrative experience, albeit for a small group of people.<br><br>*Source:* *Sector Review, Ethiopia, A Study of Health Financing Issues and Options,* February, 1987. |

**Table 3-5 (continued)**

| Country | Plan | Year | Group(s) Covered | Type of Management | Enrolled | | Services Covered | | | |
|---|---|---|---|---|---|---|---|---|---|---|
| | | | | | Number | Percent Population | Inpatient Care | Outpatient Care | Preventive Care | Drugs |
| Ghana | National health insurance under consideration. | -- | -- | -- | --[a] | -- | -- | -- | -- | -- |
| Guinea | None exists. | -- | -- | -- | -- | -- | -- | -- | -- | -- |
| Kenya | National Hospital Insurance Fund (NHIF). | 1984 | People with taxable income of Ksh 1,000 or more per month. | Public | 2,100,000 | 9.9% | Yes | No | No | If in hospital. |

[a] Potential contributors include: (i) 200-300,000 independent cocoa farmers; (ii) 2 million employees in formal labor markets; (iii) 200,000 civil servants.

123

## Table 3-5 (continued)

| Country | Unit of Enrollment | Annual Premium | Uniform Premium | Copay-ment | Deduct-ible | Total Budget | Comments and Sources of Data |
|---|---|---|---|---|---|---|---|
| Ghana ........ | -- | -- | -- | -- | -- | -- | Employers provide health care for employees, but data are scarce. As of January 1, 1989, MOH employees and trainees will have to pay the full cost of drugs that they use, as will all other persons subject to cost recovery. |
| | | | | | | | *Sources:* Ghana: *Population, Health and Nutrition Sector Review,* October, 1988; R. Vogel, *Cost Recovery in the Health Care Sector.* |
| Guinea ........ | -- | -- | -- | None exists. | | -- | Government workers are exempted from hospital admission charges (treated as an internal transfer between MOH and MOF). There are no premiums, however. |
| | | | | | | | *Source:* Guinea: *Population, Health and Nutrition Sector Review,* May, 1986. |
| Kenya ........ | Employee. | Ksh 240 | Varies by income. | Yes | No | 109.0 million Ksh | Benefits consist of fixed daily payment to hospital of Ksh 200 for 180 days per year. This covers some hospitals, but in others, patient pays the higher difference, as a copayment. |
| | | | | | | | *Source:* Kenya: *Review of Expenditure Issues and Options in Health Financing,* June, 1988. |

**Table 3-5 (continued)**

| Country | Plan | Year | Group(s) Covered | Type of Manage-ment | Enrolled | | Services Covered | | | |
|---|---|---|---|---|---|---|---|---|---|---|
| | | | | | Number | Percent Popula-tion | Inpa-tient Care | Outpa-tient Care | Pre-ventive Care | Drugs |
| Kenya (continued) | Public employees. | 1986 | Public employee fringe benefit for *private* medical care. | Public (MOH) | -- | -- | Yes | Yes | Yes | Yes |
| | Private plans (60 insurance firms). | 1984 | Private employees and some families of employees. | Private | 60,000 | .03% | Yes | Yes | Yes | Yes |
| Lesotho | No public or private health in-surance in Lesotho. | 1986 | -- | -- | -- | -- | -- | -- | -- | -- |
| Madagascar | Apparently no public or private health insurance. | | | | -- | | | | | |

125

**Table 3-5 (continued)**

| Country | Unit of Enrollment | Annual Premium | Uniform Premium | Copay-ment | Deduct-ible | Total Budget | Comments and Sources of Data |
|---|---|---|---|---|---|---|---|
| Kenya (continued) | Government employee. [a]Varies inversely with employee grade. | 0 | 0 | Yes[a] | No | 27.12 million Ksh | This fringe benefit represents 2.2% of total MOH recurrent budget. |
| | Group insurance for company employees. | Varies by company. | Varies by company. | Varies by company. | Varies by company. | | All private plans have set annual limits to claims by individuals. Private insurance benefits are in addition to those obtained under NHIF which has led to overconsumption of covered inpatient services. |
| Lesotho | -- | -- | -- | -- | -- | -- | Health insurance is not offered by any companies operating in Lesotho. Enterprises spend as much as the ministry of health does on health care for their employees. The Lesotho Civil Service Medical Aid Scheme has ceased to operate. Similar aid schemes continue to operate in Botswana and Swaziland. <br><br> *Source:   Health Financing in Lesotho, 1987.* |
| Madagascar | -- | -- | -- | -- | -- | -- | *Source:   Madagascar:  Population and Health Sector Review, July, 1987.* |

**Table 3-5 (continued)**

| Country | Plan | Year | Group(s) Covered | Type of Management | Enrolled | | Services Covered | | | |
|---|---|---|---|---|---|---|---|---|---|---|
| | | | | | Number | Percent Population | Inpatient Care | Outpatient Care | Preventive Care | Drugs |
| Malawi | There is no public or private health insurance in Malawi. | | | | | | | | | |
| Mali | Institut Nationol de Prevoyance Social (INPS). | 1986 | Public- and private-sector employees and their families. | Public | 250,000 | 3.3% | Yes | Yes | Yes | Yes |

127

**Table 3-5 (continued)**

| Country | | Unit of Enrollment | Annual Premium | Uniform Premium | Copay-ment | Deduct-ible | Total Budget | Comments and Sources of Data |
|---|---|---|---|---|---|---|---|---|
| Malawi | ........ | -- | -- | -- | -- | -- | -- | Private medical practice is limited to about thirty-five physicians in urban areas. The Private Hospitals Association (PHAM) provides about 45% of the country's health services. PHAM is church-related. Local government authorities and other agencies such as the army, police, estates, and industries provide curative and preventive services for their employees. |
| | | | | | | | | *Source:*  *Staff Appraisal Report, Malawi Second Family Health Project*, February, 1987. |
| Mali | ........ | Employee & family. | Employer contributes 2% of em-ployee's salary for health insur-ance portion of INPS. | Varies with salary. | Care provided free in INPS industrial clinics. | | 380 million FCFA | Because drugs are rarely available in public-sector facilities and INFS clinics, patients must buy them in private market. |
| | | | | | | | | *Source:*  J. Brunet-Jailly, *Le Financement des Couts Recurrents de la Sante au Mali*, Premiere Redaction, septembre, 1988. |

**Table 3-5 (continued)**

| Country | Plan | Year | Group(s) Covered | Type of Management | Enrolled Number | Enrolled Percent Population | Inpatient Care | Services Covered Outpatient Care | Services Covered Preventive Care | Services Covered Drugs |
|---|---|---|---|---|---|---|---|---|---|---|
| Mali (continued) | Government employees. | 1986 | Each ministry is expected to pay 80% of its employees' and families' health-care costs. | Public | 200,160 | 2.6% | Yes | Yes | Yes | Yes |
| Mozambique | There is no public or private health insurance in Mozambique. | | | | -- | -- | -- | -- | -- | -- |
| Niger | There is no public or private health insurance in Niger. | | | | -- | -- | -- | -- | -- | -- |

129

**Table 3-5 (continued)**

| Country | | Unit of Enrollment | Annual Premium | Uniform Premium | Copay-ment | Deduct-ible | Total Budget | Comments and Sources of Data |
|---|---|---|---|---|---|---|---|---|
| Mali (continued) | ........ | Government employee and family. | 0 | -- | Yes | No | Indeter-minate | In practice, ministries rarely pay the 80% of treatment costs, so that government health facilities end up absorbing the loss.<br><br>*Source:*  Ronald J. Vogel, *Cost Recovery in the Health Care Sector*, 1988. |
| Mozambique | ........ | -- | -- | -- | -- | -- | -- | *Source:*  Mozambique: *Staff Appraisal Report, Health and Nutrition Project*, September, 1988. |
| Niger | ........ | -- | -- | -- | -- | -- | -- | *Source:*  *Staff Appraisal Report, Health Project*, February, 1986. |

# Table 3-5 (continued)

| Country | Plan | Year | Group(s) Covered | Type of Management | Enrolled Number | Enrolled Percent Population | Inpatient Care | Outpatient Care | Preventive Care | Drugs |
|---|---|---|---|---|---|---|---|---|---|---|
| Nigeria | (1) National Insurance Corp. of Nigeria (NICON). | 1984 | Staff, wives, and children under 18. | Parastatal | 1,500[a] | [b] | Yes | Yes | Yes | Yes |
| | (2) National Electric Power Authority (NEPA). | 1984 | Staff, wives, and children under 18. | Parastatal | 28,000[a] | [b] | Yes | Yes | Yes | Yes |
| | (3) Nigerian Ports Authority (NPA) | 1984 | Staff, wives, and children under 18. | Parastatal | 22,000[a] | [b] | Yes | Yes | Yes | Yes |
| | (4) Nigeria Airways Ltd. | 1984 | Staff, family. Also treats retired staff. | Parastatal | 8,967[a] | [b] | Yes | Yes | Yes | Yes |

**Table 3-5 (continued)**

| Country | | Unit of Enrollment | Annual Premium | Uniform Premium | Copayment | Deductible | Total Budget | Comments and Sources of Data |
|---------|---|--------------------|----------------|-----------------|-----------|------------|--------------|------------------------------|
| Nigeria | ......... | Employee. | N400 per staff—paid by parastatal. | None | None | None | 600,000 Naira | Staff submits photographs of self, wife/wives, and children in order to avoid abuses. NICON uses Mount Sainair Hospital in Lagos. Retainers at weekends for admissions and child delivery. All other medical services are obtained from the Nigerian Railway Corporation Hospital which charges a minimal fee of N25 per visit. |
| | ......... | Employee. | N428.51 per staff—paid by parastatal. | None | None | None | 12,000,000 Naira | Staff submits photographs of self, wife/wives, and children. Referral letters are issued in triplicate. |
| | ......... | Employee. | N272.72 per staff—paid by parastatal. | None | None | None | 6,000,000 Naira | NPA stopped the use of retainers for private health care at the end of 1984, due to rising costs. Now the authority runs its own clinic and refers admission cases to government hospitals and the Lagos University Teaching Hospital (LUTH). |
| | ......... | Employee. | N234.62 per staff—paid by parastatal. | None | None | None | 1,400,000 Naira | Nigeria Airways had always had its own clinic prior to 1978. It referred its outpatients to Lagos University Teaching Hospital. These services became unreliable during the period of the oil boom, so in 1978 it started using retainers for private health care. |

132

**Table 3-5 (continued)**

| Country | Plan | Year | Group(s) Covered | Type of Management | Enrolled Number | Enrolled Percent Population | Services Covered Inpatient Care | Services Covered Outpatient Care | Services Covered Preventive Care | Services Covered Drugs |
|---|---|---|---|---|---|---|---|---|---|---|
| Nigeria (continued) | (5) Nigeria Railway Corp. (NRC). | 1984 | Staff, and family. Children over 18 and employed, not covered. | Parastatal | 35,000[a] | [b] | Yes | Yes | Yes | Yes |
| | (6) 2,751 private companies. | 1988 | Varies[c] | Private | 330,394[d] | [b] | Yes | Yes | Yes | Yes |

[a]Includes only staff, not data for families.
[b]Of a total population of 103 million, too small a percentage to report.
[c]Details for each private firm are not available; only averages are given.
[d]Employees and families.

133

**Table 3-5 (continued)**

| Country | Unit of Enrollment | Annual Premium | Uniform Premium | Copay-ment | Deduct-ible | Total Budget | Comments and Sources of Data |
|---|---|---|---|---|---|---|---|
| Nigeria (continued) | ........ | ........ Employee. | N282.85 per staff— paid by parastatal. | None | None | None | 9,900,000 Naira | Provides dentures but not reading glasses. NRC has always had its own clinic in Lagos. Emphasis is on maximum utilization of its medical personnel (which at present stands at 1,082), and the control of amount spent on drugs and maintenance. |
| | ........ Employee. | N200— average cost per staff family per year, or N16.67 per month. | Varies | Varies | Varies | 45,020,863 Naira (6.5% of total payroll) for the 1,031 firms that responded to this question. | There are 8,794 registered private employers in Nigeria with 1,162,854 employees (or, an average of 132.2 employees per firm). In 1988, the National Committee on the Establishment of Health Insurance Scheme in Nigeria sent out 7,400 questionnaires to private employers; 37.2% (2,751) responded. Of these, 887 employers supplied in-house care; 1,854 employers had private arrangements on doctor premises; and 1,829 employers reimbursed employees in part or in whole. The average cost of a hospital admission was N127.00. |

*Source:* Federal Ministry of Health, *Appendices to the Report of the National Committee on the Establishment of Health Insurance Scheme in Nigeria* (NCEHISN), September, 1988.

134

**Table 3-5 (continued)**

| Country | Plan | Year | Group(s) Covered | Type of Management | Enrolled | | Services Covered | | | |
|---|---|---|---|---|---|---|---|---|---|---|
| | | | | | Number | Percent Population | Inpatient Care | Outpatient Care | Preventive Care | Drugs |
| Senegal | Institutions de Prevoyance Sociale (IPS). No documentation is available for the IPS. | | | | | | | | | |
| | Private insurance is pervasive among the some 30,000 expatriates (mostly French) in Senegal, the expenditures of which largely go to finance the Hopital Principal, but no data were available. | | | | | | | | | |
| Sudan | Ministry of Health. | 1986 | All government employees. | Public | No data available. | -- | Entitles GOS employees and their families to free Class II or "B" hospital beds for duration of stay. | -- | -- | -- |
| Swaziland | Not known. | -- | -- | -- | -- | -- | -- | -- | -- | -- |

135

**Table 3-5 (continued)**

| Country | | Unit of Enrollment | Annual Premium | Uniform Premium | Copay-ment | Deduct-ible | Total Budget | Comments and Sources of Data |
|---|---|---|---|---|---|---|---|---|
| Senegal | ........ | -- | -- | Varies with salary. | -- | -- | -- | The Institutions de Prevoyance Sociale requires a 6% contribution on the part of employers and employees. There are no data presently available on the number of firms/people enrolled, nor on the finances of the Institutions de Prevoyance Sociale.<br><br>*Sources:* Senegal: *Staff Appraisal Report, Rural Health Project*, November, 1982; and R. Vogel, *Cost Recovery in the Health Care Sector*, 1988. |
| Sudan | ........ | Employee. | 1% of salary. | Varies with salary. | None | None | 5.59 million Sudanese Pounds | Due to GOS financial difficulties in 1980s, rapid growth of private sector (e.g., in 1983), there were three private hospitals in Khartoum area; in 1987 there were fifteen private hospitals.<br><br>*Source:* Sudan: *Population, Health and Nutrition Sector Review*, June, 1987. |
| Swaziland | ........ | -- | -- | -- | -- | -- | -- | *Source:* Swaziland: *Population, Health and Nutrition Sector Review*, June, 1987. |

136

**Table 3-5 (continued)**

| Country | Plan | Year | Group(s) Covered | Type of Management | Enrolled | | Services Covered | | | |
| --- | --- | --- | --- | --- | --- | --- | --- | --- | --- | --- |
| | | | | | Number | Percent Population | Inpatient Care | Outpatient Care | Preventive Care | Drugs |
| Tanzania | There is no public or private health insurance in Tanzania. | | | | -- | -- | -- | -- | -- | -- |
| Uganda | There is no public or private health insurance in Uganda for the indigenous population. | | | | | -- | | -- | -- | -- |

137

**Table 3-5 (continued)**

| Country | | Unit of Enrollment | Annual Premium | Uniform Premium | Copay-ment | Deduct-ible | Total Budget | Comments and Sources of Data |
|---|---|---|---|---|---|---|---|---|
| Tanzania | ........ | -- | -- | -- | -- | -- | -- | Tanzania has no health insurance. Per capita health expenditures have continued to decline during the 1980s.<br><br>*Sources:* *Population, Health and Nutrition Sector Review*, October, 1988; R. Vogel, *Financing the Health Sector in Tanzania: A Public Expenditure Review*, December, 1987. |
| Uganda | ........ | -- | -- | -- | -- | -- | -- | Private health insurance does exist for the expatriate community (i.e., for those employed in international concerns, e.g., the banks), but for the indigenous population, private health insurance has not emerged as a source of financing. The health insurance that does exist for the expatriates often entails expenditures abroad.<br><br>*Source:* K. Lee, W. Hull, and G. Hoare, *The Cost and Financing of Health Services in Uganda*, December 1987. |

138

**Table 3-5 (continued)**

| Country | Plan | Year | Group(s) Covered | Type of Management | Enrolled Number | Enrolled Percent Population | Inpatient Care | Outpatient Care | Preventive Care | Drugs |
|---------|------|------|------------------|--------------------|-----------------|----------------------------|----------------|-----------------|-----------------|-------|
| Zaire | Mandated coverage. | 1986 | Private sector employees and families. | Private | 7.2 million | 22.4% | Yes | Yes | Yes | Yes |
| Zambia | State mines. | 1981 | Employees and families. | Public | 342,000 | 6.1% | Yes | Yes | Yes | Yes |
| Zimbabwe | NAMAS.[a] | 1987 | Employees and families. | Private | 384,000 | 4.6%[b] | Yes | Yes | Yes | Yes |

[a]National Association of Medical Aid Societies.
[b]Percentage estimate of *total* population, the number enrolled contains only employees (384,050) *not* their family members.

**Table 3-5 (continued)**

| Country | | Unit of Enrollment | Annual Premium | Uniform Premium | Copay-ment | Deduct-ible | Total Budget | Comments and Sources of Data |
|---|---|---|---|---|---|---|---|---|
| Zaire | ........ | Person employed. | 0 | N.A. | None | None | 144.0 million U.S.$ | By law, employers are required to furnish health care or pay for the health care of their employees. In 1986, 10% of personnel expenses in the private sector went for health care. Private enterprise expenditures were $20 per person, while MOH expenditures were $0.33. *Source:* Zaire: *Population, Sante et Nutrition, Etude Sectorielle*, septembre, 1988. |
| Zambia | ........ | Person employed. | 0 | N.A. | None | None | 30.9 million Kwacha | Employees at the Zambia Consolidated Copper Mines only constitute 6.1% of the population, but have 24.1% of total country health expenditures spent upon them. There are no user fees in the public health system of Zambia. *Source:* Zambia: *Population, Health and Nutrition Sector Review*, May, 1984. |
| Zimbabwe | ........ | Employee. | Z$ 275[c] | Varies by income. | No[d] | No | 105.0 million Z$ | Insurance heavily subsidized by tax deductions for both employer and employee. *Source:* Zimbabwe: *Issues in the Financing of Health Care*, August, 1989. |

[c]*Average* annual premium paid.
[d]Only copayment required for drugs.

and the sole copayment consists of paying the difference between the maximum Ksh 200 per hospital day and any more expensive hospital care that is chosen. Only inpatient care is covered. In addition, public employees have a fringe benefit whereby 2.2 percent of the total MOH recurrent budget is used to subsidize their use of private medical care; this fringe benefit covers inpatient, outpatient, and drug care. There is no deductible, but there is a coinsurance provision where the government employee pays a coinsurance rate that varies inversely with the employee's government grade level. Finally, about 60,000 employees and their families benefit from group health insurance policies, the benefits and premiums of which vary by company. All of these private plans have set annual limits to the claims that they will pay for the individual, and these private health insurance benefits are in addition to those obtained under the NHIF, which is reported to have led to too frequent and frivolous use of covered inpatient services.

The kind of private health insurance that exists in Zimbabwe is of some interest because it very closely approximates the old Blue Cross/Blue Shield model of health insurance that prevailed in the U.S. during the 1960s and 1970s, with all of the consequent perverse efficiency effects that the model had on both the consumers and producers of health care in the U.S. Prior to the 1980s, Blue Cross/Blue Shield offered almost complete coverage of hospital care and generous physician reimbursement. Because of its service-benefit payment method, which was essentially cost based, and paid retrospectively, and because of low deductibles and coinsurance, neither consumers nor providers had any incentive to economize in the consumption and production of medical care. The National Association of Medical Aid Societies (NAMAS), which is the national association for the nonprofit medical aid societies (the analogs of the individual Blue Cross/Blue Shield plans in the U.S.) estimates that it had enrolled about 384,000 employees and their families by 1987, which was about 4.6 percent of the total population of Zimbabwe. The total enrollment was 224,000 employees in 1981 at independence, which indicates that the medical aid societies that are members of NAMAS have enjoyed rapid growth in their enrollees. Perhaps the major reason for this rapid growth is that the premiums charged do not represent the true cost of care, particularly in government hospitals and in the large and sophisticated, government-owned Parirenyatwa Tertiary Hospital, where NAMAS enrollees enjoy a large subsidy—the difference between what it costs the hospital to provide a day of care and what

NAMAS member insurers pay.  For example, only 3.5 percent of NAMAS expenditures went to government (MOH) hospitals in 1987.[13] The largest percentage, 48.6 percent, went to private physicians and dentists with whom NAMAS negotiates fee schedules, and which presumably does reflect the true marginal cost of private physician and dental practice.   NAMAS estimates that its maximum market penetration in Zimbabwe would ultimately be about 10-11 percent of the total population, given the lower income of the other 90 percent of the population.   The premiums that NAMAS member societies charge employers/employees vary with the income of the employee, so that some intraplan cross subsidization among employees does take place.   NAMAS plans do not use deductibles, but a copayment is required for the purchase of drugs.

### Analysis of the Major Issues in Health Insurance

The four tables reveal the diversity of the health insurance arrangements that exist in Sub-Saharan Africa.  One can use at least five criteria for evaluating these different forms of health insurance (Feldstein, 1988).  These criteria are:  who benefits from them; the incentives for efficiency that are built into them; the equity of the financing mechanisms; their ease of administration; and their political acceptability.

#### Beneficiaries

In the prototypical case of the Sub-Saharan countries, the majority of the population is informally insured by the ministry of health, with free care financed through the general tax fund.  If there is cost recovery, everyone but the poor, in effect, pays some deductible and/or coinsurance.  However, the distribution of health care facilities and MOH health expenditures is such that the poor do not even receive a proportional share of the health care.  This situation can be changed by redistributing the given budget for health expenditures towards the poor.  If such a direct redistributive policy is not politically possible, then government must resort to indirect means of redistribution.  One way of doing this is to mandate formal health insurance for those in the formal labor market either by (a) requiring the employer to provide health care for his/her employees, (b) requiring the employer to provide health insurance (both [a] and [b] being implicit taxes on labor), or (c) requiring the employer and the employee to contribute to a health insurance fund (the incidence of this implicit tax will depend upon elasticities of demand for and supply of labor). The proceeds from these implicit taxes then augment the total resources available for health care expenditures, and a greater percentage of the MOH budget can then be spent upon the poor.

Another strategy would be for the government to create a formal national health insurance for the formal labor market, financed by an explicit payroll tax. Again total resources for health expenditures are increased, and a greater percentage of the MOH budget can be spent upon the poor; the incidence of the explicit tax depends upon the elasticity of demand for and supply of labor. With either arrangement of financing, total demand for health care will have increased, and, depending upon medical-care supply elasticities, the price per unit of medical care should increase. How large the new subsidy for medical care for the poor should be can only be a value judgement, unless the decision is based upon a cost-benefit analysis. The basic economic argument for the subsidy is that there are externalities in the consumption of medical care by the poor,[14] and that employers/employees in the formal labor market are willing to bear the implicit or explicit taxes rather than having the preexisting MOH budget redistributed, in order that more care go to the poor.

The primary beneficiaries of the implicit (informal) kinds of national health insurance that exist in the sixteen countries where there is no formal health insurance seem to be government employees. In most cases, they receive some kind of preferential treatment over the rest of the citizenry, either in not having to pay any cost-recovery fees or in getting some kind of discount for hospital and physician services, and even for drugs in some cases (e.g., Ghana). Likewise, because most government employees tend to live in or near major cities, where most of the health-care facilities are located, their time costs for obtaining care would be lower. In the countries where there is formal health insurance, government employees again seem to receive much more favorable treatment than the rest of the population (e.g., the government-employee fringe benefit in Kenya). In most countries with employer-provided health care or "insurance," the employees in the formal labor market benefit, and to the extent that the demand for skilled labor is relatively inelastic, the employer probably bears the major burden of the "tax" for this coverage and/or insurance. As a case in point, the employees of Zambia Consolidated Copper Mines

(ZCCM) constitute only 6.1 percent of the total population of Zambia, but receive 24.1 percent of the country's total health expenditures. In none of these countries (perhaps with the exception of Tanzania [Vogel, 1987b] or Ethiopia [Ethiopia, World Bank, 1987], where the two governments have made strong efforts to provide care in rural areas) do those in the nonformal labor sector seem to benefit from either nonformal or formal health insurance, both because they are either not covered or because they live in areas of the country where the government spends very little on health care.

Also, it should be noted that public insurance efforts can compete with or even replace private insurance for some groups, which may not be a desirable outcome.  There are ways in which private insurers can be encouraged by government policy (e.g., by reinsurance or by stop-loss provisions; see Vogel, 1991), without the government becoming a provider of health insurance.  Employer-provided care at least lessens the financial burden on the public sector, for an insurable group that is willing to pay.

### Incentives for Efficiency

Considerations about efficiency center upon efficiency in the consumption of medical care and efficiency in its production. Efficiency in consumption refers to having an incentive structure that induces persons to consume health care in an economically prudent manner (i.e., the absence of "frivolous" consumption).  Efficiency in production refers to having an incentive structure that induces providers to take into account the economic costs of the treatment that they render.  Efficiency in consumption can be encouraged through insurance coverage that gives the correct insurance price signals to consumers.  If only hospital inpatient care is covered by the insurance, while out-of-pocket payment must be made for outpatient care, hospital inpatient care will be overconsumed at the margin.  Likewise, the insurance benefit structure should be such that it gives strong incentives to use the referral system.  The insured should also have insurance price incentives to seek out less costly forms of health care and not to overutilize the health care.  Deductibles and coinsurance (related to income, if administratively possible) are usually used for this purpose.

Perhaps, more important than efficiency in consumption is efficiency in production.  Fuchs (1982) shows that, although the patient-consumer initiates the health-care encounter by deciding to go for health care and to what kind of provider, the provider then begins a chain of treatment decisions for the patient that can have large cost implications.  If the insurance mechanism reimburses the provider in such a manner that the provider bears no financial risk, then the provider will behave differently than if he/she is placed at financial risk for the treatment decisions taken.  Prepaid capitated forms of insurance reimbursement are usually seen as the vehicle that is most conducive to shifting financial risk to the provider of treatment.

Because most of the health insurance reimbursement in Table 3-4 is an open-ended cost-based type (e.g., Zimbabwe), or represents transfers from ministry to ministry (e.g., Mali), the producers of the health care are at no financial risk, and therefore have no incentive to be efficient.  Consumers of health care face low or no deductibles and coinsurance (e.g., Zimbabwe or Nigeria), and they too have no financial incentive to exercise ordinary economic prudence in the consumption of medical care.  Even when there is insurance, deductibles/copayments of some type are a desirable feature to prevent moral hazard.  Insurance, therefore, does not replace a user-fee system; there should always be some form of deductible/copayments.

### Equitable Financing

Given that the objective of the formal health insurance initiative is to pool risk for everyone and to cover the externalities in the consumption of medical care by the poor (i.e., that society as a whole benefits when the poor have more access to medical care, without having to pay for it), it would always be preferable, on equity grounds, to finance the increase in total resources for the MOH with a progressive income tax, rather than with the implicit or explicit payroll taxes outlined earlier.  Payroll taxes, particularly those with an upper limit on the base of the tax rate, are regressive to income.  However, the poor are not required to pay the implicit or explicit taxes unless they participate in the formal labor market, so that the implicit and explicit taxes are not as regressive to the income of the different income classes as would be implicit or explicit payroll taxes that would be applicable to all income classes.  With respect to equity in the financing of additional health services for the poor in Sub-Saharan Africa, we can assume that a progressive income surtax earmarked for health care cannot be enacted for the same political reasons that the preexisting MOH budget cannot be reallocated more toward the poor.

Much of the informal and formal insurance is provided by government to upper- and middle-income government employees. The tax systems used to finance this insurance are, at best, proportional, and in many cases, regressive to income. Therefore, in general, these governmental health insurance systems can be judged to be regressive to income, both in who benefits from them and in who pays the taxes to finance them. Many of the private employer schemes appear to be proportional or progressive to income, to the extent that the employer bears the incidence of the "tax" (premium) in tight labor markets for skilled personnel.

### Administrative Aspects

Because the major policy goals of introducing health insurance into Sub-Saharan Africa are to mobilize more resources for health care for the poor and to create incentives for greater allocational and internal efficiency within the health care system, a major design imperative for this health insurance is that it be one that can be administered as easily and inexpensively as possible.

There is little empirical evidence on the administrative costs of health insurance in the Sub-Sahara. The costs of administration of the Prevoyance Sociale in Mali may approach as much as 50 percent of revenues (Vogel, 1988), but NAMAS in Zimbabwe indicates that its member medical aid societies' administrative costs are probably less than 10 percent of revenues. There are many practical problems to be solved in designing health insurance that is financially sustainable, including actuarial data on the costs of care and the amounts of services that will be demanded (Borch, 1990).

### Political Acceptability

Finally, the design of formal health insurance should take into account its probable political acceptability by employee-consumers, employers, providers, and government. If those employees/employers who are taxed (either implicitly or explicitly) do not believe that they benefit from the health insurance, or do not believe that the consequently freed funds in the MOH budget are used efficiently and effectively upon the poor, there will be taxpayer   resistance and noncompliance, over and above that which would have occurred with a well-designed formal health care insurance. Likewise, if the providers of health care believe that they are not treated fairly and reasonably in the transfer of financial risk, they will not respond in an optimal fashion to the incentives offered by the health insurance. Assuming that the formal health insurance is designed at the ministry of health, it will not become a reality and function smoothly for its redistributive and efficiency objectives, if it does not find approval at the ministry of finance, in the parliament and at the presidential level.

### Final Observations on Health Insurance

The larger percentage of MOH budgetary expenditures in these countries (with the possible exception of Tanzania and Ethiopia) is skewed towards a well-defined, smaller population. In all of these countries, the well-to-do pay for the "best" health care in the private sector, either out of their own pockets or through insurance policies that usually come from foreign sources, such as the French Prevoyance Sociale. The large majority of the population, which is poor, relies upon the MOH budget as an implicit or informal form of national health insurance, or upon traditional healers for whose care they must pay out-of-pocket. Because MOH per capita budgetary expenditures are relatively low in the geographical areas where the poor live or for the kinds of health care facilities that the poor use, the poor do not benefit much from these informal national health insurance systems. Indeed, fragmentary evidence indicates that the poor spend a relatively large percentage of their annual income on traditional healers and on drugs when they are available (De Ferranti, 1985).

The data and analysis in this section seem to indicate that the greatest beneficiaries, as a class, of the health insurance that currently exists in Sub-Saharan Africa is the relatively small middle class. When they are employed in the private sector, their employers either provide health care directly or on contract, which means, in effect, that they are insured. This finding is really not surprising, in view of the fact that in richer countries, such as in North America and in Western Europe, the middle and upper classes enjoy greater financial and geographic access to health care, via health insurance, even national health insurance.[15] Be that as it may, it seems safe to conclude that the development of health insurance to date in Sub-Saharan Africa has not promoted greater equity in the access to health services by the poor, nor has it permitted greater access.

When one examines the efficiency aspects of the health insurance that is in place in the Sub-Sahara, it must be concluded that the forms of health insurance that have been adopted do not, for the most part, encourage efficiency.

Reform of many of these health insurance arrangements will not be an easy task, simply because the redistribution of income is politically difficult.  In countries where there is implicit national health insurance, greater equity for the poor requires that a larger percentage of the MOH budget be directed toward the poor.  One obvious way of having some of the resources to pursue such a policy would be to eliminate any favorable treatment that government employees receive in the health-care system.  Similarly, more MOH resources could be freed in all of these countries, if there were more private health insurance available to those who could afford to pay for it.[16] Governments must carefully  examine the regulatory and incentive atmosphere to make sure that they are not inhibiting the development of private health insurance.  Nevertheless, governments must also be careful that the kinds of private health insurance that do develop are designed to foster efficiency in the production and consumption of health care.  The empirical research literature indicates that prepaid capitated health insurance fosters efficiency on the production side, and that deductibles and coinsurance have similar effects on the consumption side.

## THE ROLE OF THE PRIVATE SECTOR[17]

Few studies have focused on the private sector of Sub-Saharan Africa. Among the reasons accounting for this lack of attention is the difficulty of evaluating incomplete and often unreliable data on private expenditures.  However, the role of government in shaping and implementing health policy should not obscure the importance of the private sector, because the available data underscore the importance of private expenditures on health.

In countries where private endeavor has been actively encouraged, the importance of private expenditures does not come as a surprise. In Kenya, for example, private-sector payments by individuals account for 41 percent of total outlays for health (Kenya, World Bank, 1987). In Sudan, private expenditures represent 75-80 percent of total health expenditures (Sudan, World Bank, 1987).  In a country like Guinea where the private sector is nascent, private expenditures on health already exceed official government expenditures on health care (Guinea, World Bank, 1988).  In Benin, private expenditures are reportedly larger than the ministry of health recurrent budget (Benin, World Bank, 1986).  In drought-stricken Ethiopia, private payments account for 66 percent of the financing of modern care (Ethiopia, World Bank, 1988).  It would appear that even in countries where the private sector is not encouraged, private expenditures for health are nonetheless substantial.  Private funds are used to purchase services from missions, private providers of medical care, industrial dispensaries, commercial pharmacies, and traditional healers and herbalists.

In Cameroon, missions operate 40 percent of health facilities (Cameroon, World Bank, 1984).  In Lesotho, the Private Health Association of Lesotho (PHAL), which is comprised of missions operated by six Christian denominations, operates half of the country's hospitals and 60 percent of its clinics (Lesotho, World Bank, 1985). Typically, the mission sector recovers part of its costs through user fees.  In Lesotho these user fees represent 60-80 percent of operating costs.  In Uganda, 80 percent of the recurrent budgets of missions comes from patient fees (Uganda, World Bank, 1988).  The missions generally provide better quality services than government-owned facilities, are heavily utilized, and usually are able to maintain an adequate supply of drugs.  They are also, in some cases, instrumental in promoting the private sector, as in Chad, where the Catholic church has established 1,000 financially independent village pharmacies (Chad, World Bank, 1986).  In addition, missions are usually located in rural and underprivileged areas.

The development of private, for-profit medicine varies widely across the different countries where data are available.  In some cases, as in Guinea and Mauritania, where it has recently been legalized, private practice remains limited (Guinea, World Bank, 1986, and Mauritania, World Bank, 1987).  In Madagascar, private practitioners are relatively few as importation of medical equipment is being hampered by a shortage of foreign exchange (Madagascar, World Bank, 1987).  Low government salaries, shortages of drugs at government health facilities, and limited opportunities for employment in the private sector have often encouraged the development of a more or less clandestine parallel market.  This pattern is observed in Zaire and Uganda (Zaire, World Bank, 1988, and Uganda, World Bank, 1985).

In these cases, the lack of appropriate regulation often leads to poor quality of services.

Private physicians are concentrated in urban areas where their services are sought by the better-off members of the community. This characteristic is observed in countries as diverse as Botswana, the Cote d'Ivoire, Kenya, Sudan, and Lesotho (Botswana, World Bank, 1979; Cote d'Ivoire, World Bank, 1988; Kenya, World Bank, 1987; Sudan, World Bank, 1987, and Lesotho, World Bank, 1985). Despite the existence of fees, services are in great demand. In Cameroon, for example, private facilities have higher rates of utilization than free government clinic facilities (Cameroon, World Bank, 1984). However in Lesotho, user resistance to the higher fees has been observed, as some consumers have travelled relatively long distances to free government facilities (Lesotho, World Bank, 1987).

### Pharmaceuticals

In Madagascar and Zaire (Madagascar, World Bank, 1987, and Zaire, World Bank, 1987), private companies are very active in importing pharmaceuticals. For example, over the period 1976-1985, the share of private-sector drug sales increased from 63 percent to 80 percent of total sales in Madagascar. However, in Zaire where the government actively promotes private imports of drugs, no controls over quality or quantity are maintained. This has resulted in high prices and the development of informal channels through which salesmen without any training prescribe and sell drugs in rural areas.

Some African countries manufacture pharmaceuticals. Often, however, private manufacturing capacity is underutilized due to the shortage of foreign exchange with which to import raw materials and spare parts. This is particularly the case in Ghana and Malawi (Ghana, World Bank, 1988, and Malawi, World Bank, 1983), where the private sector capacity utilization varies between 40 and 45 percent. In some cases, private lobbying may be hindering the adoption of a rational drug policy that emphasizes generic products, as in Benin (Benin, World Bank, 1986).

Private pharmacies are located principally in urban areas. This is particularly evident in former French colonies like Cameroon, Madagascar, Togo, and Senegal where 87 percent of locally owned pharmacies are concentrated in the capital (Cameroon, World Bank,

1984; Madagascar, World Bank, 1987; Togo, World Bank, undated; and Senegal, World Bank, 1982). The lack of quality and quantity control often results in the sale of outdated drugs and the provision of exotic and expensive drugs at high prices, as observed in Senegal and Zambia (Senegal, World Bank, 1982, and Zambia, World Bank, 1984). This problem is exacerbated in countries like Mauritania, Togo, and Zaire where no essential drug list exists (Mauritania, World Bank, 1987; Togo, World Bank, undated; and Zaire, World Bank, 1987). However, in Cameroon, in the Central African Republic, and in Nigeria, distribution and procurement of drugs are efficient at least in urban areas (Cameroon, World Bank, 1984; Central African Republic, World Bank, 1988; and Nigeria, World Bank, 1983).

### Traditional Medicine

The traditional sector is important in all the countries studied here. In Zambia, it is estimated that two-fifths of the total government health budget was spent on traditional care (Zambia, World Bank, 1984). In Madagascar, 32 percent of people reported going to a traditional healer before seeking care from the modern sector (Madagascar, World Bank, 1987). However, information on traditional medicine is probably less fully reported than for modern health care; thus, the relative importance of traditional medicine is thought to be underestimated in these reports.

### Private, For-Profit Care

The large amount of private expenditure in many countries indicates that a strong demand exists for private health services in Sub-Saharan Africa. To some extent, the importance of the private sector depends upon the degree of government tolerance. Nevertheless, many World Bank reports suggest that even in those countries that actively discourage the private practice of medicine, substantial amounts of money are spent on care from this sector. Charging fees does not choke off demand because the private sector is perceived by part of the public as providing services of superior quality. However, private, for-profit health facilities tend to be located in richer urban areas.

Table 3-6 presents information on sources and uses of funds for the sixteen countries for which financial data could be obtained or

## Table 3-6
### Estimates of Sources and Uses of Recurrent Funds in Health Care Sector

| | SOURCES | | | | | | |
| | Government | | Private Sector | | | | |
| Sources | Central | Local | Church Missions and NGOs | Modern | Traditional | Donors | Total |
|---|---|---|---|---|---|---|---|
| *Botswana (1979)* | | | | | | | |
| Local Currency[a] | 13.0 | 2.6 | 2.4 | 8.0 | 3.3 | 15.6 | 44.9 |
| PPPR US$ (millions)[a] | 23.4 | 4.7 | 4.3 | 14.4 | 5.9 | 28.1 | 80.7 |
| Per Capita PPR Dollars[a] | 27.41 | 5.51 | 5.04 | 16.87 | 6.92 | 32.89 | 94.66 |
| Percent of Total | 29.0 | 5.8 | 5.3 | 17.8 | 7.3 | 34.7 | 100.0 |
| *Burkina Faso (1981)* | | | | | | | |
| Local Currency[a] | -- | -- | -- | -- | -- | -- | -- |
| PPPR US$ (millions)[a] | -- | -- | -- | -- | -- | -- | -- |
| Per Capita PPR Dollars[a] | -- | -- | -- | -- | -- | -- | -- |
| Percent of Total | -- | -- | -- | -- | -- | -- | -- |
| *Burundi (1986)* | | | | | | | |
| Local Currency[a] | 1,755 | -- | -- | 62.8 | -- | 600 | 2,983 |
| PPPR US$ (millions)[a] | 26.84 | -- | -- | 9.60 | -- | 9.18 | 45.62 |
| Per Capita PPR Dollars[a] | 5.71 | -- | -- | 2.04 | -- | 1.95 | 9.71 |
| Percent of Total | 58.8 | -- | -- | 21.1 | -- | 20.1 | 100.0 |

**Table 3-6 (continued)**

| | USES | | | | | | |
| | Government | | Private Sector | | | | |
| Sources | Central | Local | Church Missions and NGOs | Modern | Tradi- tional | Donors | Total |
|---|---|---|---|---|---|---|---|
| *Botswana (1979)* | | | | | | | |
| Local Currency[a] | 17.3 | 4.7 | 3.4 | 5.3 | 3.3 | 10.9 | 44.9 |
| PPPR US$ (millions)[a] | 31.1 | 8.5 | 6.1 | 9.5 | 5.9 | 19.6 | 80.7 |
| Per Capita PPR Dollars[a] | 36.5 | 9.91 | 7.17 | 11.17 | 6.92 | 22.98 | 94.66 |
| Percent of Total | 38.5 | 10.5 | 7.6 | 11.8 | 7.3 | 24.3 | 100.0 |
| *Burkina Faso (1981)* | | | | | | | |
| Local Currency[a] | 4,154 | 190.0 | -- | 2,555 | -- | 3,132 | 10,031 |
| PPPR US$ (millions)[a] | 33.89 | 1.55 | -- | 20.84 | -- | 25.55 | 81.83 |
| Per Capita PPR Dollars[a] | 5.47 | 0.25 | -- | 3.36 | -- | 4.12 | 13.20 |
| Percent of Total | 41.4 | 1.9 | -- | 25.5 | -- | 31.2 | 100.0 |
| *Burundi (1986)* | | | | | | | |
| Local Currency[a] | 2,104 | -- | 215 | 664 | -- | -- | 2,983 |
| PPPR US$ (millions)[a] | 32.18 | -- | 3.29 | 10.15 | -- | -- | 45.62 |
| Per Capita PPR Dollars[a] | 6.85 | -- | 0.70 | 2.16 | -- | -- | 9.71 |
| Percent of Total | 70.5 | -- | 7.2 | 22.3 | -- | -- | 100.0 |

153

**Table 3-6 (continued)**

|  | SOURCES | | | | | | |
|---|---|---|---|---|---|---|---|
|  | Government | | Private Sector | | | | |
|  | | | Church | | | | |
| Sources | Central | Local | Missions and NGOs | Modern | Tradi-tional | Donors | Total |
| *Cent. Af. Rep.* | | | | | | | |
| *(Ave 1984-99)* | | | | | | | |
| Local Currency[a] | <--------------------- | | 3,128 | | ----------------> | 2,900 | 6,029 |
| PPPR US$ (millions)[a] | | | | | | | |
| Per Capita PPR Dollars[a] | | | | | | | |
| Percent of Total | <--------------------- | | 51.9 | | ----------------> | 48.1 | 100.0 |
| *Ethiopia (1986)* | | | | | | | |
| Local Currency[a] | 79.0 | -- | 5.7 | 197.1 | 30.0 | 20.0 | 331.8 |
| PPPR US$ (millions)[a] | 126.75 | -- | 9.15 | 316.23 | 48.13 | 32.09 | 532.35 |
| Per Capita PPR Dollars[a] | 3.0 | -- | 0.22 | 7.49 | 1.14 | 0.76 | 12.61 |
| Percent of Total | 23.8 | -- | 1.7 | 59.4 | 9.0 | 6.0 | 100.0 |
| *Kenya (1984)* | | | | | | | |
| Local Currency[a] | 1,344.9 | 152.6 | 42.7 | 1,264.8 | -- | 71.0 | 2,876.0 |
| PPPR US$ (millions)[a] | 231.12 | 26.22 | 7.34 | 217.36 | -- | 12.20 | 494.25 |
| Per Capita PPR Dollars[a] | 11.79 | 1.34 | 0.37 | 11.09 | -- | 0.62 | 25.22 |
| Percent of Total | 46.8 | 5.3 | 1.5 | 44.0 | -- | 2.5 | 100.0 |

154

# Table 3-6 (continued)

| | USES | | | | | | |
|---|---|---|---|---|---|---|---|
| | Government | | Private Sector | | | | |
| Sources | Central | Local | Church Missions and NGOs | Modern | Traditional | Donors | Total |
| **Cent. Af. Rep.** | | | | | | | |
| *(Ave 1984-99)* | | | | | | | |
| Local Currency (millions)[a] | 2,486 | -- | <------------3,542------------> | | | -- | 6,029 |
| PPPR US$ (millions)[a] | | | | | | | |
| Per Capita PPR Dollars[a] | | | | | | | |
| Percent of Total | 41.2 | -- | <------------58.7------------> | | | -- | 100.0 |
| **Ethiopia (1986)** | | | | | | | |
| Local Currency[a] | 118.00 | -- | 5.7 | 178.1 | 30.0 | -- | 331.8 |
| PPPR US$ (millions)[a] | 189.32 | -- | 9.15 | 285.75 | 48.13 | -- | 532.35 |
| Per Capita PPR Dollars[a] | 4.49 | -- | 0.22 | 6.77 | 1.14 | -- | 12.61 |
| Percent of Total | 35.6 | -- | 1.7 | 53.7 | 9.0 | -- | 100.0 |
| **Kenya (1984)** | | | | | | | |
| Local Currency[a] | 1,244.2 | 160.6 | 205.7 | 1,265.5 | -- | -- | 2,876.0 |
| PPPR US$ (millions)[a] | 213.82 | 27.60 | 35.35 | 217.48 | -- | -- | 494.25 |
| Per Capita PPR Dollars[a] | 10.91 | 1.41 | 1.80 | 11.10 | -- | -- | 25.22 |
| Percent of Total | 43.3 | 5.6 | 7.2 | 44.0 | -- | -- | 100.0 |

# Table 3-6 (continued)

| Sources | Government | | Private Sector | | | Donors | Total |
|---|---|---|---|---|---|---|---|
| | Central | Local | Church Missions and NGOs | Modern | Traditional | | |
| *Lesotho (1986)* | | | | | | | |
| Local Currency[a] | 24.0 | -- | 4.9 | 31.6 | -- | 1.2 | 61.7 |
| PPPR US$ (millions)[a] | 90.23 | -- | 18.42 | 118.80 | -- | 4.51 | 231.97 |
| Per Capita PPR Dollars[a] | 59.17 | -- | 12.08 | 77.90 | -- | 2.96 | 152.11 |
| Percent of Total | 39.0 | -- | 8.0 | 51.2 | -- | 1.9 | 100.0 |
| *Madagascar (1985)* | | | | | | | |
| Local Currency[a] | 17,292 | 399 | 9.34 | 17,341 | 7,000 | 4,452 | 47,418 |
| PPPR US$ (millions)[a] | 71.45 | 1.65 | 3.86 | 71.66 | 28.93 | 18.40 | 195.94 |
| Per Capita PPR Dollars[a] | 7.03 | .16 | .38 | 7.05 | 2.85 | 1.81 | 19.28 |
| Percent of Total | 36.5 | 0.8 | 2.0 | 36.6 | 14.8 | 9.4 | 100.0 |
| *Mali (1985)* | | | | | | | |
| Local Currency[a] | 5,741 | -- | -- | 4,853 | 10,000 | 5,130 | 25,724 |
| PPPR US$ (millions)[a] | 24.88 | -- | -- | 21.03 | 43.34 | 22.23 | 111.43 |
| Per Capita PPR Dollars[a] | 3.30 | -- | -- | 2.79 | 5.74 | 2.95 | 14.78 |
| Percent of Total | 22.3 | -- | -- | 18.9 | 38.9 | 19.9 | 100.0 |

SOURCES

# Table 3-6 (continued)

| Sources | Government | | Private Sector | | | Donors | Total |
|---|---|---|---|---|---|---|---|
| | Central | Local | Church Missions and NGOs | Modern | Traditional | | |
| **USES** | | | | | | | |
| *Lesotho (1986)* | | | | | | | |
| Local Currency[a] | 23.9 | -- | 4.6 | 32.0 | -- | 1.2 | 61.7 |
| PPPR US$ (millions)[a] | 89.85 | -- | 17.29 | 120.31 | -- | 4.51 | 231.97 |
| Per Capita PPR Dollars[a] | 58.92 | -- | 11.34 | 78.89 | -- | 2.96 | 152.11 |
| Percent of Total | 38.7 | -- | 7.5 | 51.9 | -- | 1.9 | 100.0 |
| *Madagascar (1985)* | | | | | | | |
| Local Currency[a] | 20,892 | 399 | 1,967 | 16,832 | 7,000 | 328 | 47,418 |
| PPPR US$ (millions)[a] | 86.33 | 1.65 | 8.13 | 69.55 | 28.93 | 1.36 | 195.94 |
| Per Capita PPR Dollars[a] | 8.49 | .16 | .80 | 6.84 | 2.85 | .13 | 19.28 |
| Percent of Total | 44.1 | 0.8 | 4.1 | 35.5 | 14.8 | 0.7 | 100.0 |
| *Mali (1985)* | | | | | | | |
| Local Currency[a] | 10,560 | -- | -- | 4,830 | 10,000 | 334 | 25,724 |
| PPPR US$ (millions)[a] | 45.77 | -- | -- | 20.93 | 43.34 | 1.45 | 111.48 |
| Per Capita PPR Dollars[a] | 6.07 | -- | -- | 2.77 | 5.74 | 0.19 | 14.78 |
| Percent of Total | 41.1 | -- | -- | 18.8 | 38.9 | 1.3 | 100.0 |

**Table 3-6 (continued)**

| Sources | SOURCES | | | | | | |
|---|---|---|---|---|---|---|---|
| | Government | | Private Sector | | | Donors | Total |
| | Central | Local | Church Missions and NGOs | Modern | Traditional | | |
| *Rwanda (1982)* | | | | | | | |
| Local Currency[a] | 883.0 | -- | 500.0 | 432.0 | -- | 252.0 | 2,067 |
| PPPR US$ (millions)[a] | 15.46 | -- | 8.75 | 7.56 | -- | 4.41 | 36.19 |
| Per Capita PPR Dollars[a] | 2.81 | -- | 1.59 | 1.38 | -- | .80 | 6.58 |
| Percent of Total | 42.7 | -- | 24.2 | 20.9 | -- | 12.2 | 100.0 |
| *Somalia (1982)* | | | | | | | |
| Local Currency[a] | 109.9 | -- | -- | 90.7 | 128.1 | 102.1 | 430.8 |
| PPPR US$ (millions)[a] | 18.74 | -- | -- | 15.46 | 21.84 | 17.41 | 73.45 |
| Per Capita PPR Dollars[a] | 3.79 | -- | -- | 3.13 | 4.42 | 3.52 | 14.85 |
| Percent of Total | 25.5 | -- | -- | 21.1 | 29.7 | 23.7 | 100.0 |
| *Sudan (1985)* | | | | | | | |
| Local Currency[a] | 114.9 | -- | -- | 344.7 | -- | -- | 459.6 |
| PPPR US$ (millions)[a] | 108.46 | -- | -- | 325.39 | -- | -- | 433.85 |
| Per Capita PPR Dollars[a] | 5.0 | -- | -- | 14.99 | -- | -- | 19.99 |
| Percent of Total | 25.0 | -- | -- | 75.0 | -- | -- | 100.0 |

# Table 3-6 (continued)

| | | | USES | | | | |
| | Government | | Private Sector | | | | |
| Sources | Central | Local | Church Missions and NGOs | Modern | Traditional | Donors | Total |
|---|---|---|---|---|---|---|---|
| *Rwanda (1982)* | | | | | | | |
| Local Currency[a] | 961.0 | -- | 601.0 | -- | 505.0 | -- | 2,067 |
| PPPR US$ (millions)[a] | 16.83 | -- | 10.52 | -- | 8.84 | -- | 36.19 |
| Per Capita PPR Dollars[a] | 3.06 | -- | 1.91 | -- | 1.61 | -- | 6.58 |
| Percent of Total | 46.5 | -- | 29.1 | -- | 24.4 | -- | 100.0 |
| *Somalia (1982)* | | | | | | | |
| Local Currency[a] | 212.0 | -- | -- | 218.8 | -- | -- | 430.8 |
| PPPR US$ (millions)[a] | 36.15 | -- | -- | 37.3 | -- | -- | 73.45 |
| Per Capita PPR Dollars[a] | 7.31 | -- | -- | 7.54 | -- | -- | 14.85 |
| Percent of Total | 49.2 | -- | -- | 50.8 | -- | -- | 100.0 |
| *Sudan (1985)* | | | | | | | |
| Local Currency[a] | -- | -- | -- | -- | -- | -- | -- |
| PPPR US$ (millions)[a] | -- | -- | -- | -- | -- | -- | -- |
| Per Capita PPR Dollars[a] | -- | -- | -- | -- | -- | -- | -- |
| Percent of Total | -- | -- | -- | -- | -- | -- | -- |

159

# Table 3-6 (continued)

| | SOURCES | | | | | | |
| | Government | | Private Sector | | | | |
| Sources | Central | Local | Church Missions and NGOs | Modern | Tradi- tional | Donors | Total |
|---|---|---|---|---|---|---|---|
| *Swaziland (1984)* | | | | | | | |
| Local Currency[a] | 10.3 | -- | 1.10 | 6.80 | 13.0 | 2.90 | 34.1 |
| PPPR US$ (millions)[a] | 15.32 | -- | 1.64 | 10.12 | 19.34 | 4.31 | 50.72 |
| Per Capita PPR Dollars[a] | 20.99 | -- | 2.24 | 13.86 | 26.49 | 5.91 | 69.48 |
| Percent of Total | 30.3 | -- | 3.2 | 19.9 | 38.1 | 8.5 | 100.0 |
| *Uganda (1982)* | | | | | | | |
| Local Currency[a] | 1,507 | 366 | 97 | 3,150 | 6,310 | 472 | 11,902 |
| PPPR US$ (millions)[a] | 48.90 | 11.88 | 3.15 | 102.21 | 204.74 | 15.31 | 386.17 |
| Per Capita PPR Dollars[a] | 3.65 | 0.89 | 0.23 | 7.63 | 15.28 | 1.14 | 28.82 |
| Percent of Total | 12.7 | 3.1 | 0.8 | 26.5 | 53.0 | 4.0 | 100.0 |
| *Zambia (1981)* | | | | | | | |
| Local Currency[a] | 65.2 | 1.2 | 4.5 | 50.8 | 25.0 | 9.2 | 155.9 |
| PPPR US$ (millions)[a] | 87.36 | 1.61 | 6.03 | 68.07 | 33.5 | 12.33 | 208.9 |
| Per Capita PPR Dollars[a] | 15.06 | 0.28 | 1.04 | 11.74 | 5.78 | 2.13 | 36.02 |
| Percent of Total | 41.8 | 0.8 | 2.9 | 32.6 | 16.0 | 5.9 | 100.0 |

# Table 3-6 (continued)

| | USES | | | | | | |
|---|---|---|---|---|---|---|---|
| | Government | | Private Sector | | | | |
| Sources | Central | Local | Church Missions and NGOs | Modern | Tradi- tional | Donors | Total |
| **Swaziland (1984)** | | | | | | | |
| Local Currency[a] | 11.1 | -- | 4.1 | 6.0 | 13.0 | -- | 34.1 |
| PPPR US$ (millions)[a] | 16.51 | -- | 6.10 | 8.93 | 19.34 | -- | 50.72 |
| Per Capita PPR Dollars[a] | 22.62 | -- | 8.35 | 12.23 | 26.49 | -- | 69.48 |
| Percent of Total | 32.4 | -- | 12.0 | 17.6 | 38.1 | -- | 100.0 |
| **Uganda (1982)** | | | | | | | |
| Local Currency[a] | 1,619 | 533 | 520 | 2,730 | 6,310 | 190 | 11,902 |
| PPPR US$ (millions)[a] | 52.53 | 17.29 | 16.87 | 88.58 | 204.74 | 6.16 | 386.17 |
| Per Capita PPR Dollars[a] | 3.92 | 1.29 | 1.26 | 6.61 | 15.28 | 0.46 | 28.82 |
| Percent of Total | 13.6 | 4.5 | 4.4 | 22.9 | 53.0 | 1.6 | 100.0 |
| **Zambia (1981)** | | | | | | | |
| Local Currency[a] | 62.5 | 1.2 | 11.1 | 51.6 | 25.0 | 4.5 | 155.9 |
| PPPR US$ (millions)[a] | 83.75 | 1.61 | 14.87 | 69.14 | 33.5 | 6.03 | 108.9 |
| Per Capita PPR Dollars[a] | 14.44 | 0.28 | 2.56 | 11.92 | 5.78 | 1.04 | 36.02 |
| Percent of Total | 40.1 | 0.8 | 7.1 | 33.1 | 16.0 | 2.9 | 100.0 |

**Table 3-6 (continued)**

| Sources | Government | | Private Sector | | | | |
| | Central | Local | Church Missions and NGOs | Modern | Tradi-tional | Donors | Total |
|---|---|---|---|---|---|---|---|
| *Zimbabwe (1987)* | | | | | | | |
| Local Currency[a] | 287.0 | 25.0 | 7.1 | 219.7 | -- | 74.3 | 613.1 |
| PPPR US$ (millions)[a] | 355.44 | 30.96 | 8.79 | 272.09 | -- | 92.02 | 759.3 |
| Per Capita PPR Dollars[a] | 42.82 | 3.73 | 1.06 | 32.78 | -- | 11.09 | 91.48 |
| Percent of Total | 46.8 | 4.1 | 1.2 | 35.8 | -- | 12.1 | 100.0 |

SOURCES

**Table 3-6 (continued)**

| | USES | | | | | |
| Sources | Government | | Private Sector | | | Total |
| | Central | Local | Church Missions and NGOs | Modern | Traditional | Donors |
| --- | --- | --- | --- | --- | --- | --- | --- |
| *Zimbabwe (1987)* | | | | | | | |
| Local Currency[a] | 325.2 | 54.2 | 26.2 | 207.5 | -- | -- | 613.1 |
| PPPR US$ (millions)[a] | 402.75 | 67.12 | 32.45 | 256.9 | -- | -- | 759.3 |
| Per Capita PPR Dollars[a] | 48.52 | 8.09 | 3.91 | 30.96 | -- | -- | 91.48 |
| Percent of Total | 53.0 | 8.8 | 4.3 | 33.8 | -- | -- | 100.0 |

[a]See Appendix 4.

163

derived from World Bank sources.  Like the data in Table 1-9, the data in Table 3-6 provide a snapshot of recurrent expenditure at a point in time.  The data refer to years between 1979 and 1986.  Data for Botswana came from a report for 1979; data for Burundi, Ethiopia, and Lesotho were for 1986.  Data for Zimbabwe are from a recently completed health-financing study published in 1992 (Hecht, ed., 1992) and done in 1988, using data for 1987.  These data are presented in the local currency, converted to PPPR U.S. dollars,  expressed on a per capita basis, and then given as a percentage of total health-care sources or health-care uses.  The level of detail reflected in column headings results from efforts to strike a balance between presenting as much detail as possible, and summarizing the data in a consistent format.  The following column headings are used:  Government (Central and Local), Private Sector (Church Missions and NGOs, Modern, and Traditional), and Donors.  Even at this level of aggregation, not all countries can be reported adequately.  For example, the data for some countries were broken down by central and local government, but the government data for other countries were combined in the reports.  Likewise, it was possible to obtain data estimates for traditional medical care for only eight of the sixteen countries; for the other eight, the data were not available.

Table 3-6 shows that in only three of the countries does the government share of sources exceed 50 percent (Burundi, Kenya,and Zimbabwe), and then only slightly.  For two of these countries (Burundi and Zimbabwe), the government share is overstated, because there are no reports of expenditures for traditional care, which understates the denominator used in calculating the percentage.  In the case of Kenya (government share, 52.1 percent), private modern and traditional care were combined in the report and it is not clear how the traditional sector share was estimated.

Table 3-6 also reveals that the share of recurrent expenditures financed by official development assistance varies widely among countries.  External assistance accounts for only 1.9 percent of funds in Lesotho, but reaches 48.1 percent in the Central African Republic.  But even between these two extremes, donor shares vary between 2.5 percent in Kenya and 34.7 percent in Botswana.  These variations could result from variations in accounting definitions between countries; differences in each country's ability to absorb aid; preferences of individual donors, due perhaps to past colonial ties or political ideologies; or variations in the successes of some recipient countries in attracting donations.  In their study on official development assistance (ODA) for health in all of the countries of the Sub-Sahara, Orivel and Tchicaya (1988) were able to make two generalizations: the poorest countries do not receive priority from donors; and the importance of health aid per capita seems to be inversely related to the population size of the country (see Table 1-6 for all ODA).[18]   What they also found was that about $100 million of the approximately $450 million in ODA for health each year is given for water and sanitation projects, that anywhere from 10 to 20 percent of the ODA, depending upon the year, is given for hospitals, and that about the same percentage is given for public health as is given for hospitals.   These three categories of health aid account for anywhere from 50 to 60 percent of the total in any given year.   Four types of programs that Orivel and Tchicaya believe fit more into the spirit of the Alma Ata Declaration, only receive about 20 to 25 percent of the health aid. These are aid for the training of personnel (which has had a tendency to diminish), aid for vaccinations (which has increased), aid for rural health services (which has been somewhat chaotic), and aid for primary health care (which has remained relatively stable).

The data in Table 3-6 also show how large a role the private sector seems to play in a number of countries.   This phenomenon raises interesting questions.   First of all, it reminds one to be extremely cautious about coming to any conclusions about what is taking place in the health-care sector, when one's information is based solely upon government (MOH) expenditure activity.   As just one example, at independence many African governments took over health care facilities that had colonial origins; that is to say, a major hospital would have been established at a colonial trade center or along colonial trade routes for the benefit of the colonialists themselves.   When the missionaries came (as in Tanzania or in Ghana), they tended to establish their health-care facilities in the rural areas that had no modern health services.   In the case of Tanzania, missionary health-care facilities are now so heavily subsidized by the government, and the large subsidy is contained in the government budget, that government expenditure data are indicative of both levels of health-care expenditure and the geographic distribution of that expenditure.   On the other hand, in Ghana, the church missions of a number of different religious denominations are extremely autonomous and spread throughout the country.   They do receive a subsidy from government, but they also raise and receive substantial resources on their own from abroad and from user charges, so that their place in the government budget is not very indicative of the importance of their health-care activities. As mentioned previously, the modern, for-profit sector may be actually reinforcing and exacerbating governments' tendencies to spend upon urban curative care. Estimates on traditional medical expenditures must also be treated with caution, not only because of the differing methodologies used to derive them, but because the traditional healer performs many functions, some of which can only tangentially be considered health care.

Beyond these considerations, however, are questions about the origins and growth of the modern private health-care sector in Sub-Saharan Africa. Certainly, the widespread lack of local health insurance places some upper limit upon the profitability of private medical practice. In Zimbabwe and in the Cote d'Ivoire, health insurance has grown rather rapidly, as has the private health-care sector. Can the growth of the private practice be attributed to the growth in the health insurance? Or, is it the other way around? Both Zimbabwe and the Cote d'Ivoire are more economically prosperous than many of their neighbors in Africa. Does a certain stage of economic growth need to be reached before either the private sector or health insurance emerge? Or, is it that in very poor countries, such as in Guinea-Bissau, health-care personnel are so badly paid by government that they are forced to moonlight and set up their own private practices? Or, is it, as in some states in Nigeria, that government health care is so badly managed and of such poor quality, that the private sector is forced to come forth in order to respond to the latent demand for pharmaceuticals and for quality health care?

Analysis of the modern, nonmission private sector also raises additional questions. The recent World Bank study on financing health services in developing countries (Akin, Birdsall, and De Ferranti, 1987) advocated, as one of four general reform measures, the encouragement of nongovernment health-care services. While hardly anyone could disagree with this policy prescription as a general proposition, given the inherent advantages in efficiency that the private sector possesses, caution must be used to distinguish between what the private sector does do well and what it cannot be expected to do. One of the most difficult equity problems with modern health care services in the countries of Sub-Saharan Africa is their uneven geographical distribution, and, hence, their availability to all people. To a certain extent, private, for-profit traditional healers have filled this gap in many rural areas and even in some parts of urban areas. Part of this gap is due to the low-income problem and part of it is not. As Golladay (1980) and De Ferranti (1985) have shown, the clientele of traditional healers sometimes spends a surprisingly high percentage of its annual family income on these services. It is, nonetheless, a high percentage of a low income. And, while these low incomes may be able to support the unsophisticated and even primitive capital and cost-of-living requirements of a traditional healer, they do not very well support the more expensive capital and labor requirements of modern health care, without some form of subsidization. The church missions have also filled part of the gap to provide modern health care. Although the church missions do charge fees to those who can pay, they could not survive financially without help from foreign charity or without help from the government. In some countries (such as Ghana and Tanzania) government subsidization has been fairly extensive, but in other countries (such as Mali) it has been negligible. Only in extremely isolated instances is private, for-profit health care subsidized by any country in Sub-Saharan Africa.[19] As a result, the for-profit sector has established itself and expanded in those geographical areas where the population concentration is dense and where incomes are higher, that is, where there is a reasonable chance of making a profit.

Reasoning along these lines naturally leads to the question of how one should interpret the percentage shares of the private, for-profit sector in Table 3-6 that range from 59.4 percent in Ethiopia to 17.8 percent in Botswana. One interpretation could be that, in countries where per capita income is both low and evenly distributed, and the population is primarily rural, one would not expect to see a high for-profit percentage share; or, alternatively, where per capita income is low, but the distribution of income is skewed toward urban areas, one would expect the private, for-profit sector to have a higher percentage share. Conversely, in countries where per capita income is both high and evenly distributed, and the population is primarily in rural areas, one would tend to see a higher private, for-profit share than in the previous two cases, but then an even higher for-profit share in countries that have both high per capita income and the distribution of income skewed toward urban areas.

These interpretations then raise the question of the proper role of government in the health-care sector, once the for-profit share of the sector is taken into account. In general, the theory of public finance answers this question for the health sector (see De Ferranti, 1985). Government should finance the eradication of external effects and nonexclusion situations and, depending upon the normative judgment, government should finance health care for those who do not have a high enough level of income to finance it for themselves. But, government need not necessarily be the provider of health care, *if* the health care can be more efficiently provided by some other entity or entities (e.g., the private, for-profit sector), *if* there are no capital and labor market imperfections, and *if* political considerations do not enter into the choice.  On a priori grounds, economists would argue that the private sector can produce health care more efficiently, but that there are, more or less, capital and labor market imperfections and shortages in these countries, and that there is the question of government credibility in the eyes of the private sector.  Therefore, in most of these countries, the private sector would not expand capital facilities on the promise that government would or could pay for the health-care costs of the poor who would use the expanded capital (which, however, *does* happen in places like the U.S., with the Medicare and Medicaid programs).  For these reasons, government does then have to become both the financier *and* provider of last resort, except for the higher-income groups. The economic counsel then would be that government provide as neutral an economic environment as possible, in order to encourage private-sector investment in the health-care sector; however, it must also be realized that such investment will be limited by both income and population density constraints (even in a country as rich as the U.S., the private provision of rural health care has remained a continuing policy dilemma).  This being realized, government must confine itself to financing and providing the most cost-effective forms of health care for the poor, within the limits of its health budget constraint.

If government devotes a disproportionate share (relative to the distribution of the population) of its budget to urban hospitals, then it is simply reinforcing the natural economic tendency of the private sector to locate in more affluent urban areas.  The government facilities do not usually treat the affluent, but they do provide "unfair" competition in the urban market for the middle class that does exist, a market down into which some private sector efforts might be directed; the competition is "unfair" because the government facilities usually do not charge fees.  The economic environment is not neutral, and government finances and provides health care for the middle class and some urban poor, to the detriment of the rural and some urban poor.  In light of these considerations, the for-profit share of sources and uses of funds should probably be interpreted as the share going to affluent urban areas; in and of itself, it cannot be interpreted well, unless more information is known about how and where government is spending its percentage share.    Chapter 2 showed that a large percentage of government health-care resources go into urban curative care.    From the point of view of those interested in the welfare of rural populations, then the really important percentage shares in the "snapshots" in Table 3-6 are those of the missions, traditional care, and donor funds, to the extent that donor funds go to rural areas, and these shares are not always very large.

Finally, there is only indirect evidence about how much some of these percentage shares can change over time:    As has already been noted, private sector drug sales in Madagascar increased from 63 percent of the total in 1976 to 80 percent in 1985.    Another piece of evidence comes from the Cote d'Ivoire, and is only for the import of pharmaceuticals (see Vogel, 1988).    According to the Bureau of Organization and Management in the Ministry of Health, the Cote d'Ivoire imported 5.4 billion nominal FCFA worth of pharmaceuticals in 1977.    By 1985, the total had grown to 24.2 billion nominal FCFA. The composition of the purchasers of these imports has changed dramatically in the nine-year period.    The Cote d'Ivoire purchasers are divided into three groups: the MOH and its pharmacy division (pd); purchasers with the permission of either the MOH or pd (presumably, the private sector); and other.    In 1977, these purchasers imported 20.8 percent, 79.2 percent, and .01 percent of the total respectively. By 1985, the respective percentage shares had changed to 3.2, 96.7, and .09.    At least in the Cote d'Ivoire, the private share changed dramatically in the nine-year period.


## DECENTRALIZATION IN ADMINISTRATION

On an a priori basis, it would seem that the need (from an efficiency perspective) for decentralization would be a positive function of the size of the country, both in population, population dispersion, and geographic size.    In this respect, Nigeria would be a better candidate for efforts at decentralization than would be Lesotho.    In the literature on organizational theory and public administration, decentralization is usually considered under the heading of delegation. As an organization becomes more complex and geographically dispersed, leaders at the top of a highly centralized organization lose touch with workers at lower levels, and the necessary information for the functioning of the organization and for the decision-making process becomes progressively more filtered and loosely translated as it moves up the chain of command.  Decision making becomes delayed and opportunities for progress are missed.  In the last few years, much has been said, done, and written about the positive value of the decentralization of organizations.

On the other hand, while many functions can probably be usefully decentralized, there are other functions that should be centralized, on purely economic grounds.  For example, there may be large economies of scale in the purchase and distribution of pharmaceuticals.    In Tanzania, a NORAD-UNICEF pharmaceutical project for the procurement of pharmaceuticals for all of Tanzania was able to stretch an original $30 million, three-year project into four years (Vogel, 1987b).  This was possible simply because of the fact that international competitive bidding on an essential drugs package produced such savings that there were enough funds left over to purchase sufficient pharmaceuticals for a fourth year of the project.  Likewise, it would seem that planning, manpower policy, and budgetary policy should be done at the central level.

Decentralization in the public health-care sector does, however, go hand-in-hand with cost-recovery policy.  In the section of this chapter where we considered the financial implications of cost recovery, particularly for the poorer countries within Sub-Saharan Africa, it was made clear that it is at the hospital level where cost recovery is most feasible and desirable, both from a revenue-raising perspective and from the perspective of creating internal efficiencies within the referral system.   The MOH will "tax" some of these revenues in order to mobilize funds or drugs and supplies, for the lower-level health centers and health posts.  But, if the hospitals are going to create the kind of quality care that will induce patients to pay their fees, then the hospitals must enjoy a certain amount of autonomy in spending in order to meet the quality demands of their patients, demands that the hospitals are better able to judge than the MOH, particularly when the hospitals are in far-flung areas.   In Vogel (1988), the hospitals in Senegal and Mali that seemed to have the most autonomy were the ones that raised the most revenue, with due attention to the needs of the poor.  As was shown earlier, health centers and health posts do not receive much financial autonomy, simply because the additional "revenue" that they receive from the MOH, as the result of successful cost recovery at the hospitals, comes in in-kind MOH shipments of pharmaceuticals and supplies, due to the economies of scale in centralized purchase and distribution.

Because of the scarcity of skilled administrative manpower in most of the Sub-Sahara, decentralization should probably not go further down than the district level.  But if even the district hospitals are in areas that are too poor to support cost recovery, as in some districts in Kenya and Tanzania, most decentralization should stop at the provincial hospital level.  In this regard, it is difficult to generalize, because of the vast differences in the sizes of the countries.   Nigeria is huge relative to Gambia.  Many of the twenty-one states in the Federal Republic of Nigeria are larger in population and in geographic area than many of the countries in the Sub-Sahara; that is why the Nigerian states and local governments bear so much of the responsibility for financing and managing health care.

## NOTES

1.  By "inappropriate" care, we mean care that could have been just as well and more cheaply given at lower-level facilities.

2.   Although these ratios are expressed as percentages of the MOH budget, other bases have also been used.  For example, in Morocco, in North Africa, hospital administrators at the two university medical centers have now established a target cost-recovery ratio of 50 percent of *nonpersonnel* recurrent costs.  Also, Table 3-1 excludes Zaire, which uses a decentralized cost-recovery system and a definition of the cost-recovery ratio that is similar to that in Morocco.  However, the fragmentary evidence on Zaire makes it difficult to calculate a national cost-recovery ratio.  In Zaire, financial control resides in eighty-five health zones that have been created.  Each zone has a hospital and a network of health centers.  The zones are autonomous and each develops its own cost-recovery policies.  In several of the zones, a large proportion of operating and maintenance expenses (excluding salaries) is financed by operating revenue.  In ten zones that were studied, the reference hospitals achieved between 49-99 percent coverage of operating costs, while health centers were able to cover between 81-110 percent (Bitran et al., 1986).  A welfare economics argument could be made for making the government responsible for paying personnel costs, while payment of nonpersonnel costs would be the responsibility of the user of the health-care facility.  If one is willing to assume that personnel costs constitute the fixed costs of providing "the existence of the health-care facility" to which citizens in the society assign an option value, then the citizens cannot be excluded

from consuming this option value. The option value could then be considered to be a public good that ought to be publicly financed. However, it is possible to exclude persons from the use of the *services* of the health-care facility, so that the person-oriented curative services that are performed there are truly private goods that can be rationed by prices which could be set equal to their marginal nonpersonnel costs (Over and Denton, 1988).

3. From an incentive point of view, it is not clear what form this particular tax ought to take. If we assume that the MOH acts simply as a passive transfer agent between the hospitals and the MOF, then it would seem not to matter whether the MOF tax on the MOH were lump-sum, proportional, or progressive.

4. That is to say, within the relevant price range, the percentage decrease in the quantity demanded will be smaller than the percentage increase in the price charged, which means that a price increase will increase total revenue.

5. However, there are many unresolved problems with respect to the drug supply. For some of the dimensions of the problem, see Cross et al. (1986), Gray (1986), Vogel and Stephens (1989), Foster (1988 and 1990) and Hammer (1991).

6. There may be some tradeoff in level of fees versus structure of fees, from the point of view of revenue maximization, but, presumably, the MOH would be trying to balance the two goals of equity and revenue maximization.

7. Vogel (1988) observed a striking example of this phenomenon in the Cote d'Ivoire. The Hopital Protestant de Dabou is located in a rural area, seventy miles east of Abidjan. There is also a government hospital in Dabou. The Hopital Protestant covers 45 percent of its recurrent costs with cost recovery. Administrators there have complete confidence that they never turn away a poor person who is unable to pay, and yet they charge most of their patients a fee or some portion of the fee. Indeed, most patients are willing to pay because they know that drugs will be available and that they will be treated with respect and dignity. The Hopital Protestant has a large outpatient clientele for its different clinics. For example, the well-baby clinic was operating at 120 percent of its stated capacity. Meanwhile, the small government hospital in Dabou does not charge fees, has no drugs, and has very few patients.

8. However, some entries in Tables 3-3, 3-4 and 3-5, that will be discussed shortly, do try to give some estimate of the extent to which this arrangement exists, in countries where data are available.

9.   In Zimbabwe, the National Association of Medical Aid Societies (NAMAS), which is the national association of private insurers, estimates that eventually it will be able to reach about 10 percent of the population of Zimbabwe, meaning only about 10 percent of the population can afford to pay for private health insurance.  The 2.1 million persons covered by the compulsory NHIF in Kenya is approximately 10 percent of the population of Kenya.

10.   As an example, see the discussion in Brunet-Jailly (1988).

11.   These estimates come from the source documents listed in the last column in Table 3-5.

12.   One estimate puts the number of expatriates at about 30,000.

13.   Private hospitals and nursing homes received 15.3 percent of total NAMAS expenditure.  The small percentage going to government hospitals can be attributed to (a) below marginal-cost prices in the government hospitals, particularly at Parirenyatwa, and (b) inefficient billing on the part of the hospitals.  For example, Parirenyatwa is months behind in its billing because of an unworkable arrangement that it has with the government central computing office in Harare.

14.   These externalities in the consumption of medical care arise when society makes a collective judgement that the poor do not have enough medical care, because the poor cannot afford to pay for the medical care.  Therefore, society *as a whole* benefits from transferring resources to the poor in order to enable them to consume more medical care.

15.   For example, in Sweden, where income is more equally distributed than in most countries and where there is a well-funded national health insurance, the Swedish government has a great deal of difficulty in finding physicians to serve in the rural areas of the north.

16.   It could be argued that more private health insurance would increase the demand for health care on the part of the well-to-do who could afford the health insurance, and thus make the distribution of access to health care even more inequitable.  This result need not necessarily follow.  First of all, if the private health insurance is well designed (such as being capitated, and/or only catastrophic), then the demand for health care by the well-to-do need not necessarily increase.  Second, even if the health insurance is not well designed, the existence of the health insurance should bring forth a private health-care supply-side response, which, if the MOH budget is not cut back, should increase total national resources going to health care.  Finally, if the well-to-do no longer use MOH facilities, or use them less than in the past, the MOH can spend more per capita on the poor.  Therefore,

depending upon the design of the private health insurance and/or the private health-care supply response, the poor may actually capture a greater share of total and/or government health-care resources than they did in the past.

17.  Lewis (1988) offers a good general summary of the definition, experience, and potential of the private sector and health care delivery in developing countries.

18.  In a previous study, they found a similar pattern for aid to education.

19.  For example, in Zimbabwe, expenditures for private health insurance are partially deductible under the income tax law. Because the health insurance pays on a fee-for-service basis, government directly subsidizes the purchase of private health insurance, and indirectly subsidizes the overconsumption of medical care by the affluent, who can afford to purchase private health insurance.

# 4

# Health Financing
# Reform Options

Geographically, Sub-Saharan Africa occupies a large part of a large continent. The forty countries in the Sub-Sahara exhibit a great deal of diversity with respect to both economic capacity and economic development and with respect to culture and tradition. Their health-care systems also show large differences, mainly in levels of finance and in levels of health status attained. Nevertheless, there are also common elements that all of the countries share to one degree or another. From a health financing perspective, perhaps the single most important common element is their colonial heritage that left them with health-care systems dominated by hospitals that, as a consequence, could have had little effective impact upon the prevailing epidemiologies of these countries. Most of these countries are now struggling to rectify this imbalance. If implemented, the health financing reform options outlined in this chapter should provide the means to make that struggle less onerous. Table 4-1 furnishes the framework for discussion.

In Table 4-1, there are the two major categories of financing reform: resource efficiency and resource mobilization. These will be discussed in turn. Because these changes cannot take place in a vacuum, three time frames (short, medium, or long term) are given along the top row of Table 4-1, as well as what actors would be involved in the decision-making process (within MOH, MOH and other ministries, MOH and NGOs and/or private sector), and what the likely effect (slight, moderate, or significant) the reform would have upon the country's objectives for efficiency and equity.

In one sense, increased resource efficiency and increased resource mobilization in the health-care sector are two sides of the same coin. Increased resource efficiency frees more resources for other uses. For example, the resource efficiencies brought about by the adoption of an

**Table 4-1**
**Health Financing Reform Options**[a]

| REFORM OPTIONS | ESTIMATED TIME FRAME | | | DECISION PROCESS | | | EFFICIENCY AND/OR EQUITY EFFECTS | | |
|---|---|---|---|---|---|---|---|---|---|
| | Short Term (Less than 1 year) | Medium Term (1-3 years) | Long Term (3-5 years) | Within MOH | MOH & Other Ministries | MOH & NGOs and/or Private Sector | Slight | Moderate | Significant |
| I. Resource Efficiency | | | | | | | | | |
| A. Allocative efficiency | | | | | | | | | |
| (1) Shifting the facility-based "patient" budget for tertiary/secondary/primary care to 50%/30%/20%. | X | X | | X | | | | X | |
| (2) Raising the share of the MOH budget devoted to preventive health programs to meet specified targets. | X | X | | X | | | | X | |
| B. Technical efficiency | | | | | | | | | |
| (1) Enhancing efficiency of hospital inpatient and outpatient care | | | | | | | | | |
| (a) The substitution of outpatient care for inpatient care | | X | | | | | | X | |
| (b) Adopting measures to increase bed-occupancy rates in district and mission hospitals, and to decongest central and provincial hospitals | | X | | X | | | | X | |

| REFORM OPTIONS | ESTIMATED TIME FRAME | | | DECISION PROCESS | | | EFFICIENCY AND/OR EQUITY EFFECTS | | |
|---|---|---|---|---|---|---|---|---|---|
| | Short Term (Less than 1 year) | Medium Term (1-3 years) | Long Term (3-5 years) | Within MOH | MOH & Other Ministries | MOH & NGOs and/or Private Sector | Slight | Moderate | Significant |
| (c) Reducing length-of-stay in selected hospitals | | X | | X | | | | X | |
| (d) Reducing hospital costs per patient day and per admission: | | | | | | | | | |
| - Analyzing hospital cost structures | X | | | X | | | X | | |
| - Adopting cost-saving measures | X | | X | | | | X | | |
| (2) Improving efficiency of drug supply and utilization | | | | | | | | | |
| (a) Adopting an essential drugs program | X | | X | X | | | | X | |
| (b) Rationalizing procedures for allocating foreign exchange | X | X | | | X | | | X | |
| (c) Developing regulations and incentives for private sector to utilize essential drugs | X | X | | | | X | | | X |
| (d) Limiting the number of drugs prescribed at each outpatient visit | X | | | X | | | | X | |
| (e) Monitoring physicians' prescribing practices | | X | | X | | | | X | |

# Table 4-1 (continued)

| REFORM OPTIONS | ESTIMATED TIME FRAME — Short Term (Less than 1 year) | Medium Term (1-3 years) | Long Term (3-5 years) | DECISION PROCESS — Within MOH | MOH & Other Ministries | MOH & NGOs and/or Private Sector | EFFICIENCY AND/OR EQUITY EFFECTS — Slight | Moderate | Significant |
|---|---|---|---|---|---|---|---|---|---|
| (3) Management of health expenditures | | | | | | | | | |
| (a) Revising MOH budget and expenditure formats | X | | | | X | | | | X |
| (b) Continuing to decentralize responsibility for preparing budgets, incurring expenditures, and effecting payments | | X | | X | | | | | |
| (c) Developing an integrated MOH budget covering all capital and recurrent spending | | X | X | X | | X | | X | |
| (d) Strengthening MOH health manpower planning capacity | | X | | X | | | | | X |
| (e) Improving accounting skills and systems in MOH and local government health facilities | | X | | X | X | | | X | |
| (f) Decentralizing procurement of goods and services that can be efficiently purchased at local level | | X | | X | X | | | | X |
| C. Marshalling donor coordination | | | X | | X | | | X | |

| REFORM OPTIONS | ESTIMATED TIME FRAME | | | DECISION PROCESS | | | EFFICIENCY AND/OR EQUITY EFFECTS | | |
|---|---|---|---|---|---|---|---|---|---|
| | Short Term (Less than 1 year) | Medium Term (1-3 years) | Long Term (3-5 years) | Within MOH | MOH & Other Ministries | MOH & NGOs and/or Private Sector | Slight | Moderate | Significant |
| **II. Resource Mobilization** | | | | | | | | | |
| A. Adopting a cost-recovery policy and/or improving it | | | | | | | | | |
| (1) Introducing means-testing procedures: requiring patients to demonstrate income (through pay slips, letters from social services, etc.) or submit to an interview to determine ability to pay | | X | | X | X | | | | X |
| (2) Pegging the level of fees to the consumer price index | X | X | | X | | | | X | |
| (3) Increasing inpatient and other charges for patients with health insurance to cover the full cost of services | | X | | X | | | | | X |
| (4) Imposing a nominal outpatient fee | | X | | X | | | | X | |
| (5) Charging separately for drugs prescribed | | X | | X | | | | X | |

**Table 4-1 (continued)**

| REFORM OPTIONS | ESTIMATED TIME FRAME | | | DECISION PROCESS | | | EFFICIENCY AND/OR EQUITY EFFECTS | | |
|---|---|---|---|---|---|---|---|---|---|
| | Short Term (Less than 1 year) | Medium Term (1-3 years) | Long Term (3-5 years) | Within MOH | MOH & Other Ministries | MOH & NGOs and/or Private Sector | Slight | Moderate | Significant |
| (6) Developing incentives for health facilities to improve their revenue collection efforts | | X | | X | | | | X | |
| (7) Strengthening hospital billing and collection procedures | | X | | X | | | | | X |
| B. Expanding and/or reforming existing health insurance | | | | | | | | | |
| (1) Requiring through legislation that firms over a certain size provide a minimum level of health benefits to their employees in HMOs | | X | X | | X | X | | | X |
| (2) Promoting greater competition among health insurance firms (HMOs) | | X | X | | | X | | X | |
| C. Decentralizing financing of health services | | | | | | | | | |
| (1) Revenue-sharing between central and local government | | X | | X | X | | | X | |

| REFORM OPTIONS | ESTIMATED TIME FRAME | | | DECISION PROCESS | | | EFFICIENCY AND/OR EQUITY EFFECTS | | |
|---|---|---|---|---|---|---|---|---|---|
| | Short Term (Less than 1 year) | Medium Term (1-3 years) | Long Term (3-5 years) | Within MOH | MOH & Other Ministries | MOH & NGOs and/or Private Sector | Slight | Moderate | Significant |
| (2) Revenue-sharing between MOH and church-mission health institutions | | X | | | | X | | X | |
| (3) Community support for local health facilities | | X | | X | | | X | | |
| (4) Local drug revolving funds | | X | | X | X | | X | | |
| D. Changes in tax legislation | | | X | | X | X | | X | |
| E. Creating a National Health Development Fund | | X | | | X | | | | X |

aThis table is a reconstructed version of the recommendations that were sent separately to the government of Zimbabwe, as the result of Hecht, ed. (1992). The author was a member of the World Bank team that produced that study. Hecht developed the original table from the analytical input of all of the team members.

essential drugs program, with competitive bidding for the drugs on international markets, frees more resources for the purchase of additional drugs and/or for the purchase of gasoline for ambulances. Likewise cost recovery, as a resource mobilization strategy, will also generate more resources.  Therefore, increased resource efficiencies are, in effect, increased resource mobilization, by economic definition. However, the converse need not necessarily be the case; increased resource mobilization may not lead to increased resource efficiency. For example, if the MOH cost-recovery ratio increases from 5.2 to 12.1 percent, as it did in Ghana between 1985 and 1987 (Vogel, 1988), and then the proceeds of the cost recovery sit in ministry coffers, because of bureaucratic indecision, and few steps are taken by the MOH to increase resource efficiency, as apparently happened (Waddington and Enyimayou, 1989), more resources have been raised for the MOH account, but they have not been used efficiently.  In fact, there is the danger that increased resource mobilization could even become a substitute for increased resource efficiency.  That is why the heading I.B.3 in Table 4-1 also considers the *management* of health expenditures.

## RESOURCE EFFICIENCY

Resource efficiency consists of two dimensions, allocative efficiency and technical efficiency.  Under the first heading in Table 4-1 (I.A.1) it is recommended that the prevailing allocation of MOH budgetary resources spent upon tertiary/secondary/primary patient care be reallocated from, say, an average 60%/30%/10% to some other proportion, such as 50%/30%/20%.  This would decrease the tertiary share by 17 percent but raise the primary share by 100 percent. Secondly (I.A.2), the share of the MOH budget that is used for preventive purposes should be increased in order to meet specified concrete targets, the formulation of which were discussed in Chapter 2 of this study.  The implementation of both of these options would be a significant step toward changing the existing large discrepancy between epidemiological patterns and expenditure patterns in many of the countries of the Sub-Sahara.  Both options could be implemented in the short and medium term, be effected within the MOH decision process, and have a moderate to significant impact upon the efficiency and equity objectives of the country.

The three most important aspects of technical efficiency are shown in Table 4-1.  They are:   enhancing the efficiency of inpatient and outpatient hospital care; improving the efficiency of pharmaceutical and drug supply and utilization; and managing health expenditures, including manpower analysis and planning, given the importance of the personnel component in MOH budgets.

Hospital efficiency (I.B.1) is particularly important because so many MOH resources in so many of these countries are spent upon hospitals.  The bulk of any hospital's costs are related to inpatient care; however, modern medical technology has now made it possible to perform many procedures on an outpatient rather than an inpatient basis.  The removal of cataracts is just one example.  The MOH, and the hospitals (B.1.a), should carefully study the economic feasibility of performing more procedures on an outpatient basis; within the Sub-Saharan context, economic feasibility would be a function of the relative scarcities and costs of capital and labor (and kinds of labor), and foreign exchange shadow-costs.  As explained in Chapter 3, one of the most important tools for increasing bed occupancy rates (B.1.b) at lower levels of the hospital system would be the hierarchical structure of prices chosen for the cost-recovery reform; the more discipline that the price structure imposes upon the referral system, the more we would expect congestion at tertiary facilities to decline.  This recommendation once again reminds the policy maker how inseparable and intertwined are resource efficiency and resource mobilization strategies.  Likewise (B.1.c), reducing average length-of-stay, is both a function of substituting outpatient for inpatient care, and careful analysis and monitoring of outlier patients by type of medical case.[1]

Finally (B.1.d), hospitals should try to reduce their cost per patient day and per discharge.  The two most important means of doing this are, first, analyzing hospital cost structures, using data that are systematically and regularly collected; such data permit the identification of high unit costs of hospital operation for such items as the laundry, food services, cleaning, etc.  Second, once identification has taken place, the adoption of cost-saving measures can be pursued. For example, if, after careful study, it was determined that laundry services performed within the national hospital had seemingly high unit costs, competitive bids for the performance of the hospital laundry services could be sought in the private sector.  The results of these bids would also provide the hospital with information about what the unit cost of laundry "ought" to be.  Again, all of these hospital efficiency reforms could be achieved within the short-to-medium term; the decision process occurs within the ministry of health, and they would produce slight to moderate, but principally moderate effects upon efficiency and equity goals.

The second set of reform options, with respect to technical efficiency, is directed at improving the efficiency of drug supply and utilization (I.B.2).  First (B.2.a), and foremost, substantial savings can be achieved with the adoption of an essential drugs program for government health-care facilities.   Although some Sub-Saharan countries have made substantial progress (WHO, 1988) in adopting this reform option (e.g., Zimbabwe), others have not (e.g., Mali).  Second, (B.2.b), most of these countries have limited or no drug production capacity.[2]  Therefore, they must rely upon the importation of drugs and pharmaceuticals, and must have the foreign exchange to do so.  Given the internal, within-country competition between ministries for the acquisition of foreign exchange, it is particularly important that the MOH be able to demonstrate to the ministry of finance (MOF) and/or to the central bank that the MOH is using its own allocation of foreign exchange efficiently.  The first step in doing this would be to adopt the essential drugs program, but in many countries, the MOH is viewed by the MOF as the "weak sister" among ministries, because of past MOH inefficiencies.  In these countries, it may be necessary to set up foreign exchange allocation rules among the ministries so that the MOH receives its "fair share" of the scarce foreign exchange.  Third, (B.2.c), it makes little sense for the government to adopt an essential drugs program, if the private sector is not required to adhere to the same program.  Within the context of the scarcity of foreign exchange and health resources in general, and the fact that the WHO-assisted essential drugs programs represent a floor-coverage for the epidemiology of each individual country, the importation of name-brand or so-called "designer drugs" represents a luxury that most of these countries cannot afford, particularly in countries where the private health-care sector is large relative to the public health-care sector (e.g., Kenya).  Fourth, (B.2.d), there is a great deal of anecdotal evidence from many countries in the Sub-Sahara that "too many" (inappropriate for the medical condition) drugs are prescribed and injections given in both inpatient and outpatient settings.  In this regard both health-care providers and patients must be educated by the MOH regarding the overuse of a good thing, particularly the overuse of injections with the consequent danger of acquiring AIDS if needles are not properly sterilized.  On the health-care provider side this education could be partially accomplished by providing a prescription manual to every health-care worker who comes into treatment contact with patients;

their supervisors would do spot checks to make sure that the manuals were being consulted.  On the patient side, wall posters at treatment sites could warn of the dangers of overprescription, and the possible AIDS risk from injections;[3] also, if patients complain about what they perceive to be an underprescription of drugs, health-care workers can show the patient the contents of the manual and the recommendations therein for the prescription of drugs for specific diseases.  Fifth, (B.2.e), and finally, some attempt should be made to monitor physicians' prescribing practices, particularly at hospitals, where they can be most easily monitored.  As has been shown earlier in this study, as the captain of the team, the unsupervised physician is in the position of being able to do a great deal of financial harm (or good) to the health-care system, because he/she makes so many of the treatment decisions on behalf of the patient.  In this regard, peer pressure can be a powerful stimulus.  Many hospitals in developed countries now circulate monthly computer printouts with the amounts and kinds of prescriptions issued by each *named* physician to all of the staff physicians.  In Sub-Saharan countries that do not yet have computers in the hospitals, there is no reason why a staff person could not produce a similar list that was compiled using a desk calculator.  Of course, if a country has already adopted an essential drugs program and adheres to it strictly, the financial urgency of this last recommendation for pharmaceutical reform would be less than for a country that had not done so.

All of the drug and pharmaceutical reform options could be accomplished in the short-to-medium term, although for countries that have not had any experience with an essential drugs program, the drug policies might only be accomplished in the long term, about three to five years.  Also, unlike with the previous options considered in Table 4-1, the decision process for rationalizing procedures for allocating foreign exchange would have to be done with the MOF and/or with the central bank; likewise the options of developing regulations and incentives for the private sector to utilize the essential drugs list might have to be negotiated with the NGOs and the private sector.  The two reform options that deal with an essential drugs list could have a substantial impact upon efficiency objectives, not only in terms of saving money, but also because, in just about every country, drugs are in short supply, thus considerably diluting the treatment-of-illness process.  The other three drug-reform options would have a moderate effect upon efficiency objectives.

The third set of reform options with respect to technical efficiency in Table 4-1 bears upon the management of health expenditures

(I.B.3). In most of the countries studied, the budgets that are used are not appropriate instruments for analyzing the finances and efficiency of the health-care sector. For example, it is usually not difficult to obtain time-series data for a country's public health sector; the analytical problem with the data, however, is that they show what was budgeted for the sector as a whole and for its various components (e.g., personnel, drugs and supplies, capital expenditures) on an *ex ante* basis. It is never possible to ascertain the total amount that was *actually* spent by the MOH in any given year, nor what was actually spent upon the components.

Because of this and other related analytical problems, the first three reform options for the management of health expenditures concentrate upon budget formulation and preparation. Reform option B.3.a recommends revising MOH budget and expenditure formats in an analytically meaningful way; consistent with this recommendation, perhaps the African Development Bank or the World Bank could promulgate a best-practice budget formula that could be used by all of the Sub-Saharan countries. With respect to this recommendation, all of the countries could benefit from the budgetary expertise that these two international institutions possess. An extremely useful by-product of a common format would be the creation of a tool for comparative analysis for the countries themselves; for example the minister of health in the Cote d'Ivoire could compare his/her budgetary experience with that in Cameroon. Reform option B.3.b recommends decentralizing responsibility for preparing budgets, incurring expenditures, and effecting payments. This option is particularly important for large countries (in population and/or in geographic size) for all of the reasons given in Chapter 2, but also in order to be able to achieve reform option B.3.a above in an accurate and meaningful way. The third budgetary reform option (B.3.c) is the formulation of an integrated budget that covers all capital and recurrent expenditure spending. Some of the countries already have this kind of budget (e.g., Kenya), but in other countries, it is virtually impossible to ascertain the country total for either capital or recurrent budgets (e.g., Nigeria).

The last three reform options in I.B.3 are equally important from the perspective of managing health expenditures. Competent manpower planning (B.3.a) at the MOH needs careful attention because the health-care sector is so labor intensive. But, more than that, manpower training requires a long and expensive gestation period, particularly for physicians, and planning mistakes made today can have disastrously expensive budgetary and health consequences in the longer term.  Physician/population and nurse/population ratios recommended by the WHO have no economic content, because they ignore country epidemiology and the relative costs of differing kinds of health-care labor and capital in each country.  Careful health manpower-planning in each of the Sub-Saharan countries will have to take these economic factors into account.  Therefore, health manpower-planning training, whether at universities inside or at outside the countries should contain a balanced curriculum of economics, planning, and public health.

Reform option B.3.e recommends improving accounting skills and systems in MOH and local government health facilities.  This reform option  is easier prescribed than done in countries where accounting skills are scarce, and where the private sector can easily absorb all new accounting graduates at salary levels that are much higher than the public sector can afford to pay.  But, the question can be posed in another fashion:  can the public sector afford *not* to pay competitive salaries to accountants, given the large sums of MOH funds that may be in the process of being lost annually due to the present lack of financial accountability in the health sector of many of the Sub-Saharan countries?  Perhaps a compromise solution to this problem would be to create a salary structure where the salary of four or five chief accountants would be high enough to make them unsusceptible to the financial attractions of the private sector; they, in turn, would train and supervise the work of accountant-practitioners much in the same manner that physicians in some countries train and supervise the work of physician-extenders or nurse-practitioners.

Reform option B.3.f recommends decentralizing the procurement of goods and services that can be efficiently purchased at the local level.  While this recommendation has its basis in common economic sense, it is not always practiced in many countries, possibly because of problems of corruption (Gould and Amaro-Reyes, 1985).  As explained in Chapter 3, it does not make economic sense to decentralize the purchase of imported health-care inputs such as pharmaceuticals (for the purchase of which there are large economies of scale), with bulk purchase in international competitive bidding.  On the other hand, it seems economically difficult to justify the purchase of food or laundry services for a district hospital from an office in the MOH in the far-off capital of the country.  If corruption is a problem, it is probably because the accounting recommendations in reform option B.3.e above have yet to be implemented.

The estimated time frame for the options included under the management of health expenditures requires a fair amount of training and preparation and is, therefore a medium-term time-frame option.

Four of the six options require that the MOH collaborate with other ministries in implementing the reform option. It is expected that three of the six options will have a significant impact upon the efficiency objectives of the MOH, two will have a moderate effect, and one (the development of an integrated budget) will have a slight effect.

Finally, something needs to be done about donor coordination (I.C.). It is not clear whether this should be done at the individual country level or at a higher level (such as at the United Nations), but the lack of donor coordination creates large inefficiencies in these health-care systems, both in the often inappropriate kinds of donations that donors give and in the amounts of time that upper-echelon MOH officials spend in dealing with the individual donors.

## RESOURCE MOBILIZATION

Again, it must be emphasized that the reform-option issues of resource efficiency and resource mobilization are inextricably intertwined. For example, all of the reform options for increasing technical efficiency within the hospitals in I.B. above depend in one way or another upon the adoption of, or the existence of, a well-designed cost-recovery system that has the teeth in it to discipline the referral system. Therefore, the first recommendation for resource mobilization is the adoption of a cost-recovery reform (II.A.), or, if one is already in existence in the country, improving it along the lines laid out in Chapter 3.

In Table 4-1, there are seven different aspects of cost recovery that need emphasis. The first, (II.A.1), strongly recommends the introduction of means testing as an essential component for equity within the cost-recovery system. One of the largest obstacles to the adoption of cost recovery in Sub-Saharan Africa has been the very real fear that the poor might be priced out of the use of the health-care system. But, this need not be the case at all. Given the way that many health-care systems in the Sub-Sahara are presently structured and financed, the needs of the poor are almost totally ignored. The bulk of government health-care funds are spent upon hospitals that cater to middle- and upper-class government employees in the capital or in other large urban areas; where there are health-care facilities for the poor, the facilities more often than not are bereft of drugs and supplies so that the effective real health care delivered in them often asymptotically approaches zero. As explained at length in Chapter 3, one of, if not the major, objectives of a combination of resource efficiency and resource mobilization policies is to redistribute health care toward the poor. Therefore, means testing must be done; Griffin (1989) contains an extended discussion of sensible and sensitive ways of conducting means testing. Vogel (1988) shows many examples of successful means testing procedures in government hospitals (e.g., the Hopital St. Louis in Senegal) and in church-mission hospitals (e.g., the Hopital Protestant de Dabou in the Cote d'Ivoire).

The second recommendation (II.A.2) is that the fee structure needs to be pegged to the consumer price index or to some other index of national inflation. The use of this reform option has both a resource efficiency dimension and a resource mobilization dimension. If the structure of fees remains constant and prices elsewhere in the national economy are increasing at even a moderate rate, the real value of fees as a rationing device and as a fortifier of the referral system erodes. Likewise, if the structure of fees remains constant for too long, given inflation, the usefulness of the cost-recovery system for resource mobilization diminishes.

Reform option II.A.3 recommends increasing inpatient and other charges for patients with health insurance to cover the full cost of services. In some countries (e.g., Cote d'Ivoire, Kenya, Zimbabwe) government hospitals levy the same charge to the insured as to the uninsured. Because the charges only represent approximately 10 percent of the cost of the services rendered, the private health insurance system, and the relatively more affluent citizens who buy the health insurance, are being subsidized by the rest of the population, including the poor who pay taxes. In other countries (e.g., Mali) other government ministries are supposed to pay the MOH for health services rendered by the MOH hospital to the other ministry employees; they rarely do so, and if they do, they pay only a fraction of the costs of treatment.[4]

Because the hospital is seen as the ultimate referral point, within the efficiency context, reform option II.A.4 recommends also charging a nominal outpatient fee for those who use the hospital outpatient departments. Again, from an efficiency perspective, these outpatient fees should, at the margin, deter some people from going to a hospital outpatient department for the treatment of a condition that could have been treated at a health post or health center for a smaller fee or at no fee. In his 1988 study, Vogel found that the preponderance of user-fee revenue in the four countries studied (Cote d'Ivoire, Ghana, Mali, and Senegal) came from the sale of drugs and pharmaceuticals; in their 1991 study in Nigeria, Akin et al. found that demand for health care in government facilities was particularly responsive to the percentage of time that drugs and pharmaceuticals were available. These and other studies indicate that the demand for drugs and pharmaceuticals in the Sub-Saharan countries is strong and that people are willing to pay for them.  Therefore, reform option II.A.5 recommends charging separately for drugs prescribed, not only because such charges are excellent sources of revenue for resource mobilization, but also because drugs are usually the single most important health-care input that is in short supply in these Sub-Saharan health-care systems; the drug charges then also serve to ration drugs from frivolous use.

Reform option II.A.6 recommends developing incentives for health facilities, particularly hospitals, to improve their revenue collection efforts.  Exhortation by MOH officials is one method that has been tried in order to achieve the objective of improved revenue collection and it seems to have been effective in Ghana, due to the strong efforts and personality of the director of medical services in the MOH (Vogel, 1988).  But financial incentives can be equally, or more, compelling. It is quite clear that hospitals will not be able to improve their quality, which will draw additional paying patients, if they are not allowed to retain a substantial portion of the revenues that they collect; on the other hand, the MOH will not be able to perform its redistributive function towards the poor, if it cannot have a large portion of the additional revenues.  Vogel and Frant (1992) show that an MOH lump-sum levy on the hospitals' cost-recovery revenues is the least incentive-distorting method of raising revenue for both the hospitals and the MOH.  Finally cost-recovery reform option II.A.7 recommends the strengthening of hospital billing and collection procedures, which also depends upon the accounting recommendations in I.B.3.e above.

All of these cost-recovery reform options can be put into place in the short or medium term.  In countries that have already made a good beginning with cost recovery, such as Ghana, short-term fine-tuning of the system may be all that is necessary.  For example, Waddington and Enyimayou (1989) found that, at least in one area of Ghana, the rural poor seem to have been priced out of the market; perhaps Ghana should charge more at the hospitals, with means testing of course, and charge nothing at rural health posts and at rural health centers.  In countries where cost recovery has not yet been tried on any large scale or where cost recovery is newly nascent, a medium-term view may be more appropriate.  One important aspect of a medium-term view is to alert the population to the necessity of resource efficiency and resource mobilization efforts on the part of the MOH, in order to forestall any vocal opposition to cost recovery. For example, in 1989, the MOH in Kenya attempted to initiate a technically well-planned and ambitious cost-recovery program; however, political and press reaction was so negative that the MOH was forced to retrench the program. In retrospect, many observers have concluded that the MOH in Kenya should have better publicized its well-meaning intentions and educated the public about the nature of the reforms that it hoped to achieve, before it had embarked upon such an ambitious overhaul of the financing of its health-care system. With respect to the decision process, the MOH needs to confer with the MOF concerning how the MOF will treat the MOH budget, once cost recovery has begun, and what portion, if any, of the cost-recovery proceeds will go to the MOF. As Vogel and Frant (1992) show, any MOF actions need to be sensitive to the incentives for revenue collection, or lack of it, that the MOF might pose. For means testing, the MOH may want to confer and to collaborate with the ministry of social welfare or any other analogous agency that deals with the poor; one would expect large economies of scale in means testing, and duplication of effort should be avoided. Six of the seven cost-recovery options have moderate to significant efficiency and equity effects, but careful means testing will cause the most significant equity effect.

There are two recommendations under heading II.B.; expanding and/or reforming existing health insurance. Formal national health insurance is probably not suitable for most of the countries in the Sub-Sahara at this stage of their economic development (Vogel, 1990a). The health financing that comes from the social security systems in some of the Francophone countries is inefficient and inequitable. Zimbabwe and Kenya probably have the most advanced private health insurance systems in Sub-Saharan Africa, in terms of the percentage of the population covered, but, like many private health insurance systems in the West, the systems in Zimbabwe and Kenya have serious structural defects, from the point of view of efficiency in the consumption and production of health care. What are basically needed for consumption and production efficiencies are locally adaptive forms of capitated, prepaid health insurance plans, built upon the basic model of the Health Maintenance Organization (HMO).

One way to begin such an effort is for government to provide seed money for farmers' cooperatives or for marketing boards to form such organizations. The most important prerequisite for the financial survival of an HMO is that it not suffer adverse selection; thus, another way that government might encourage the private formation of HMOs is to provide stop-loss insurance protection, on a sliding scale in the early years, for any HMOs that form.  Reform option II.B.1 recommends requiring through legislation that firms over a certain size provide a minimum level of health benefits to their employees in HMOs.  This might encourage larger firms to form their own HMOs or to band together with other large firms (thus lowering the possibility of adverse selection) to form HMOs.  At the very least, such legislation would create a demand for HMOs; there is no reason to believe that a private-sector supply response would not be forthcoming, at least in the more developed countries such as in the Cote d'Ivoire and in Zimbabwe, and possibly in Nigeria.  Also, teachers' unions and other similar organizations might be interested in such an arrangement. Reform option II.B.2 calls for promoting greater competition among insurers, and, in the light of the discussion about HMOs, the insurers would be HMOs.  The best means of promoting competition is a minimum of government interference which would allow them to compete through innovative ways of delivering health care and through lower prepaid capitated prices.

The reform options in II.B would require medium to long-term preparation and significant cooperation between government and the private sector, at least initially.  By promoting private health insurance of the HMO type, there could be moderate to significant effects upon efficiency objectives, and, to the extent that more responsibility for providing health care to workers in the formal labor sector was removed from the government, government would have more resources per capita to devote to the health care of the poor.  This could create a significant equity effect.

The four reform options in II.C have to do with the decentralization of the financing of health services.  The first two (II.C.1 and 2) deal with revenue sharing between the central government and local government, and between the MOH and the church mission health-care facilities.  Both reform options must take into account the fact that while some local governments and church missions have a certain amount of revenue-generating capacity (the former through local taxes and the latter through cost recovery and foreign-donor assistance), they are often located in the poorer regions of the country.  In the case of local governments, the public administration principles that underlie decentralization (and democracy) give legitimacy to their conducting their own health-care facilities. Likewise, some countries (e.g., Ghana and Tanzania) have a substantial reliance upon the church missions for the provision of health care in the poorer areas of the country and often at the primary- and secondary-care level. Thus, revenue sharing from the central government and from the MOH is highly desirable. However, care must be taken in the construction of the revenue-sharing formula not to attenuate any incentives that local government or the church missions might have to engage in their own cost-recovery activities, again, with proper attention to the needs of the poor.

Reform option II.C.3 recommends fostering community support for local health-care facilities. While rural communities in many of these countries are too poor to pay some, or any cost-recovery fees, some countries (e.g., Senegal, Kenya, Tanzania) have been highly successful in promoting community support in the voluntary building and maintenance of local health posts, and even health centers. Again, at the margin, such efforts free MOH financial resources for the purchase of other health-care inputs, such as locally produced supplies and dressings.

With two caveats, option I.C.4 recommends the creation of local drug revolving funds. The first caveat is that drug revolving funds have not been remarkably successful in Sub-Saharan Africa (Vogel and Stephens, 1989) but then again, in some regions of Zaire they seem to have succeeded; the reason for failure in many cases partially seems to stem from mismanagement. The second, more important caveat is that in many regions of most of the countries, people are simply too poor to pay for any percentage of the costs of the drugs, let alone the full costs, and, for this reason, to expect a revolving drug fund to be completely self-sustainable, as many of the USAID revolving drug funds in rural Senegal were expected to do, is somewhat unrealistic.[5] On the other hand, there is no reason to believe, except for management problems, that revolving drug funds could not be successful in more affluent urban areas. Some cross subsidization between the rich and the poor would have to take place in the price structure, the upper price limit for the rich being the price of the same pharmaceuticals or drugs in private pharmacies. Even this kind of revolving drug fund might have to be partially subsidized by the MOH. Another line of argument might hold that the sale of pharmaceuticals at the retail level in urban areas should be left to the private, for-profit sector; consistent with previous reasoning in this study, the MOH (or some private-sector regulated monopolist) would be the wholesaler, in order to take advantage of the economies of scale of bulk purchase in internationally competitive markets.

The estimated time frame for implementing the reform option recommendations for the decentralization of the financing of health services would be the medium term, principally because the design, and possible testing, of a revenue-sharing formula demands some thought and because the central government and MOH need to negotiate rules of jurisdiction and conduct with local governments and church-mission officials. The efficiency and equity effects would be slight to moderate.

Reform option II.D recommends changes in tax legislation, and would only be applicable to a few countries, such as Zimbabwe, where the tax treatment of health insurance premiums seems to have had the same pernicious effects upon the purchase of health insurance and medical care as it has had in the United States.[6] In brief, if employer and employee contributions to health insurance plans are deductible under the income tax laws, employers and employees receive, in effect, a discount on the after-tax purchase of health insurance. As a consequence, they purchase more health insurance coverage than they would have, had they had no discount. In turn, the "overinsurance" that they possess enables them to purchase more medical treatment (some perhaps frivolous) than they would have had they not had "too much" health insurance. These kinds of tax treatments tend to favor people in upper-income groups. Thus, such tax treatment tends to produce both perverse efficiency effects (at the margin, "too much" health insurance is purchased and "too much" medical care is consumed) and perverse equity effects (those in higher income tax brackets benefit more than those in lower income tax brackets and those who are too poor to have to pay any income taxes). Adoption of this policy reform may require a long-term time frame, because once such subsidies become embedded in the law, they are difficult to remove, and because complex and prolonged negotiations might be necessary with the MOF and with the health insurance industry.

The final, and possibly the most controversial (because it has never before been tried in Sub-Saharan Africa) reform option recommendation is the creation of a National Health Development Fund (NHDF). The idea rests upon a simple principle in economics, that of the notion of negative "externalities." When some people engage in some forms of behavior that affect other people in a negative fashion, government can either forbid that behavior by making it illegal, such as forbidding the private ownership of firearms, or government can tax the behavior, such as levying pollution taxes on an industry that pollutes the rivers. If, for political reasons, government chooses to tax rather than to forbid, then the tax revenues can either be put into the general tax fund, or they can be earmarked for particular uses, such as cleaning the polluted rivers. When people smoke, drink alcohol excessively, and drive their automobiles, they create direct and indirect negative externalities.  The direct negative externalities are that nonsmokers end up becoming secondary smokers, nondrinkers end up in automobile accidents caused by excessive drinkers, and nondrivers end up inhaling the carbon monoxide that automobile exhaust produces.  The indirect negative externalities arise because smokers, drinkers, and those who inhale too much polluted air have a much higher probability of contracting lung cancer, cardiovascular disease, and cirrhosis of the liver and thereby impose the cost of paying for their earlier and longer illnesses upon others.[7]  Given the negative externalities of these kinds of behavior, a good case can be made that the behavior be taxed, and that the proceeds of the taxes be used to pay for preventive or curative care.

Therefore, for reform option II.E the recommendation is that each Sub-Saharan country establish a NHDF that would be financed from the proceeds of an earmarked sales tax upon tobacco products, alcoholic beverages, and, possibly, even upon gasoline and diesel fuel. Because the demand for these products is relatively price inelastic (Manning et al., 1989), the earmarked tax would be a good source of revenue for the MOH that could use the funds for educating the public about the nefarious consequences of smoking, drinking excessively, and causing air pollution.[8]  The tax funds would also be another source of additional funds for primary and preventive care for the poor.  Because of the expected opposition of producers and vendors of these products, the estimated time frame for the creation of the NHDF would be the medium- or long-term.  The MOH would have to coordinate the tax and the fund legislation with the parliament and with the MOF.  The NHDF could have a significant effect upon both efficiency and equity objectives.


## CONCLUSION

The reform options that are contained in Table 4-1 and that have been discussed in this chapter should be viewed as a comprehensive and interdependent package for the reform of financing health-care systems in Sub-Saharan Africa.  As explained in the introduction to this chapter, the public health sector in each individual country has some of its own unique financing and incentive problems, but the common problem seems to be the role of the hospital vis-a-vis the epidemiology of the country, and the financial drain that the hospital represents when trying to address the epidemiology adequately.  The program of reform advocated in this study would systematically downgrade the role of the hospital in the public sector, and thus eventually provide the financial means for delivering better health for all.

## NOTES

1.    The diagnosis related grouping (DRG) system now used by Medicare to pay hospitals for the care of the elderly in the United States gives strong incentives to monitor length of stay.  Every hospital is paid a set fee for each of 470 separate medical and surgical diagnoses.  If, for example, a given diagnosis has an implicit length-of-stay reimbursement for five days, and the patient stays in the hospital ten days, the hospital is forced to absorb the costs of the additional five days.   Therefore, the hospitals have a strong incentive to monitor their physicians.  Of course, the DRG system also gives hospitals significant incentives for undertreatment and thus the hospitals must be carefully monitored by government.

2.    Indeed, it is arguable whether, at the stage of economic development where many of these countries stand, it is desirable to have *any* internal drug manufacturing capacity (Vogel, 1988).

3.    One possible problem arising from this counsel is that many mothers might not be willing to bring their babies to facilities for immunizations.  This potential problem needs further thought.

4.  Of course, in many of these countries, the hospital accounting systems are in such disarray that it is now virtually impossible to ascertain what are the true costs of treatment.  See reform option I.B.3.e above.

5.  That is why the Bamako initiative could not possibly have been successful, if it had been implemented.

6.    For an excellent treatment of the economic theory and summary of empirical studies of such tax treatment, see Pauly (1986).  Although the subject matter in this reference pertains to the U.S., its economic content is sufficiently general that it applies to any country in the world.

7.    In an interesting study done in the U.S., Manning and his colleagues at the RAND Corporation (1989) found that smokers do pay their way, because they die at earlier ages than do nonsmokers and leave a surplus in their retirement accounts for others to use; drinkers, on the other hand, do not pay their way.

8.  Ironically, because the demand for these products is so price inelastic, higher taxes on them would not necessarily cause a large decline in their use.   However, there may be an interaction between income and price.   For example, Manning et al. (1989) found that doubling the tax on beer in the U.S. would cause a substantial reduction in teenage drunken driving and automobile accidents.

# Appendix 1

# Basic Data for Calculation of Health Welfare Ratios in Table 1-11

**Table A1-1**
**Basic Data for Calculation of Health Welfare Ratios in Table 1-11**[a]

| Country | 1975 | 1980 | 1985 |
|---|---|---|---|
| Botswana | 14.3 | 24.4 | 39.6 |
| | 711 | 893 | 1,072 |
| Burkina Faso | 14.7 | 21.0 | 22.2 |
| | 5,596 | 6,161 | 6,662 |
| Cameroon | 42.0 | 50.8 | 112.3 |
| | 7,439 | 8,701 | 10,190 |
| Ethiopia | 83.7 | 103.1 | 154.9 |
| | 32,954 | 37,717 | 42,234 |
| Gambia | 3.7 | 8.4 | 8.6 |
| | 536 | 652 | 762 |
| Ghana | 38.8 | 42.5 | 86.3 |
| | 9,970 | 11,500 | 13,513 |
| Kenya | 143.3 | 223.2 | 208.8 |
| | 13,707 | 16,642 | 20,414 |
| Liberia | 19.6 | 20.3 | 20.6 |
| | 1,582 | 1,871 | 2,210 |

**Table A1-1 (continued)**

| Country | 1975 | 1980 | 1985 |
|---|---|---|---|
| Malawi | 30.5 | 48.5 | 54.0 |
| | 5,213 | 6,123 | 7,137 |
| Mauritius | 23.0 | 28.9 | 33.0 |
| | 891 | 957 | 1,020 |
| Niger | 15.2 | 18.5 | 18.4 |
| | 4,766 | 5,532 | 6,418 |
| Nigeria (unadjusted) | 258.3 | 321.1 | 197.6 |
| | 74,884 | 84,732 | 99,753 |
| Rwanda | 10.7 | 12.7 | 13.4 |
| | 4,358 | 5,139 | 6,034 |
| Senegal | 41.6 | 45.5 | 34.3 |
| | 4,960 | 5,696 | 6,560 |
| Sierra Leone | 17.7 | 21.2 | 15.3 |
| | 3,045 | 3,296 | 3,657 |
| Swaziland | 7.9 | 12.3 | 20.3 |
| | 535 | 633 | 757 |
| Tanzania | 113.5 | 117.2 | 103.6 |
| | 15,942 | 18,757 | 22,241 |
| Uganda | 23.0 | 13.8 | 49.3 |
| | 11,102 | 12,630 | 14,695 |
| Zaire | 49.3 | 36.2 | 17.6 |
| | 24,965 | 28,893 | 33,494 |

**Table A1-1  (continued)**

| Country | 1975 | 1980 | 1985 |
|---------|------|------|------|
| Zambia | 106.2 | 93.3 | 112.4 |
| | 4,846 | 5,647 | 6,704 |
| Zimbabwe | 100.5 | 119.0 | 156.4 |
| | 6,050 | 6,976 | 8,394 |

[a]The first-row entry for each country is real government health expenditures (in millions of $) and the second-row entry is population (in thousands)

*Sources*:  Expenditure data from Gallagher (1988); population data from Summers and Heston (1988).

# Appendix 2

# The Range of Life Expectancies

Table A2-1 contains data on life expectancy at birth and at age forty for males and females for six countries, two of them Sub-Saharan, at three levels of economic development. Japan and the United States are at the highest level of development, Mexico and Thailand are at midrange, and Malawi and Liberia are at a low level. For males, life expectancy at birth ranges from a high of seventy-six years in Japan to a low of forty-six years in Malawi; the percentage difference between the two, using Japan as the base, is 39.5 percent. For women, the range of life expectancy at birth ranges from a high of eighty-two years in Japan to a low of forty-seven years in Malawi, or, a 42.7 percent difference. At age forty, the range in life expectancy narrows. For men, it goes from a high of 36.5 years in Japan to a low of 26.2 years in Liberia, or a 28.2 percent difference. For women, the range is 41.1 years in Japan to 28.4 years in both Malawi and Liberia, or a 30.9 percent difference. Thus, for men, there is an 11.3 percent difference in the contrast between life expectancy at birth and at age forty; for women, an 11.8 percent difference in the contrast.

**Table A2-1**
**Life Expectancy at Birth and at Age 40:  Selected Countries,**
**by Level of Economic Development**

| Country | Life Expectancy at Birth | | Life Expectancy at Age 40 | |
| --- | --- | --- | --- | --- |
| | Men | Women | Men | Women |
| Japan | 76 | 82 | 36.5 | 41.1 |
| U.S. | 73 | 80 | 34.1 | 40.2 |
| Mexico | 66 | 73 | 32.4 | 35.4 |
| Thailand | 63 | 68 | 30.3 | 34.3 |
| Malawi | 46 | 47 | 26.4 | 28.4 |
| Liberia | 53 | 56 | 26.2 | 28.4 |
| % Difference Highest/Lowest | 39.5 | 42.7 | 28.2 | 30.9 |

*Sources*:  Life expectancy at birth, World Bank (1992); life expectancy at
age 40, Gray (1990).

# Appendix 3

# Improvement in In-County Water and Sanitation Efficiency

There is some disagreement in the literature about the efficacy and cost effectiveness of water and sanitation (WS) as instruments for the prevention of morbidity and mortality. After having stated that access to clean water is necessary for social development, Patel (1989) concludes with the observation: "However, the case for considering increased access to water, on its own, as an efficient contributor to health and child survival, is still very weak. Interactions with sanitation and health education have been noted, and future research may improve on this result." On the other hand, Okun (1988) and Koch-Weser (1988) both make the explicit point that cost comparisons between ORT and WS can be misleading. ORT is a curative technology that has a direct and immediate effect; it cures an episode of diarrhea. It has no effect on the causes of morbidity. WS is preventive; it is part of the health infrastructure, and, as such, partakes in many interactions over time. For example, a mother of five children, who spends three or four hours each day carrying water, will have less time to devote to her children's care and probably no time or energy left for her own health education. She will not have the time to read and/or discuss with a health promoter the basic preventive WHO pamphlet, "Facts for Life," and be aware of valuable information pertaining to prevention for herself and for her children. The opportunity costs of the water-carrying activity are then more diarrhea for her children, more malnutrition, and further susceptibility to other diseases and problems, including more diarrhea. Early childhood malnutrition leads to learning disabilities and other problems in later life. Okun concludes that without WS "and hygiene education, ORT programs are not likely to effect long-term improvement in child health status." Barnum et al. (1980) show a model of how these interactions work via direct and indirect effects. These effects are, however, notoriously difficult to measure, and, as a consequence, the true cost effectiveness of WS has yet to be measured.

Meanwhile, studies of how WS is provided, funded, and used in many developing countries indicate that the same inefficiencies and inequities that exist in the formal health-care sector also exist in the WS sector (World Bank, 1988). That is to say, WS is much more widespread in urban areas and in the affluent sections of urban areas than it is in rural areas and in the poor sections of urban areas. Even though the practice of charging user fees for WS is much more common than charging for health care in the health-care sector, average charges are often below average costs for WS, particularly in Africa (WHO, 1987). Thus, the general tax system subsidizes the affluent who are able, and most probably, willing to pay. Many of the poor buy water from vendors. World Bank (1988) shows the ratio of water-vendor to public-utility prices for water in a number of capital cities in the developing world. In many of these cities, the water-vendor price is several times higher than the public-utility price, indicating that those who do not have access to piped water, value clean water highly because of the relatively higher price that they are willing to pay for it.

Even though water can be viewed as a preventive technology for health purposes, it has all of the economic characteristics of a purely private good. Therefore, it is not clear that the framework for discussion about WS policy should be divorced from considerations about amortizing investments in WS over time through user charges. As with curative hospital care, provisions for exempting the poor from payment for WS must be made. However, once such a discussion framework is adopted, the relevant concept of the costs of WS becomes the *net* cost of providing WS, that is, the difference between the time-stream of user-fee revenues and amortization and operating costs that measures the yearly subsidy necessary to pay for WS for the poor from public funds. As Patel (1989) points out, it makes no difference whether the public sector or the private sector *provides* the WS; the only necessary factor is that the subsidy for the poor be financed by the public sector. To the extent that user fees encourage efficiency in the consumption and production of WS, more national resources are freed for other uses (including formal health care). Likewise, the imposition of user charges on those who can afford to pay, and WS subsidies for those who cannot afford to pay has the effect of improving equity in a country.

# Appendix 4

# Currency, Exchange Rates, PPPR Conversion Factors, and Population for Countries Listed in Table 3-6

**Table A4-1**

**Currency, Exchange Rates, PPPR Conversion Factors, and Population for Countries Listed in Table 3-6**

| Countries | Currency (millions) | Exchange Rate to the U.S. Dollar | PPPR Conversion Factor | Population (thousands) |
|---|---|---|---|---|
| Botswana | Pula | 0.815 | .6823 | 853 |
| Burkina Faso | FCFA | 271.730 | .4511 | 6,258 |
| Burundi | FBu | 120.690 | .5418 | 4,702 |
| Central Af. Republic | FCFA | --- | --- | --- |
| Ethiopia | Birr | 2.070 | .3011 | 42,234 |
| Kenya | K Shilling | 14.414 | .4037 | 19,604 |
| Lesotho | Maloti | 2.191 | .1214 | 1,525 |
| Madagascar | FMG | 662.480 | .3653 | 10,164 |
| Mali | FCFA | 898.520 | .2568 | 7,545 |
| Rwanda | RWF | 92.850 | .6151 | 5,490 |
| Somalia | S Shilling | 10.750 | .5456 | 4,945 |
| Sudan | S Pound | 2.288 | .4630 | 21,784 |
| Swaziland | E | 1.438 | .4675 | 730 |
| Uganda | U Shilling | 94.338 | .3267 | 13,451 |
| Zambia | Kwacha | .868 | .8598 | 5,844 |
| Zimbabwe | Z Dollars | 1.612 | .5009 | 8,394 |

# References

**BOOKS AND ARTICLES**

African Development Bank. 1987. *Health Sector Policy Paper*. Abidjan. African Development Bank.

Akin, John S. 1989. *Economics of Health Insurance: Theory and Developed Country Experience: A Proposal*. Washington, D.C. World Bank. Latin America Technical Department. Human Resources Division.

Akin, John S., N. Birdsall, and D. De Ferranti. 1987. *Financing Health Services in Developing Countries: An Agenda for Reform*. Washington, D.C. World Bank.

Akin, John S., H. Denton, D. K. Guilkey, R. J. Vogel, and A. Wouters. 1991. *Federal Republic of Nigeria: Health-Care Cost, Financing and Utilization, a Subsector Report*. Washington, D.C. World Bank Report No. 8382-UNI.

Barnett, Tony, and P. Blaikie. 1992. *AIDS in Africa: Its Present and Future Impact*. New York. The Guilford Press.

Barnum, Howard, R. Barlow, L. Fajardo, and A. Pradilla. 1980. *A Resource Allocation Model for Child Survival*. Cambridge, Massachusetts. Oelgeschlager, Gunn and Hain.

Barnum, Howard, and J. Kutzin. 1990. *Public Hospitals in Developing Countries: Resource Use, Costs and Financing*. Washington, D.C. World Bank.

Birdsall, Nancy. 1987. *Strategies for Analyzing Effects of User Charges in the Social Sectors*. PHN Technical Note 87-1. Washington, D.C. World Bank.

Bitran, Richardo A. 1988. *Health Care Demand Studies in Developing Countries: A Critical Review and Agenda for Research*. Arlington,

VA.   John Snow, Inc. Project REACH.   U.S. Agency for International Development.

Bitran, Ricardo A., M. Mpese, S. Bavugabgose, M. Kasonga, N. Nsuka, T. Vian, and K. Wambenge. 1986. *Zaire Health Zones Financing Study*. Arlington, VA. John Snow, Inc. Project REACH. U.S. Agency for International Development.

Borch, Karl. 1990. *Economics of Insurance*. Amsterdam.   North Holland.

Brunet-Jailly, J. 1988. *Le Financement des Couts Recurrents de la Sante au Mali* Premiere Redaction. Geneve. Organisation Mondiale de la Santé.

Creese, Andrew L. 1990. *User Charges for Health Care: A Review of Recent Experience*. SHS Paper Number 1. Geneva. World Health Organization.

Cross, Peter N., M. A. Huff, J. D. Quick, and J. A. Bates. 1986. "Revolving Drug Funds:  Conducting Business in the Public Sector." *Social Science and Medicine* 22: 355-343.

De Ferranti, David. 1985. *Paying for Health Services in Developing Countries: An Overview*. Washington, D.C. World Bank. World Bank Staff Working Papers No. 721.

Diop, Francois, K. Hill, and I. Sirageldin. 1991. *Economic Crisis, Structural Adjustment, and Health in Africa*. Washington, D.C. World Bank. Working Paper Series 766.

Dor, Avi, P. Gertler, and J. van der Gaag. 1989. "Non-Price Rationing and the Medical Care Provider Choice in Rural Cote d'Ivoire." *Journal of Health Economics* 8: 291-304.

Dunlop, David W.   1983.   "Health Care Financing:   Recent Experiences in Africa." *Social Science and Medicine* 17: 2107-2025.

Ellis, Randall P. 1987. "The Revenue Generating Potential of User Fees in Kenyan Government Health Facilities." *Social Science and Medicine* 25: 995-1002.

Feldstein, Paul J. 1988. *Health Care Economics*, 3rd ed. New York. Wiley.

Foster, Susan D. 1988. *Cost Savings from Essential Drug Policies: The Evidence So Far*. Geneva. World Health Organization.

Foster, Susan D. 1990. *Improving the Supply and Use of Essential Drugs in Sub-Saharan Africa*. Washington, D.C. World Bank. Working Paper Series 456. June.

Fuchs, Victor R. 1982. *Who Shall Live?* New York. Basic Books.

Gallagher, Mark. 1988. "Real Government Expenditures per Capita: 1975-1985." United Nations Development Programme and World Bank Working Paper. Washington, D.C. World Bank. June 23.

Golladay, Frederick. 1980. *Health*, Sector Policy Paper. Washington, D.C. World Bank.

Gould, David J., and J. A. Amaro-Reyes. 1985. *The Effects of Corruption in Administrative Performance: Illustrations from Developing Countries*. Washington, D.C. World Bank. Staff Working Paper No. 580.

Gray, Clive S. 1986. "State-Sponsored Primary Health Care in Africa: The Recurrent Cost of Performing Miracles." *Social Science and Medicine* 22: 361-368.

Gray, Ronald H. 1990. "Life Expectancy after 40 Years: The Influence of Economics." *Journal of the American Medical Association* 263: 3332.

Griffin, Charles C. 1989. *Means Testing in Developing Countries*. University of Oregon, Department of Economics. Paper prepared as a background document for the Rockefeller Foundation.

Griffin, Charles C. 1990. *Health Sector Financing in Asia*. Washington, D.C. World Bank. Report No. IDP 68.

Grossman, Michael. 1972. *The Demand for Health: A Theoretical and Empirical Investigation*. New York. National Bureau of Economic Research.

Gwatkin, Davidson R. 1980. "Indications of Change in Developing Country Mortality Trends." *Population and Development Review* 6: 615-644.

Gwatkin, Davidson R. 1983. "Does Better Health Produce Greater Wealth?" Washington, D.C. Overseas Development Council. Mimeo. August.

Gwatkin, Davidson R. 1992. "The Distributional Implications of Alternative Strategic Responses to the Demographic-Epidemiological Transition," forthcoming in Samuel H. Preston, ed., *The Policy and Planning Implications of the Epidemiological Transition in the Less-Developed Countries*. Washington, D.C. National Academy of Sciences.

Hammer, Jeffrey S. 1991. *To Prescribe or Not to Prescribe: On the Regulation of Pharmaceuticals in Developing Countries*. Washington, D.C. World Bank. Working Paper Series 589. February.

Hecht, Robert., ed. 1992. *Zimbabwe: Financing Health Services*. Washington, D.C. World Bank.

Herz, Barbara, and A. R. Measham. 1987. *The Safe Motherhood Initiative: Proposals for Action.* Washington, D.C. World Bank. World Bank Discussion Papers No. 9.

Hill, Kenneth, and A. Pebley. 1988. "Levels, Trends and Patterns of Child Mortality in the Developing World." Baltimore. Johns Hopkins University. Mimeo.

International Monetary Fund. Various years. *Government Financial Statistics.* Washington, D.C. International Monetary Fund.

Jimenez, Emmanuel. 1987. *Pricing Policy in the Social Sectors: Cost Recovery for Education and Health in Developing Countries.* Baltimore. Johns Hopkins University Press.

Koch-Weser, Dieter. 1988. "Water Supply and Sanitation (WS & S) and the Quality of Life," *American Journal of Public Health* 78: 1411-1412.

Lewis, Maureen A. 1988. *The Private Sector and Health Care Delivery in Developing Countries: Definition, Experience, and Potential.* Arlington, VA. John Snow, Inc. Project REACH.

Lindauer, David L., O. Meesook, and P. Suebsaeng. 1986. *Government Wage Policy in Africa: Summary of Findings and Policy Issues.* Washington, D.C. World Bank. CPO Discussion Paper No. 1986-24.

Manning, Willard G., E. B. Keeler, J. P. Newhouse, E. M. Sloss, and J. Wasserman. 1989. "The Wages of Sin: Do Smokers and Drinkers Pay Their Way?" *Journal of the American Medical Association* 26(11): 1604-1609.

Menzel, Paul J. 1983. *Medical Costs, Moral Choices.* New Haven, Conn. Yale University Press.

Musgrave, Richard A., and P. B. Musgrave. 1980. *Public Finance in Theory and Practice.* New York. McGraw-Hill.

Mwabu, Germano. 1990. *Financing Health Services in Africa: An Assessment of Alternative Approaches.* Washington, D.C. World Bank. Working Paper Series 467. June.

Mwabu, Germano M., and W. M. Mwangi. 1986. "Health Care Financing in Kenya: A Simulation of Welfare Effects of User Fees. *Social Science and Medicine* 22: 763-767.

Mwabu, Germano, J. K. Wang'ombe, and V. N. Kimani. 1992. *Health Service Pricing Reforms and Health Care Demand in Kenya: June 1989 to March 1991.* Nairobi. Nairobi and Kenyatta Universities Health Policy Analysis and Development Group.

Newhouse, Joseph P.  1987.  "Cross National Differences in Health
    Spending:  What Do They Mean?"  *Journal of Health Economics*
    6: 159-162.
Nigeria.  Federal Ministry of Health.  1988.  *Report of the National
    Committee on the Establishment of Health Insurance Scheme in
    Nigeria*.  Vol. I. Lagos, Nigeria.  MOH.  September.
————.  *Appendices to the Report of the National Committee on the
    Establishment of Health Insurance Scheme in Nigeria*.  Vol. II.
    Lagos, Nigeria.  MOH.
Okun, Daniel A.  1988.  "The Value of Water Supply and Sanitation
    in Development:  An Assessment."  *American Journal of Public
    Health* 78: 1463-1467.
Organization for Economic Cooperation and Development.    1987.
    *Financing and Delivering Health Care:  A Comparative Analysis of
    OECD Countries*.  Paris.  OECD.
Orivel, Francois and A. Tchicaya.  1988.  *L'Aide a la Sante en Afrique
    Sub-Saharienne*.  Dijon.  Institut de Recherche sur L'Economie de
    l'Education.  octobre.
Over, A. Mead, Jr.  1991.  *Economics for Health Sector Analysis:
    Concepts and Cases*.  Washington, D.C.  World Bank.  Economic
    Development Institute.
Over, A. Mead, Jr., and H. Denton.  1988.  *Nigeria:  The Financing of
    Health Care in a Federal System*.  Washington, D.C.  World Bank.
    April.
Ozgediz, Selcuk.  1983.  *Managing the Public Service in Developing
    Countries: Issues and Prospects*.  Washington, D.C.  World Bank.
    Staff Working Paper No. 583.
Parkin, David, A. McGuire, and B. Yule.  1987.  "Aggregate Health
    Care Expenditures and National Income:  Is Health Care a
    Luxury Good?"  *Journal of Health Economics* 6: 109-127.
Patel, Mahesh S.  1989.  *Eliminating Social Distance between North and
    South:  Cost-Effective Goals for the 1990s*.  New York.  UNICEF.
    Staff Working Paper No. 5.
Pauly, Mark V. 1986. "Taxation, Health Insurance, and Market Failure
    in the Medical Economy."  *Journal of Economic Literature* 24: 629-
    675.
Saunders, Margaret K.  1989.  *Analysis and Summary of World Bank
    Activity in Health Insurance*.  Washington, D.C.  World Bank.
    Economic Development Institute.

Selowsky, Marcelo, and L. Taylor.    1973.    "The Economics of Malnourished Children:  An Example of Disinvestment in Human Capital." *Economic Development and Cultural Change*  22: 17-30.

Stephens, Patience W., E. Bos, M. T. Vu, and R. A. Bulatao.  1991. *Africa Region Population Projections.*    1990-1991 Edition. Washington, D.C.  World Bank.  Working Paper Series 598. February.

Summers, Robert, and A. Heston.  1988.  "A New Set of International Comparisons of Real Product and Price Levels Estimates for 130 Countries, 1950-1985." *Review of Income and Wealth* 34: 1-25.

United Nations (UN).  Various years. *Yearbook of International Trade Statistics*  New York.  United Nations

United Nations Childrens Fund (UNICEF).  1992. *The State of the World's Children.*  New York.  Oxford University Press.

United Nations Development Programme (UNDP).  1980 and 1989. *Demographic Yearbook.*  New York.  United Nations Development Programme.

———.  1991. *Human Development Report 1991.*  New York.  Oxford University Press.

United Nations Food and Agriculture Organization (FAO).  1990. *Production Yearbook.*  Rome.  Food and Agriculture Organization.

U.S. Department of Health and Human Services (USDHHS).  1991. *Health: United States 1990.*  Hyattsville, MD.  U.S. Public Health Service.

Vogel, Ronald J.    1987a.    "A New Framework for Evaluating Recurrent Costs in a Developmental Context:   The Case of Health Care in Senegal."  University of Arizona Working Paper. December.

———.  1987b. *Financing the Health Sector in Tanzania: A Public Expenditure Review.*  Washington, D.C.  World Bank.  December.

———.  1988. *Cost Recovery in the Health Care Sector: Selected Country Studies in West Africa.*  Washington, D.C.  World Bank.  Technical Paper No. 82.

———.  1989. *Trends in Health Expenditures and Revenue Sources in Sub-Saharan Africa.*  Background paper prepared for *Africa Health Policy.* Washington, D.C.  World Bank.  Population and Human Resources Health and Nutrition Department (PHRHN).  March.

———.    1990a.    "An Analysis of Three National Health Insurance Proposals in Sub-Saharan Africa." *International Journal of Health Planning and Management* 5: 271-285.

————. 1990b. "The Costs of Health for All: An Exploratory Economic Analysis." Background paper prepared for *Human Development Report 1991*. New York. United Nations Development Programme. October.

————. 1990c. *Health Insurance in Sub-Saharan Africa: A Survey and Analysis*. Washington, D.C. World Bank. Working Paper Series 476. August.

————. 1991. "Cost Recovery in the Health-Care Sector in Sub-Saharan Africa." *International Journal of Health Planning and Management* 6: 260-281.

Vogel, Ronald J., and H. B. Frant. 1992. "On the Allocation of Revenues from User Fees: The Case of Health Budgeting in Sub-Saharan Africa." *Public Budgeting and Financial Management* 4: 171-194.

Vogel, Ronald J., and B. Stephens. 1989. "Availability of Pharmaceuticals in Sub-Saharan Africa: Roles of the Public, Private and Church Mission Sectors." *Social Science and Medicine* 29: 479-486.

Waddington, Catriona, and E. K. Enyimayew. 1989. "A Price to Pay: The Impact of User Charges in Ashanti-Akim District, Ghana." *International Journal of Health Planning and Management* 4: 17-47.

Weisbrod, Burton A. 1991. "The Health Care Quadrilemma: An Essay on Technological Change, Insurance, Quality of Care and Cost Containment." *Journal of Economic Literature* XXIX: 523-552.

World Bank. 1988. *World Development Report, 1988*. New York. Oxford University Press.

————. 1992. *World Development Report, 1992*. New York. Oxford University Press.

World Bank and United Nations Development Programme. 1989. *Africa's Adjustment and Growth in the 1990s*. Washington, D.C. World Bank and United Nations Development Programme.

World Health Organization. 1986. *Basic Documents*. Geneva. World Health Organization.

————. 1987. *The International Drinking Water Supply and Sanitation Decade, Mid-Decade Review*. Geneva. World Health Organization.

————. 1988. *The World Drug Situation*. Geneva. World Health Organization.

## WORLD BANK:  UNPUBLISHED DOCUMENTS

Benin:          *Review of Public Expenditures, 1985-90*, Africa Regional Office, September 21, 1987, Report No. 6951-BEN.

Benin:          *Population, Health and Nutrition Sector Memorandum*, April 3, 1986.

Botswana:       *Staff Appraisal Report, Family Health Project*, Population, Health and Nutrition Department, April 11, 1984, Report No. 4820-BT.

Burkina Faso
(formerly
Upper Volta):   *Health and Nutrition Sector Review*. Population, Health and Nutrition Department, November 12, 1982, Report No. 3926 UV.

Burundi:        *Population and Health Sector Review*, Population, Health and Nutrition Department, July 15, 1983.

Cameroon:       *Population, Health and Nutrition Sector Review* Population, Health and Nutrition Department, October 1984, Report No. 5296-CM.

Central African
Republic:       *Republique Centrafricaine, Rapport Preliminaire sur L'Anlayse des Contraintes Sectorielles et des Sources de Financement*, CEDES. Mission Effectue du 1/06 au 27/06, 1988.

Chad:           *Le Developpement Des Services De Sante Dans La Republique Du Tchad*, Soumise A La Banque Africaine De Developpement, Abidjan, Cote D'Ivoire, Health Policy Institute, Boston University, avril 1986.

Cote
d'Ivoire:       *Analyse du Systeme de Sante et Financement de Son Fonctionnement*, CHUL International, Rapport de Mission en Cote d'Ivoire, aout 1988.  (2 vols.)

Cote
d'Ivoire:       *Staff Appraisal Report, Republic of the Ivory Coast, Health and Demographic Project*, Population, Health and Nutrition Department, August 29, 1985, Report No. 5636-IVC.

Ethiopia:       *Staff Appraisal Report, Family Health Project*, East Africa Department, Population and Human Resources Division, May 12, 1988, Report No. 6742-ET.

Ethiopia:       *Sector Review, A Study of Health Financing Issues and Options*, Population Health and Nutrition Department, Division 1, February 9, 1987, Report No. 6624-ET. (2 vols.)

Ethiopia:       *Population, Health and Nutrition Sector Review*, Population Health and Nutrition Department, Division 1, September 30, 1985, Report No. 5299-ET.

Gambia:         *Staff Appraisal Report, National Health Development Project*, Population, Health and Nutrition Department, January 23, 1987, Report No. 6340-GM.

Ghana:          *Population, Health and Nutrition Sector Review*, West Africa Department, Population and Human Resources Division, October 21, 1988.

Ghana:          *President's Report*, December 24, 1985, Report No. P-4157 GH.

Guinea:         *Population, Health and Nutrition Sector Review*, Population Health and Nutrition Department, May 15, 1986.

Kenya:          *Review of Expenditure Issues and Options in Health Financing*, Population and Human Resources Operations Division, Africa Country Department II, September 30, 1987, Report No. 6963-KE.

Lesotho:        *Health Financing in Lesotho*, 1987.

Lesotho:        *Staff Appraisal Report, Health and Population Project*, Population, Health and Nutrition Department, April 1, 1985, Report No. 5437-LSO.

Madagascar:     *Population and Health Sector Review*, Country Department III, Africa Regional Office, July 7, 1987, Report No. 6446-MAG.

Malawi:         *Staff Appraisal Report, Second Family Health Project*, Population, Health and Nutrition Department, February 26, 1987, Report No. 6471-MAI.

Malawi:         *Population Sector Review*, Population, Health and Nutrition Department, Division I, March 10, 1986, Report No. 5648-MAI.

Malawi:         *Staff Appraisal Report, Republic of Malawi*, Population, Health and Nutrition Department, March 24, 1983, Report No. 4342-MAI.

Mali:             *Le Financement des Couts Recurrents de la Sante au Mali*, OMS (Geneve), Premiere Redaction, septembre 1988.

Mali:             *Staff Appraisal Report, Health Development Project*, Population, Health and Nutrition Department, November 15, 1983, Report No. 4465-MLI.

Mali:             *Health Sector Memorandum*, Projects Department, West Africa Regional Office, Education Division, August 24, 1979, Report No. 2618a-MLI.

Mauritania:       *Health Sector Memorandum* (draft), June 10, 1987.

Mozambique:       *Staff Appraisal Report, Health and Nutrition Project*, Southern Africa Department, Population and Human Resources Division, September 30, 1988 (revised), Report No. 7423-MOZ.

Niger:            *Staff Appraisal Report, Health Project*, Population Health and Nutrition Department, February 26, 1986, Report No. 5937-NIR.

Nigeria:          *Staff Appraisal Report*, Sokoto Health Project, February 21, 1985, Report No. 4599-UNI.

Rwanda:           *Staff Appraisal Report, Family Health Project*, Population, Health and Nutrition Department, March 6, 1986.

Rwanda:           *Population, Health and Nutrition Sector Review*, Population, Health and Nutrition Department, August 21, 1984.

Senegal:          *Population Sector Report*, Population, Health and Nutrition Department, June 24, 1987, Report No. 6510-SE.  (2 vols.)

Senegal:          *Staff Appraisal Report, Rural Health Project*, Population, Health and Nutrition Department, November 29, 1982, Report No. 4003-SE.

Sierra Leone:     *Staff Appraisal Report, Health and Population Sector Support Project*, Population, Health and Nutrition Department, April 22, 1986, Report No. 5995-SL.

Somalia:          *Population, Health and Nutrition Sector Review*, Population, Health and Nutrition Department, September 5, 1985.

Sudan:            *Population, Health and Nutrition Sector Review*, Population, Health and Nutrition Department, Division I, June 4, 1987.

Swaziland:      *Population and Health Sector Review*, Population, Health and Nutrition Department, May 31, 1985, Report No. 5338-SW.

Tanzania:       *Population, Health and Nutrition Sector Review* (draft), Southern Africa Department, Population and Human Resources Operations Division, October 11, 1988.

Togo:           *Rapport* (undated).

Uganda:         *Population, Health and Nutrition Sector Review*, Population, Health and Nutrition Department, June 17, 1985, Report No. 5262-UG.

Zaire:          *Population, Sante et Nutrition, Etude Sectorielle*, Department des pays des Grands Lacs et de l'ocean Indien, Division des operations, population et resources humaines, 1 septembre 1988, Rapport No. 7013 ZR.

Zaire:          *Population, Health and Nutrition Sector Review*, November 17, 1987, Report No. 7013-ZR.

Zaire:          *Health Zones Financing Study*, The Resources for Child Health Project, June-October 1986 (USAID/Kinshasa).

Zambia:         *Population, Health and Nutrition Sector Review*, Population, Health and Nutrition Department, May 16, 1984, Report No. 4715-ZA.

Zimbabwe:       *Population, Health and Nutrition Sector Review*, Vols. I and II, Population, Health and Nutrition Department, June 17, 1983, Report No. 4214-ZIM.

# Index

**About the Author**

RONALD J. VOGEL is a professor in the School of Public Administration and Policy and in the Department of Economics, College of Business and Public Administration at the University of Arizona. He has published widely in the fields of health-care finance and health economics.